PRAISE FOR *REACH*

"Arthur's story is the perfect read to inspire, entertain, and inform. A kid with an insatiable love of TV makes his dreams come true by not only becoming a giant in the industry but becoming a trailblazer for others."
—HOWIE MANDEL

"Arthur Smith is a reality TV pioneer and maverick.... His insight into TV is unmatched and you'll learn so much in this book, just like I have over many years of *Hell's Kitchen*."
—GORDON RAMSAY

"The 'peeks behind the curtain' that Arthur reveals in his memoir will prove particularly thrilling for TV enthusiasts, but the life lessons he shares are priceless gems that anyone with a dream will be grateful to have!"
—ZURI HALL,
cohost of *Access Hollywood* and *American Ninja Warrior*

"An absolutely fascinating and engaging book about the workings of the television and entertainment world by an insider who has led the field."
—ROBIN SHARMA,
#1 worldwide bestselling author of
The Monk Who Sold His Ferrari and *The 5 AM Club*

REACH

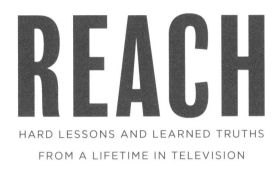

REACH

HARD LESSONS AND LEARNED TRUTHS

FROM A LIFETIME IN TELEVISION

ARTHUR SMITH

WITH DANIEL PAISNER

BLACK STONE

PUBLISHING

Copyright © 2023 by Arthur Smith
Published in 2023 by Blackstone Publishing
Cover design by Luis Alejandro Cruz Castillo

Printed in the United States of America

First edition: 2023
ISBN 979-8-200-97726-0
Biography & Autobiography / Entertainment & Performing Arts

Version 1

Blackstone Publishing
31 Mistletoe Rd.
Ashland, OR 97520

www.BlackstonePublishing.com

To my parents,
Goldie and Saul Smith,
who made me feel special every day,
giving me the confidence to . . . reach.

And to the five special women in my life—
Wendy, Rachel, Leah, Marylin, and Sheryl—
for giving me a reason to keep reaching.

"I am always doing that which I cannot do, in order that I may learn how to do it."

—Vincent van Gogh

CONTENTS

OPEN

Chances are you never heard of me before picking up this book. I'm not exactly a name-above-the-title kind of guy. However, I *am* a name-below-the-title kind of guy.

I didn't set out to become one of the top producers in television. My goal starting out was straightforward: I wanted to work in the entertainment business. I loved television most of all. I was a child of the '60s and '70s, and I used to sit for hours in front of the set, watching reruns, game shows, and old movies. I watched everything: *Gilligan's Island*, *Happy Days*, *All in the Family*, *Dallas*, and as an avid fan of all sports, I especially loved *Hockey Night in Canada*—but also, strangely (especially for a ten-year-old!), a steady diet of *60 Minutes* and national news.

Television kept me informed—and just as important, it kept me company. I tore through the *Montreal Gazette* every Saturday for the syndicated "TV Times" supplement and planned my viewing for the coming week. This was back before VCRs and DVRs, before on-screen programming guides and search functions. You had to work to make sure you didn't miss anything. If two shows you wanted to watch were on at the same time, you had to do a kind of triage to determine which show might be repeated sometime soon so you could maybe watch it at a later date.

My parents were naturally a little concerned about my excessive television watching, but as long as I did my homework and got good grades, they never put any restrictions on what I watched and, for the most part, left me alone to do my thing. In this, I suspect, they were unlike most parents of that generation, who saw the medium as an invasive, pervasive influence. They never told us kids to sit six feet from the color television—house rules in most households where mothers and fathers had been conditioned to believe their newfangled color sets could cause radiation poisoning or sterility . . . or something. From time to time, my parents would even sit down and watch with me— my father most often, when our beloved Canadiens were playing—or maybe my sisters would join me if we could all agree on a show. I spent an inordinate amount of my childhood watching prime-time entertainment shows with my head resting on my mother's shoulder. And as I watched, I imagined myself working in some way to amuse or engage or enlighten some family in some other part of the world at some other point in time.

I made a run at acting professionally toward the end of high school and into college. I thought I could ride a couple early successes to a career in front of the camera. However, the more I worked in front of the camera, the more fascinated I became with what was happening on the other side of the camera: producing, directing, writing . . . *creating.* I was drawn to the many ways television was made, and I set out to learn what I could about the business—from the ground up, if that's what it took, although I wasn't exactly inclined to pay my dues. I wanted to hit the ground running, bypass the grunt work that comes with most first jobs, and jump straight to the top. This wasn't arrogance on my part so much as ignorance. I didn't know how the business worked—or how it didn't.

I only knew that I wanted in. That led me to a lifelong career in television. I've produced a few thousand hours of prime-time (and lately, streaming) television. Prior to that, I produced tens of thousands of hours of live sports programming, first for the Canadian Broadcasting Corporation (CBC) and later for FOX Sports. I produced entertainment programming for Dick Clark Productions—variety programming, special events, awards shows. I even worked briefly as a senior studio executive at MCA/Universal. So even though you might not know my name, it has come to mean something in my corner of the entertainment industry, and I bet you know some of my work: *Hell's Kitchen, American Ninja Warrior, Kitchen Nightmares, Paradise Hotel, Trading Spaces, The Swan, The Titan Games, Mental Samurai, Pros vs. Joes, Welcome to Plathville, Ellen's Design Challenge, I Survived a Japanese Game Show, American Gangster, Unsung, UFC Countdown, The Floor is Lava*, and many more . . .

Watch at the end (or the beginning) of any of my shows, and you'll see my name. You'll also see the name of my production company, A. Smith & Co., which I started in 2000. Since then, we've produced more than two hundred shows for more than fifty networks and platforms. Along the way I've learned a thing or two about what it takes to connect with an audience, overcome a variety of obstacles, collaborate with some of the biggest stars and most creative minds in the entertainment industry, produce a body of work that has come to define a genre, and, ultimately, reach beyond what I ever thought possible.

There's something I need to get out of the way before we get going: I hate the term *reality television*. Or at least I hate how the term has been used in recent years and how it's applied with such broad strokes to pretty much every non-scripted or nonfiction show. It's confusing.

Consider: when television executives, critics, or audiences talk about a sitcom, the genre fits into a neat little box. We're all clear on the one-hour drama. Of course, there are multicam sitcoms and docu-drama series, but for the most part, we know what we're getting when we tune in to one of these shows. There's a familiar construct. We get it.

With *reality*, all bets are off. The label now includes documentaries, game shows, talk shows, variety shows, cooking shows, music shows, competition shows, sports-entertainment shows, docu-soaps . . . you get the idea. A lot of outlets avoid the term *reality* entirely. At NBC, for example, shows that fall outside the traditional half-hour sitcoms or hour-long dramas are called *unscripted content*. At FOX, they call them

alternative entertainment and specials. At HBO, it's *nonfiction* programming. At Netflix, I deal with the folks in the *unscripted and documentary
series* department.

Lately, the term has become so pervasive that it frames our expectations for these shows before we even sit down to watch them. When
I think of reality television, I think of shows like *Keeping Up With
the Kardashians* or *The Bachelor*. Nothing against those shows—I have
a ton of respect for anyone who's able to produce a long-running,
money-printing hit. (My goodness—a juggernaut by any other name
is still a juggernaut!) The producers of these shows do a certain thing,
and they do it well.

The shows we produce at A. Smith & Co. represent a wide variety
of genres, yet almost all of our shows are placed beneath the same tent.
There are so many subgenres to the so-called *reality* genre: *American Idol*
is widely thought of as a reality show, but so is our own *American Ninja
Warrior*, despite the fact that they're very different shows built on very
different templates. And can we really make the argument that either
of those shows should be categorized in the same genre as *Jersey Shore*,
90 Day Fiancé, or *The Amazing Race*?

Perhaps a little history is in order. Some television historians suggest
that the reality television genre goes back nearly fifty years, to the 1973
premiere of the groundbreaking PBS series *An American Family*, which
chronicled the daily life of the Loud family of Santa Barbara, California, but nobody used the term *reality television* back then. The first time
the phrase really seeped into the culture was with the launch of *Survivor*
and *The Real World*. These two landmark shows signaled a sea change
in the television landscape. They not only changed the ways we watch
television, they changed the ways we talk about what we're watching,
and I consider them the forebearers for the two primary subgenres of
all reality shows.

The Real World is the pioneer in the category of *unstructured reality*,
which has grown to include such shows as *Keeping Up With the Kardashians*,
Real Housewives of Beverly Hills, and our own hit TLC show *Welcome to
Plathville*. You might also classify these shows as docu-soaps, occu-soaps

or docu-follows. They tend to be observational shows about the lives of the famous and the not-so-famous; they can be comedic, dramatic, soapy, and inspiring, but they usually have some element of conflict.

The other subgenre is *structured reality*, and this is where *Survivor* led the way, and where you can now find such shows as *Big Brother*, *The Bachelor*, and our own long-running FOX series *Hell's Kitchen*. These entries all have a structured format and can include competition, makeover, lifestyle, and relationship shows.

Let's call it what it is: *American Idol* is a variety show; *Deal or No Deal* is a game show; *American Ninja Warrior* is a sports-entertainment series . . . I don't consider any of these shows to be part of the reality genre because they belong to a history of programming that came long before the reality boom. Game shows predate reality shows by fifty years, so let's show some respect and not refer to *Who Wants to Be a Millionaire?* as a reality show. Let's recognize *American Idol* as an outgrowth of, say, *Star Search* or, going back even further, *The Original Amateur Hour*, one of the first variety series on television. Similarly, *Ninja* is following in the tradition of other sports-entertainment series like *American Gladiators* and *Superstars*—different formats, to be sure, but they are all made-for-television athletic spectacles.

It's not just the fact that *reality television* has become a catchall phrase that gives me pause. I also avoid the term because, for some reason, the term has taken on a negative connotation. I'll sometimes hear a comment like, "Oh, you do reality television. I never watch that stuff." Most times, they'll say *crap* instead of *stuff*—you know, just in case it isn't clear how they really feel about these shows. Usually, that signals that the person is thinking of some of the trashiest, *dish*iest reality fare out there and not the mainstream programming that often accounts for some of our most popular shows.

Whenever I hear a line like that, I try to keep the conversation pleasant and get people to tell me what shows they *do* like to watch. If they give me answers like *Shark Tank* or *Top Chef*, I'll push back and say, "Wait, I thought you said you didn't watch reality television." That's usually enough to get the person to open their eyes and see that some of their favorite shows fit squarely into the category of programs they'd been so quick to disregard.

So what *can* we call these non-sitcom, non-drama programs? I don't like the term *unscripted*, which gets kicked around a lot, because there are surely scripts that Jeff Probst follows on *Survivor*, and as good an ad-libber as Steve Harvey appears to be on *Family Feud*, we can be sure he follows a loose script from time to time. I'm not a fan of the term *alternative programming* either because so many of these shows, like *The Voice* or *America's Got Talent*, are far from alternative—they're in the mainstream.

I've always embraced *nonfiction programming* as an umbrella term to describe the kinds of shows we produce. It's not the best term, but it gets closest to what we do and pretty much covers all the genres and subgenres. Plus, I like it because I've always been a nonfiction junkie: I love newsmagazine shows, documentaries, true-crime stories. I used to read the encyclopedia as a kid . . . for fun. It's one of the reasons I was drawn to sports when I got my start in television. Sports is the greatest reality show ever, packed with real emotion, real human drama, real stories of struggle and triumph.

At the end of the day, what we producers set out to do is make television. Good television. Compelling television. Unpredictable television. As a consumer I never discriminate against certain types of shows, and as a producer I approach every concept with an open mind. If it holds my interest, it holds my interest. If it doesn't, I'll switch the channel or turn my attention to another show in our development pipeline. As long as a show gives me the chance to tell real human stories in exciting new ways, I'm in.

My passion for television was not the only factor in launching my career. There's another key element—one I can trace to a specific, pivotal moment in my childhood—the dividing line that separated the shy, skinny kid I was from the outgoing, hard-charging person I would become. That line was drawn when I was nine years old, and something happened that turned my life around.

It started when my parents moved our family from a small bungalow in the Montreal suburb of Saint-Laurent to a sprawling, three-story home in the upscale neighborhood of Hampstead, about nine miles away.

Moving sucks.

When you're a kid and the reasons for moving have nothing to do with you, it sucks most of all. It pushes you from what you know at a time when all you care about is what's on television or how your favorite team is doing or which friends are playing in the street.

The move was a big deal—a dream fulfilled for my parents, Saul and Goldie. But for me . . . well, I was traumatized. Completely unsure of myself. Worried I'd never fit in. Despite my shyness, I'd somehow managed to collect a bunch of friends in my old neighborhood. That's how it goes when you're a little kid. You look around one day and realize there are all these other little kids just like you in the same place, doing a lot of the same things, and without even trying to, you've made friends. And yet the idea of making *new* friends seemed so impossible. I didn't have the first idea how to navigate this new environment among kids who'd known each other their entire lives.

My parents could see that I wasn't myself, so of course they worried. They'd see me staring out my new bedroom window, sometimes for hours, with a lost look on my face. For weeks, I refused to go outside to play with the neighborhood kids, even with a steady push from my parents—*especially* my mom! I was miserable, and I hated that I was miserable because my mood affected the whole house.

The move had been a nightmare for my sisters as well. Marylin, the oldest, was going into her last year of high school and felt like she was leaving her whole world behind at the worst possible time. Sheryl, next in line, had it the easiest of the three of us. She was the extrovert, quick to make friends, about to start high school. Both were able to make the best of it before long.

I could only sit and stare out the window, making the worst of it, and there was nothing my parents could do or say to make me feel any better about my situation. That didn't keep them from trying, so one day they signed me up to play in a youth hockey league.

It's impossible to overstate the importance of hockey in my life at the time. In Montreal, in the 1960s and 1970s, when the Canadiens were almost always making it to the Stanley Cup Finals, hockey was like a life force—and at nine years old, I felt this keenly. Some of my most cherished memories were watching my beloved Canadiens with my dad at the old Montreal Forum or on the Saturday night telecasts of *Hockey Night in Canada*—the highest rated show in the country. Guy Lafleur, Yvan Cournoyer, Ken Dryden, Jean Béliveau . . . these were the heroes of my childhood.

My parents thought an organized activity would shake me from my funk, and that if anything could get me out of the house, it would be hockey. Me and my friends in my *old* neighborhood, we lived and breathed the stuff. I'd started playing about three years earlier, and I was a competent defenseman—solid but nothing special. I could skate well enough. I could handle the puck and push people around. I understood the game. Mostly, I loved being on the ice with my teammates, working together toward a common goal.

I went to the chilly outdoor rink for our first practice, nervous about joining a new team with kids who'd probably played together year after year, but also excited as hell. I was determined to power past my nerves and get out on the ice. Trouble was the coach said he didn't need any more defensemen, and since I knew I was just an average defensive player (and was only nine years old), I couldn't really argue with him.

The coach took one look at me and said, "We could use you at center."

He didn't ask me if I'd be comfortable leading our front line. He hadn't even seen me skate. He just sized me up and said this was where I would play, and that was that.

My first game, I was just there. The best you could say about the way I played was that I hadn't made any mistakes or called any unwanted attention to myself. I felt good about getting back out on the ice but at the same time disappointed that I hadn't managed to actually impact the game. I still hadn't made any new friends—as far as I knew, none of my teammates even knew my name—but at least they didn't know me as the kid who'd botched a fast break or messed up on a line change. I breathed a small sigh of relief.

In my second game, I started to feel more comfortable. It was wicked cold that day, and my devoted dad was bundled up in the stands, watching me play. I thought about how things had gone in my first game, building on the few positives that had come my way by virtue of not screwing up. But my small sigh of relief was about out of air. It was time for me to breathe deep and find a new level of resolve. As a shy kid, in the past I had gravitated naturally to being a stay-at-home defenseman. It fit with my personality. I was happy to be a role player and not a star.

Now at center, that had to change.

I was no longer just *there* . . . I was *present*. There's a big difference. I took my shifts like I belonged on the ice.

With less than a minute to go, the score tied, the puck found my stick. Somehow, I managed to wrist the puck. It sailed past the goalie's gloved hand, right into the back of the net. Next thing I knew, I was caught in a swirl of backslaps and congratulations from my new teammates. It was exhilarating, to be so suddenly accepted and validated on the back of this one play. Sports can do that, don't you think?

The feeling of being lost and alone magically lifted, and I let myself think this move wouldn't suck quite so hard. Not only that, I went from thinking of myself as a role player on defense to someone who could make things happen. I took in the lesson that I had it in me to do so much more, to *be* so much more. My sense of self transformed, and I went from shrinking from the action to *wanting* to be out in front. I went on to become one of the leading scorers in the league. My personality and sense of what I could accomplish was completely changed. I went from a defenseman to a center, not just on the ice but in my mind.

That confidence followed me into every aspect of my life. Somehow, I fell in with a group of good friends, and I started to excel at other sports. I enjoyed the spotlight. I wanted the ball, the puck . . . the moment. I wanted to be *the guy*. It was like a switch had flipped.

I look back on that moment as a template for the way I've lived my life ever since. When you're part of a team, lost in the rhythm of the game, you're able to step outside yourself, beyond what you've become, past your own limiting expectations. Of course, I could not yet fully understand this at the time. I was just a kid trying to shake the *new kid* label. But over time, I saw lessons to be mined from the ways I pushed myself. From the ways I resolved to lift myself from a hole I'd been digging.

From the ways I *reached*.

That's the core of this book. On the surface, it's about my life and career. You don't work in television for forty years without collecting some great stories—I could fill a couple books with the things I've seen, the experiences I've shared, the people I've met—but I have no interest in holding court and spinning a bunch of wild tales. After all, what's the value of a great story if it doesn't come with a lesson? What's the value of a life well lived if there isn't something to be learned from it?

And so I'll keep the focus not just on the *teachable* moments that have marked my days, but on the *reachable* moments. I'll share the stories about when I was up against long odds, the stories that confirmed my belief in myself, the stories that shaped me, humbled me, or lifted me up in ways big and small. I'll tell the stories that might have some take-away value for you, that might help you grow your own games and find your own way and reach toward your own defining moments.

Because I'd had no choice but to reach, because my parents had pushed, because my coach had made me vulnerable . . . I had a whole new outlook. I would never need to be pushed again. I would never again underestimate myself or let fear get in the way of putting myself out there.

When we reach, we find out what we're capable of.

When we reach, we discover new solutions to old challenges.

When we reach, we learn the difference between a pipe dream and what we haven't dared to try yet.

When we reach, and *only* when we reach, we achieve our full potential.

Stay with me through these pages, and I'll share turning-point stories that helped me appreciate the sustaining power of reach. Taken together, they've taught me that there can be a downside to being overly ambitious, but also that ambition can be a positive thing if you understand how to tap into it and recognize the right time to extend yourself.

Of course, it's much easier to reach from a strong foundation, and I was blessed with parents who went out of their way to lift their children up. They encouraged me to think big, to take chances, to stretch myself beyond what I thought possible on my own. Their belief in me pushed me to believe in myself. (Hey, if you keep telling a kid he's special, he might come to believe it!)

They also taught me to always do the right thing. My father often said, "There's never a wrong time to do the right thing, and there's never a right time to do the wrong thing"—a line that may or may not have been original to him, but he made it his own. He made it clear that I would find my successes on the back of hard work and discipline, not by taking advantage of someone else.

That afternoon on the ice, I put myself out there, pushed myself from whatever comfort zone I'd allowed myself to fall into. I reached for something better, something bigger, something *more*. Everything changed for me on the back of that one goal. It absolutely did. At nine years old, I wasn't fully aware how the trajectory of my life might flow from this one moment, but as I look back on it, the through line is clear.

My view of the world and my place within it would never be the same.

1
THE FAMILY BUSINESS

My father, Saul Smith, was born in a place that no longer exists—a region of Eastern Europe called Bessarabia that now sits mostly in Moldova and partly in Ukraine. When he was born, it was under Romanian rule, and like it was for many Jews in the region at the time, life became more and more untenable for my grandparents and their children. Their friends and family were under attack, so my grandfather, Samuel, fled with his family to North America.

Of course, Zaida Sam didn't simply snap his fingers and fashion a new life from the one he left behind. Like many immigrants, he struggled. Assimilation is hard. Building a life out of no life at all: also hard. My father was just two years old when his family moved to the other side of the world to reach for a better life, and he remembered that they were desperately poor. They ended up in Montreal, where there was a small but dedicated Jewish community. For the longest time, my grandfather was unable to find steady employment, so he worked as a painter, picking up jobs here and there. It was honest work, but it was dispiriting, uncertain, difficult. He knew he could not go on like that forever—but still he kept at it—until the hard road he was on took him to where he was meant to be.

Eventually, my grandfather started selling leather coats, and out of that he began a small fur-manufacturing business with an enterprising friend who was also looking for a way up and out of his own rough patch. They made coats and accessories—presumably drawing on some of the knowledge and experience they'd brought with them from the old country. The work was still difficult, and early on there was nothing to indicate that these new partners would be successful, but here at least they were working in pursuit of a shared goal, and over time the business grew. My grandfather was able to provide for his family and settle into the life he and my grandmother had imagined when they came to Canada.

As my grandfather was building up his business in the usual, painstaking ways, my father was developing the industrious, overachieving, dutiful personality that would come to have a profound impact on me. Growing up, I'd hear stories of how my father used to scrub the floors for my grandmother, how he'd be the first to help out around the house, how he was always going above and beyond what was expected of him. He was the middle child, sandwiched between two sisters, and it fell to him to fill some of the spaces where the money from my grandfather's business didn't quite reach. As a kid, he had a paper route—and believe me, it's no easy thing to distribute ninety copies of *The Montreal Star* in the dead of winter for next to nothing, but he was relentless, and he never complained.

My father was self-reliant to the extreme. He put himself through school, studying to be an accountant. He could close his eyes and picture the life in front of him: a good job, a nice house, a family. But then World War II happened, and he served as a sergeant in the Canadian army. When he was done, my grandfather went to him with a different prospect. My grandfather's partner in the fur business had moved to Arizona, and my grandfather got it in his head that his son, the returning army sergeant and aspiring accountant, would be the perfect person to take his place. My father, looking ahead to the rest of his life and wanting nothing more than to please *his* father, set aside his own ambitions to help sustain the family business.

In a lot of ways, this was a concession for my father, because he certainly had other options he'd been looking forward to, but my father accepted his father's offer because he thought that's what was expected of him. Always, he wanted to do the right thing, and in the moment, this felt like what he was meant to do.

Cut to just a couple years later, S. Smith & Son was thriving. My father, as it turned out, was a born salesman with a dynamic, charming personality. I learned more about selling from him than anybody I'd go on to meet in television: the way he made people feel comfortable, got them to laugh and let their guard down, helped them to see the value in the purchase they were considering, built and nurtured relationships with his customers over time. My grandfather ran the factory end of the operation while my father tended to sales and the business side. They complemented each other perfectly.

My father would learn as much as he could about whatever he was doing—to reach for more than he already knew—so it wasn't long before he knew every aspect of production and design. He learned to design a coat and every aspect of manufacturing. He studied the fashions to think ahead of the curve and figure out what women would be buying a year or two down the road. This might not have been the life he imagined, but he was all in.

I'm the same way. After a lifetime in television, I've become an expert in every element of the business, from deal-making to development to production to editing to marketing. I got that from my dad, I like to think. From his example, I learned that in order to do a thing well and truly, you must first commit to doing it fully.

My father and grandfather were incredibly close. They'd been close going into their partnership, but after working side by side every day, they became closer still. They did everything together. If my grandfather was in the market for a television set, he would buy two—one for him and one for my dad. If my dad wanted a dishwasher, he would pick up one for my grandfather as well. My mother used to say they should have changed the name of the business because they were more like brothers than father and son.

Sadly, my grandfather died suddenly just a few years into their partnership, and my father was bereft. Zaida Sam was on vacation in Florida when he had a heart attack. He was fifty-nine years old. I wasn't born yet, but the date of my grandfather's death was an important marker in our family: February 3, 1955. Every year, when the date came around on the calendar, my father would be quiet and emotional, not quite himself. Twenty, thirty, forty years afterward, I'd catch him shaking his head and saying, "I can't believe he's gone." He never got over it.

Years later, long after I'd moved from Canada to California, my father got out of the fur coat business. I flew home to help him clear out his personal effects and came across a memorial plaque that my dad had made to honor my grandfather after he'd died. I remembered the plaque, which was displayed prominently in the reception area of the office, from the almost weekly visits my sisters and I used to make to help out with customers and keep our father company, but I hadn't seen it in years.

I turned to my father and said, "Do you mind if I keep this?"

"Why would you want this?" my father said. "It weighs about a hundred pounds."

"It's our history," I said. "I just want it."

I don't even remember how I got that plaque home to Los Angeles, because it really was ridiculously heavy, but it's become one of my most meaningful possessions. In my previous house, it hung in a prominent place in my study, but here in our new house, it simply leans against the wall in my office because I haven't figured out where to hang it just yet. (Have I mentioned that this thing is heavy?) Still, every time I look at it, I think of the sacrifices my grandfather made to come to North America and how he built a successful business—all because it felt to him like he had no choice but to try. To *reach*.

For the longest time after my grandfather's death, my father couldn't bring himself to go to the office. He was crushed, devastated, and I later learned that my mother did the most remarkable thing to ease him past his grief. She started going to the office with him to keep him company. There was nothing for her to really do at the office, but she wanted to be there for my father. He never asked. She just went. She didn't want him to be alone—that's the kind of selfless person she was, and that's how deeply my father mourned the loss of my grandfather. Incredibly, she did this for about a year, until my father found his footing.

My mother, Goldie, was one of five children, and she was wired in a tough but nurturing way. She was raised with a certain code on how to behave. There was only black and white, right and wrong. But there was one rule that trumped all the others: family first. She was a world-class caregiver, devoted to her family, as is clear from the way she stood by my father's side after my grandfather died.

She was a first-generation Canadian, born in Montreal, but raised in a similar way to my dad, with a deep respect for the ties of family and the points of connection that bind the generations. My maternal grandfather, Paul, was a cantor, and yet I don't think her family was particularly religious. They were practicing Jews, of course, and they observed the holidays and lit the Shabbos candles, but my mother never mentioned that Judaism played any kind of defining role in her childhood. Her father just happened to have an unbelievable voice and a deep respect for the music and the rituals.

In another era, in different circumstances, my mother would have been the CEO of a major company. She was exceptional in so many ways. She was bright and driven . . . and ultimately frustrated because she seemed to want more from her days. Oh, she loved being a mom to me and my sisters, and she was great at it, but I think she resented that there weren't other opportunities available to her. More than that, I think she felt that there should have been more expected of her. Instead of reaching, a part of her believed that she had settled—at least in terms of a career. As a mom, she went above and beyond always. Her ability to reach and pull opportunities from thin air was apparent everywhere, but I'm sure she wanted to be a working mom and set a different example for us kids, her daughters especially. Plus, she had such a sharp mind and so much to offer, I know she would have blossomed in an office setting. Before she was married, she'd worked a number of jobs, but the custom in those days—in our community, at least—was for women to keep house and look after the children, so she stopped working as soon as she married and focused on the care and feeding of our little family.

She was an extremely devoted mother—so much so that she sometimes drove us crazy with how involved she was in our lives. For what it's worth, I was her favorite. (Believe me, this was worth *a lot*! It was every-thing!) In a lot of families, this is just something to say—a running joke used to tweak a sibling or punctuate a story—but everyone in my family would agree with me on this. Our father loved all of us kids equally, and I suppose, on some level, my mother did too. But then, on another level, she loved me *just a little bit* more. She said as much, often pretending to say it in a joking way, but she wasn't kidding. My sisters knew it. Their husbands knew it. Everybody knew it. In my mother's defense, she never said these things when we were little kids. She waited until we were older, but by the time I started college, it wasn't unusual for her to turn to me and say, "You're my whole life, Arthur," or "I love you more than anybody else on Earth."

And do you want to know something? It wasn't weird. In fact, it was kind of special. Her love made me feel special. I was close to my father too, so I was doubly blessed on the parent front—and happily, that connection continued when I moved across the continent to California. I used to speak to my mother every night at eleven o'clock her time. It was eight o'clock on the West Coast, so there was often something else going on—dinner or a production of a show or a night out with friends—but I always made the time. Later on in life, she'd get on the phone and say, "I wanted to make sure I speak to you tonight in case I don't wake up in the morning." She spoke to my sisters every day as well, but they lived in Montreal and were able to see each other regularly, so those calls weren't scheduled. But the two of us spoke religiously. Most nights, my father would get on the phone for a moment or two, but there was no denying that these calls were meant for my mother and me.

I used to joke that I should change my legal name to My Arthur, because that was how my mother always referred to me. My mother and I were so close that when I flew to Los Angeles for a job interview with entertainment legend and mogul Dick Clark, she went with me for moral support.

Really.

I had a big job as the head of CBC Sports. I'd been all over the world, covering the Olympics and other major sporting events, leading huge production teams and delegations, and being responsible for all elements of the telecast. By every outward measure, I'd arrived. But my mother decided I needed her to hold my hand on this one interview. Who knows—maybe I did.

Later, I'll write more about that interview with Dick Clark and how it sent my career in a whole new direction, but first I want to focus on what it meant to be so deeply and wholeheartedly loved by my mother, and how that unlikely road trip stands out in my memory as the perfect example of her devotion.

Throughout my life, my mother was my coach. I spent the first part of my career covering sports and saw up close how the greatest coaches got the most out of their players—how they inspired them, drove them, lifted them to a place where they could play at a whole new level. That was my mother. She got the most out of her kids—her *players*. I saw myself through her loving eyes. My dad was my role model and mentor, but my mom was my coach. She was always in my ear, reminding me of everything I needed to do, not at all shy about telling me how exactly I needed to do it. When I told her about the interview, she simply announced that she was coming with me. There was no discussion. She flew from Montreal and met me in Toronto, and we flew out to Los Angeles together. It might have looked like we were off on a regular mother-son adventure, but to her it was so much more than that. To me too.

We did manage to squeeze in a family visit on our breeze through Los Angeles. My mother's first cousin was Dr. Art Ulene, who for the longest time was the health and medical expert for NBC News and a regular on *The Today Show*. He was the Sanjay Gupta of his day, "America's Doctor," and we had a lovely visit over breakfast. I can't help but think that, in his own way, Art played a small role in my early career objectives as well. This was the first time I'd met him, as I recall, but I certainly knew who he was and that we were named for the same relative. This connection in my mind as a TV-mad kid must have gotten me thinking of how television is made and how our careers are determined. Art had gone to medical school at UCLA and had become a doctor, and yet instead of practicing medicine, he'd wound up on this unusual path as a medical reporter. On some level, this showed me that: 1) a career in television was within reach, and 2) there was no way to know where that career might take me.

When I left for the Dick Clark interview the next morning, I suggested a couple things my mother might want to do while I was gone—you know, as long as she was in town. We were staying at the Century City Plaza, so it would have been nothing for her to set out and explore Beverly Hills or Santa Monica. But she said she wouldn't be able to enjoy herself knowing I was in the middle of a big meeting with a Hollywood legend. Instead, she decided to accompany me on the morning of the interview, and I dropped her off at the Universal Sheraton, which was close to Dick Clark's office, where she waited for me until I was done.

I was gone for almost three hours, and when I got back, she was right where I'd left her.

I said, "Mom, what did you do with yourself all this time?"

She said, "I paced. I held my locket. I held my Jewish star. I waited for you and kept hoping things were going well."

That's something, huh?

That locket was something too. It had my picture in it—not a picture of me and my sisters . . . just *me*. My mother wore it on a chain with her cherished Jewish star. And it's not like I'd given her the locket and she felt she had to honor the gift by placing my picture inside. Nope. It was just some locket, and she found a picture of me and cut it up to make it fit and wore it for the rest of her life. (My sisters were probably in the original picture with me, and my mother cut them out to make it fit—kidding, Marylin and Sheryl! KIDDING!) I still have the locket. I keep it in my *tallis* bag along with my father's Masonic temple ring. Every time I take out my *tallis* and lay *tefillin*, I hear the jingle of my mother's necklace and my father's ring and I'm taken back to the important roles they played in my life when they were here—and the important roles they continue to play now that they are gone. I don't look at the locket or the ring every time I open the bag, but I can hear them in there. I can feel them. I know they're there. Over the years, they've become essential touchstones, connecting the child I was, at the heels of my two wonderful parents, to the person I have become.

———————

Because my father had some health issues as a relatively young man, Coach Mom orchestrated weekly treks to S. Smith & Son for me and my sisters. At first, our job was to keep my father company when he visited customers, back when he made house calls. She didn't want him driving at nine or ten o'clock at night without another set of eyes on him. He had an enlarged pituitary gland. He'd been in the hospital for a stretch, and the doctors were worried he could have a sudden loss of vision or a stroke, so my mother's solution was to have one of us drive with him. When it was my turn, I'd usually sit in the car and wait for him when he went inside to deliver a coat, but sometimes I'd go with him to the front door.

I cherished those times with my father. During the winter season, there were many nights when he would work until midnight. His work ethic was staggering, and it made an impression. It was no chore or drudgery to help him out. My father was a whole lot of fun. Nothing made him happier than delivering a new fur coat to an old customer, and nothing made me happier than the pride in his voice whenever he introduced me as his son.

By the time I was ten, my father's health improved, so instead of driving around with him after dinner, my sisters and I started going into the office with him on Saturdays. Very quickly, those Saturdays became the highlight of my week, a chance to see my father do his thing in his element. He'd get us up early—like, *really* early—because he opened up around eight. Marylin and Sheryl and I would be half asleep on the car ride into town. But Dad's chipper mood and excitement for the day would eventually rub off on us, and by the time we got there, we were full of his energy. Some mornings he'd burst into song while he was driving, just to coax a smile from us kids. On other mornings he'd entertain us with jokes or silly stories about our relatives. First thing he'd do each Saturday when we got to the office was order us breakfast. Then he'd get to work while the three of us pitched in as his assistants in whatever ways were appropriate to our age or patience or interests at the time. We'd answer the phone, take down my father's notes, visit with customers . . . whatever needed doing.

Saturdays were a special time at the office. During the week, it was a hustling, bustling, thriving scene, with bookkeepers, designers, assistants, and buyers coming in from various accounts. The factory floor was always busy with cutters, sewers, and tradespeople filling orders and completing my father's latest design ideas. On Saturday mornings, though, we had the place mostly to ourselves. The day was reserved for my father's private clients. No store reps, no retailers . . . just regular people who'd come to rely on my father's services over the years. He didn't advertise his work with private clients—his relationships with department stores and boutiques were essential to his business—but he liked dealing directly with his customers, so these Saturday hours were filled by word of mouth.

I loved watching my father interact with his customers. They loved him, which was great for me to see as a little kid, but as I got older, I began to appreciate how the feeling was mutual. He really cared about his regular customers. He used to tell me and my sisters that when people came to him for a fur coat, they were trusting him on a major purchase, and he wanted to earn that trust. He'd say, "When you're buying something like a diamond or a car, you really need to have faith in the person you're buying it from. What do most people know about the quality of a diamond? What do most people know about the quality of a fur coat? They know who they trust, that's all."

In the late '60s and early '70s, when I started going to work regularly with my father on those Saturday mornings, a custom coat could cost up to $10,000—a lot of money, then as now—but Dad never focused on the money. It was always about the look and fit of a coat, the quality and practicality, and the people who shopped with him knew there was no cutting corners—that's why they were there.

Every Saturday, we got to see a master class in people skills. My father had incredible charisma, but it came from an organic place. It's not like he could flip a switch and turn it on; he was *always* on. He was charming and warm. Sometimes people would wait for hours to see him for a fitting or a consultation because most of his private customers were walk-ins, but they didn't seem to mind the wait. If they did mind and became agitated, their demeanor would soften the moment my father was able to see them. He greeted them in English or in his perfect French, and he found a way to make each customer feel special—like they were worth the wait.

That was the magic of Saul Smith. My sisters and I used to say Dad put the *show* in showroom. He loved to make people laugh. He didn't care how much time he spent with each customer or that there were people waiting. He lived in each interaction. One of my jobs was to deal with the customers who were waiting to see him, and every so often I'd have to go to him and say, "Dad, you've got to get to the next person."

But there was no moving my father along. He did things in his own time.

At the office, my sisters and I were sometimes able to figure out who my father was talking to just by listening to his voice. My father was very good with languages, so whenever we heard him speak a little Chinese from the other room, we had a pretty good idea he was talking to Mr. Wong, who owned a Chinese restaurant in town. That one was always easy because he didn't have too many Chinese customers, but Montreal was an international city, so there were many languages spoken in the office, and when my father couldn't keep up, he switched to English and raised his voice. It was one of his foibles: whenever he was trying to make himself understood, he spoke louder.

After a while, one of us would say, "Dad, why are you yelling?"

He had this one customer whose eyebrows would dance up and down when she spoke—like something from a cartoon. And my father, being my father, would speak to her and make his eyebrows dance in the same animated way. I didn't know if he was doing this to make us laugh or amuse himself, or if he was subconsciously mirroring this woman's behavior. She never knew, of course, and my father would have been mortified if she ever figured it out, but he kept this up for years. We all called her the Eyebrow Lady—my father too—and whenever she came to the office, I'd have to run out as soon as my father got going because I didn't want to burst into laughter in front of her.

My father was a pathological joker. He made jokes about everything. He even made a joke after my mother died when the funeral director approached him to cut his tie in the ancient Jewish ritual that requires the mourner to rend their garments as an expression of grief. Of course, my father was a mess—he and my mother had been married for over sixty years—but you could see the joke alight in my father's eyes and he couldn't help himself.

"What are you doing?" my father said. "It's a new tie."

To the end of his life, my father was telling jokes. He was in his nineties, firing off jokes I'd never heard before.

I'd laugh and say, "I can't believe I've never heard that one."

And then he'd laugh and say, "I can't believe I've never told you that one."

Within the family, my father's jokes were a constant—as natural as breathing. Sometimes he'd use humor to make a point while keeping us laughing, like the time my mother was on him about a shirt he'd worn a few times too many. She was the style maven in our house and always had something to say about our clothes. Most times my father didn't question her judgment and wore what she told him to wear. But one time he came home after a long day, and my mother started in on his shirt, which was not to her liking.

"What's wrong with this shirt?" he said.

"I really don't like it," my mother said. "You have shirts that are so much nicer."

"Okay. So I won't wear it again."

"That's fine, Saul. But you wore it today. How could you go out of the house with a shirt like that?"

"Fine. You don't like the shirt. I get it." Without skipping a beat, he tugged at one of the sleeves and, with one aggressive pull, ripped it cleanly at the seams. Then he grabbed the other sleeve and tore it off as well. Then he went back to his dinner like nothing had happened.

My sisters and I were laughing so hard we were in tears. My mother started laughing as well, while my father sat there in his sleeveless shirt, cutting his meat, deadpan.

It was like a sitcom in our house, but like in every good sitcom, there was a message, and the message that came through was that funny was a kissing cousin to kindness. My father was funny to the core, but with his customers, his sense of humor served a purpose. My father's constant joking created a lasting bond with his customers—an essential element in building a lasting business. He might have been in the fur-coat business, but he was also in the relationship business.

I grew up watching my father go out of his way to kill his customers with kindness and good cheer. I saw him being good to people in every interaction. Even when a store owner was struggling and couldn't pay his invoices on time, my father would smile and find a way to work things out. His thing, always, was to have a customer for life. It was never about this one coat or this one transaction.

I've applied this aspect of my father's personality to my own career. To this day, I tell my business-affairs people to treat their counterparts with grace. It's a constant battle because most lawyers are taught to "win" every deal. I had one lawyer who wanted me to squeeze every last dollar out of every last deal, especially if he thought I had some kind of leverage—or, at least, if there was the perception I had some kind of leverage.

"Arthur, there's money left on the table," he'd say.

And I'd say, "Close the deal."

"You have more leverage; you can get more."

"I know. Close the deal. I'll sell them another show tomorrow."

At this point the lawyer might get excited about a new project I've yet to share with him, and he'd ask, "What show?"

"I don't know," I'd say. "There's always another show."

This is true. It's never about this one show or this one coat. It's always about the *next* coat you'll make for someone—and the one after that and the one after that. It's about your reputation and building lasting relationships.

I got all of that from Dad.

2
READY FOR MY CLOSE-UP

I was a shy kid, but sports helped me break out of my shell. And it wasn't just hockey. I also played baseball, football, basketball, tennis—you name it.

The confidence I got from sports helped me to find my way at summer camp—an annual rite of passage I dreaded at first but came to cherish. I decided to audition for the camp play. Maybe my weird and endless fascination with television was a part of it. I wasn't what you'd call a ham as a little kid, not even in my own family. Still, I must have picked up something from all that time listening to my father's jokes and watching him entertain his customers. I also loved the spirit of competition, and since I had to try out for a part in the play, acting was just another way to see if I had what it took to stand out. It turned out I did—or, at least, I had enough to land a role.

My debut as Kenickie in *Grease* was like a firestarter. I came out of the experience thinking I would turn performing into a full-time gig. Oh, I wasn't so confident or full of myself to think I could launch myself as an actor from the Pine Valley camp stage, but I did catch myself fantasizing more and more about pursuing a career in the entertainment business. I never said anything to anybody; even I could tell it was a crazy idea. Other than my mom's cousin Art, we didn't know anybody who worked in television, and I wasn't about to follow in his footsteps and go to medical school just for the chance to be a health-and-science reporter. But my antennae were up.

I continued to audition for plays and watch a ton of television. When I was older, I began looking to make money on the back of my interest. At sixteen, I started a mobile DJ company with my friends Arnold Fox and Ian Gorski. We called ourselves Cosmic Sound, but in retrospect I don't think we were all that otherworldly—we played just three parties before we disbanded.

That same year I enrolled in the National Institute of Broadcasting— one of the great (or, I should say, not-so-great) scams of the broadcasting industry. At the time the National Institute of Broadcasting ran ads in the back pages of magazines and comic books, promising susceptible young people like myself a career in the world of radio and television. For the low, low price of $1,000, they'd send you a series of cassettes teaching you how to be an announcer from the comfort of your home. Before they'd send you the tapes, you had to submit a recording of yourself doing a mock broadcast—you know, so the powers that be at the "institute" could determine if you had what it took to make it in the business. I was thrilled when I passed the test and way too naive to think that everyone who sent in their money had what it took.

I was on a mission, and I conscientiously completed my assignments and mailed in the recordings of me reading the news, reading commercials, narrating scenes. Each assignment was graded and critiqued, and at the end of the course, we received a diploma, proof that we were good and ready for a career in broadcasting. (I still have mine!)

It was a lot of money, to be sure, but I was determined to do *something* to put me on a path to my future and saw this as my ticket into the entertainment business. I didn't ask my parents to pay for it because I had it covered. I'd saved enough from my job as a tennis instructor at the YMHA and from delivering newspapers and working for my dad. Also, I didn't want them to know about it at first. Once I got good feedback from the faculty and was proud of how I sounded, I played them one of my tapes. They didn't know what to make of it at first, but then my mother gushed that I sounded "very nice," and my father said

I sounded "very professional." They started asking questions, and when it came out that I'd spent $1,000 to enroll in this program, they were livid. There was yelling and crying.

(Just to be clear, they did the yelling and I did the crying.)

They were right to be upset with me, of course, and in the end they would turn out to be the most supportive people on the planet as I set off on my actual career, but at the time I felt like I'd let them down—probably because they told me so, over and over.

It looked like the end of the world to me then, but it wasn't. I continued to act in camp plays—and soon school plays—very often in the lead role, and the silver lining to the dressing down I received from my parents was that it opened up a dialogue with them about what I wanted to do with my life. Forget for the moment that they thought what I wanted to do with my life was stupid and believed I'd eventually come to my senses and go to law school. They understood where I was coming from, even if they had no idea where the hell I was headed.

My sister Sheryl had been down a similar road with my parents a couple years earlier. She was in every camp play, every school play— she was a phenomenal performer. She was Dolly in *Hello, Dolly!*, the Wicked Witch of the West in *The Wizard of Oz* . . . always the lead or in a prominent, showstopping role. She always killed. She was so talented, in fact, that she was accepted to the Banff School of Fine Arts, which was a very, very big deal. However, somehow, my parents managed to convince Sheryl that an acting life was too uncertain and that she should study something more substantial. They sweetened the deal with a new car, and Sheryl took the car instead of holding out to see what was behind Door Number Three. I was too young to pay close attention to the family conversation, and yet it registered for me that we were meant to pursue a more "serious" course of study. Acting was fine as a hobby, just as sports were fine as a hobby, but college was for learning a profession and setting us up for a predictable career—a career within reach.

I'm happy to report that it all worked out for Sheryl. She earned her Ph.D. and now helps to lead the education department at McGill University, and one of the reasons she's such a good professor is because she's so entertaining. She puts on a show when she teaches, and it helps her to stand out. I guess you could say her acting experience paid off as she's found a way to call on those skills in her career. Nevertheless, the way my parents talked her down from her hopes and dreams made an impression on me.

High school in Quebec ended after eleventh grade. The expected progression after high school was to go to CEGEP—from the French term *Collège d'enseignement général et professionnel*, although nobody ever called it that—a publicly funded postsecondary program intended to prepare us young Quebecois for college. I ended up going to Vanier College for my two years of CEGEP, which turned out to be a fortuitous choice.

For one thing, it was about ten minutes from home. For another, it had a working campus radio station, CSNO, where I quickly got a gig as a disc jockey and eventually became the program director. (Thanks, National Institute of Broadcasting!) And for still another thing, the students put on a sketch comedy review that year called *Vanier Live*, and I acted, sang, and performed a monologue to open the show, reaching in ways I never could have imagined just a few years earlier.

In almost every respect, I came into my own during my two years at Vanier. I'd long since come out of my shell, thanks to sports and camp plays, but here I had a whole new outlet for my interests. My work at the radio station and on the comedy review got me more focused on the path ahead than anything I learned in the classroom, even though I managed to make the dean's list each year, and I started to look ahead to where I might go to college and what I might study.

I was still intent on working in entertainment, so I focused on schools with strong film, radio, and television arts programs. When I shared this focus with my parents, they were relieved that I wasn't majoring in theater and appreciated that I was out to learn as much as I could about the media business while maintaining my interest in performing as a kind of sideline. Looking back, I suspect they might have been indulging me, because they knew I could study entertainment as an undergraduate and still find my way to law school, which my mother believed was my destiny, owing primarily to what she always referred to as my "amazing persuasive skills."

My parents really wanted me to consider Concordia or McGill, which were both in Montreal, but I wanted to go to Ryerson, which at the time was known as Ryerson Polytechnic Institute. Ryerson had a program in radio and television arts (RTA) that was by far the best program in the country for students looking to pursue a career in broadcasting or entertainment. They had state-of-the-art facilities and an all-star lineup of professors who were accomplished working professionals across the entertainment industry. McGill had more of a world-class reputation, but its TV and Film Studies programs were theoretical, not at all hands-on. Concordia had a better program than McGill, but Ryerson was the leader. However, the RTA program was super competitive: there were thousands of applicants for just 135 spots. Before I could get in, I'd have to be invited for an on-campus interview, so I told myself that as long as I could get my foot in the door, I'd find a way to be invited all the way inside.

As my second and final year at Vanier was winding down, I'd gotten an early acceptance at McGill, but I was holding out for Ryerson. The only thing I didn't love about the school was its location: Toronto. Despite my blossoming self-confidence and willingness to push myself in a public way, I knew being away from home would be a tough adjustment.

Meanwhile, I made plans for what I thought would be my last summer in Montreal. I still hadn't heard from Ryerson, but I was hopeful—tentative, but hopeful. I needed to earn extra money for college, so I made plans with my father to work for him full time once school let out—a natural outgrowth of all those Saturdays my sisters and I had spent with him at the office. Over the years I'd been given greater responsibilities around my father's office. Though I couldn't design a coat to save my life, he told me I was a natural, especially with people.

Now, my father wasn't prone to serious talks—he was more comfortable cracking jokes or breaking into song for no apparent reason—so when he sat me down one night after dinner and I saw the serious expression on his face, I became concerned.

"Son," he said, "I know you have your heart set on going into television and film, but there is something you need to know before you start college."

I panicked, thinking maybe my father was sick once again with those pituitary gland issues that had plagued him when I was little and would need me to help out at the office. I told myself I would be there for him in whatever ways he needed. But that wasn't it. Instead, he told me how important my education had always been to him and my mother, how proud they both were that I'd done so well in school, how much they were looking forward to me receiving the very best university education.

Then he said that when I was done with college, he wanted me to become a partner in his business. "On day one, we'll be fifty-fifty partners," he said. "Someday, it will be all yours."

I was stunned—and stumped. Whatever I was expecting to hear, I wasn't expecting . . . *this*. I was only eighteen years old. It was my turn to be on the receiving end of the same talk my father had received from *his* father after the war. The last thing I wanted to do was tie myself to a career before I'd even had a chance to figure out what I was meant to do, but I also couldn't bear to disappoint my father. He looked at me with tears in his eyes, waiting for my answer, and at first I couldn't think what to say.

Finally, with tears in *my* eyes, I said, "Dad, you and Mom are the most amazing parents. I love you both so much. But I genuinely feel a calling that this is something I have to try."

This was the mother of all my reach moments. (The *father* of all reach moments?) Why? Because what I was reaching for was so vague, so amorphous, and in reaching for it, I was pushing away from a path that would have meant so much to my parents. I was betting on myself instead of playing it safe and going into my father's business. It felt like I was rejecting the love and safe harbor of a predictable life in Montreal with my close-knit family in favor of a lonely, uncertain life far from home.

And yet I swallowed hard and *reached*.

My father wiped away his tears and tried to smile. He took a deep breath and said, "I thought that's what you might say, but I had to ask."

"I'm sorry, Dad." And I really, really was.

"What, sorry?" he said. "You have nothing to be sorry about. I understand, and you have my full support."

In that moment, I could not have loved him more.

Then he found his smile and said, "And if this entertainment thing doesn't work out, the door is always open."

A couple days later, I got a letter inviting me to interview for the RTA program, and a part of me thought that unexpected conversation with my father had been a kind of test—a trial by fire I'd somehow passed. But I was only halfway to my goal. I knew from everyone I'd spoken to about Ryerson that this interview was all-important. They would assess our inter-personal skills and our personalities alongside the recommendations and essays we'd provided with our application and transcript. In some ways it was like an audition—that's how I tried to think of it, forgetting for the moment that I always got nervous at my auditions.

My mother immediately declared she would come to the interview with me, and I welcomed the support. She didn't just accompany me on the flight to Toronto or the drive in the rental car from the airport to campus. No, she literally walked me up to the door of the interview. And get this: when we were sitting in the waiting area in the admissions office, one of the prospective students struck up a conversation with my mother and asked her what she was thinking of studying at Ryerson. He wasn't being ironic: he honestly thought she was an older student apply-ing to the school—that's how unusual it was to bring your mommy to an admissions interview.

The interview went well enough that an offer of admission came in the mail a few weeks later. I was overjoyed. School wasn't due to start for another five months, so I was determined to make the most out of the summer ahead and to enjoy the time working with my father, living at home, and hanging out with my high school buddies. But then some-thing happened to derail these wistful, last-hurrah-type plans. I saw a notice in the newspaper about a film being shot in Montreal. This alone wasn't uncommon. There'd been an influx of film and television shoots in Canada, owing to a variety of factors: the value of the Canadian dollar, access to quality crews, the ability of certain urban areas to pass as American cities, and generous tax breaks being offered to American studios as an incentive to move their productions to Canada.

What made the notice stand out was the casting call that went with it. The producers were looking for extras for a teen-themed movie between the ages of eighteen and twenty-five, so I immediately thought the notice was meant for me. That calling I'd mentioned to my father when I turned down his offer to join him in business—I could feel in my bones that this casting notice was connected to it in some way. So I asked my father for the day off so I could head downtown for the open auditions.

I made sure to arrive a half hour early, but when I got there, I was discouraged to see hundreds of people already in line. It was an unseasonably warm day, and the thought of standing in line and baking in the sun was not pleasant, but there was no way I was leaving. After I'd stood there a good long while, I noticed a couple official-seeming people walking up and down the line with clipboards, talking conspiratorially to each other, and making notes as they looked out across this sea of hopeful, sweaty faces. One of them approached and asked me to follow, so I did.

It's amazing to me now that I didn't question these people or ask where they were taking me. I mean, anyone could walk through a crowd of people with a clipboard and pretend to be in a position of authority, right? Weirdly, they didn't say a word to me as we made our way through the crowd into a nearby building. When we finally reached a small room inside a maze of offices, one of them turned to me and asked if I'd like to read for a part.

It was just about the last thing I was expecting to hear. "But you pulled me from the extras line. There must be some mistake."

The great lesson here? Never question a person with a clipboard who seems determined to offer you an unexpected opportunity.

"There's no mistake," they told me. "You have the look we want for a certain role."

"And what look is that?"

"A John Travolta type. Like in *Saturday Night Fever*."

I thought, *Hmm . . . I can see that.* I was handed a script and told I'd have a minute to look it over. By *a minute* they meant just that: one minute.

The movie was a light teen comedy called *Pinball Summer*. I was reading for the part of "John T." The character's name alone should have told me something about the freshness and originality of the script. Of course, it would have helped if I'd been able to bring some freshness and originality to my reading, but about the best I could do was pronounce each word correctly.

The audition took five minutes, and I was sure my performance had been underwhelming, although someone with a clipboard did ask for my phone number. On the way out, I resisted the impulse to ask if I could reclaim my spot in the extras line. I realized this would make it seem like I wasn't fully committed to the role of John T., despite the fact that my reading might have just suggested the same.

The next day, I got a phone call from the casting director inviting me to screen test for the part, with instructions to come dressed as a John Travolta wannabe. This was a reach and a stretch and a pipe dream, all rolled into one moment. I'd never been in a movie, never auditioned for a movie—and yet here was this opportunity right in front of me.

I sprang into action. I immediately called all my friends to see if anybody had a white suit I could borrow. (Someone did—hey, this was 1979, the height of the disco era!) I had a black shirt, and I borrowed a pair of slick black shoes from my father to complete the outfit.

When I got to the screen test, I was surprised to see four guys about my age dressed the same way. When it was my turn, I did my best Travolta impression. I walked like him, talked like him . . . and eventually, even tried to dance like him. Nobody really said anything, and I left thinking I'd made a complete fool of myself.

After a couple weeks of trying to forget my nothing-special audition, I got a call from the casting director offering me the part. The shoot (my end of it, anyway) was scheduled to last less than two weeks, and they would pay me more money than I was due to make working with my father for the entire summer. I thought that was cool. Also cool: one of my big scenes was shot at a Montreal club called Oz, where I hung out a lot with my friends. I knew everyone there, so I got to strut my stuff in front of all my people and really play the part of being a movie star—forget for the moment that I was no such thing. It got me thinking that I should maybe take this acting thing more seriously. I decided that once I got to Toronto, I'd try to get an agent and start going out for more parts.

Turned out I didn't have to wait. The casting director from *Pinball Summer* recommended me for another movie that was scheduled to begin shooting in Montreal later that summer. This one was another teen movie—about a misfit motorcycle gang that torments a bunch of high school kids. The movie was called *Hog Wild*, and they wanted me for the part of one of the bikers—one of the leads. I thought, *Could this really be happening?* All I had to do was meet with the director, Les Rose, and manage to not make a fool of myself, so of course I very nearly did just that.

The character they wanted me to play was called Shadow, a Fonzie-like juvenile delinquent—gruff on the outside with a heart of gold on the inside. I spent some time thinking about the character and all the different ways I could approach this meeting. The casting director told me very specifically that this wasn't an audition, but I knew on some level that's exactly what it was. No, I wouldn't be reading from the script, but I would be auditioning just the same, so I decided to go to the director's office *as* Shadow. Arthur Smith would not be taking that meeting. I would go in character.

I put together an outfit with my leather jacket and tight jeans and walked into that meeting with swagger. Then I sat down and put my feet on the director's desk. I knew I was taking a big risk, perhaps even overplaying my hand.

There was a long, awkward pause, and I thought I was about to be shown the door. Then Les Rose started to laugh. *Okay,* I thought. *So far, so good.* We talked for about an hour, and the whole time I stayed in character. I had no idea if it was going well, but I was in too deep to double back and be myself. I would ride or die as Shadow.

At the end of the meeting, Les Rose asked for my phone number, which I took as a good sign. He also asked if I'd ever ridden a motorcycle before—a reasonable question and one I should have anticipated. Still, I hesitated. I knew that if I was honest, it might cost me the gig because even if I had the right look and attitude for the part, that look and attitude would start to appear pretty damn foolish if I couldn't ride a motorcycle. I also knew that if I passed myself off as an experienced rider, I'd eventually show up on set and look pretty damn foolish for a whole other reason. Either way I was screwed.

So I said, "Of course," shook the director's hand, and thought, *What could possibly go wrong?*

With time and perspective I can't help but see this summer before college as one giant *reach*—that emotional conversation with my father when he told me he wanted me to join him in business, putting everything I had into gaining admission to my dream school, my almost impulsive decision to land a spot as an extra in a movie that led to so much more. Each experience was a clear reminder that if you don't try, you can't expect to succeed. You can't win the lottery unless you buy a ticket!

3

SCHOOL DAYS AND THEN SOME

Some white lies come back to bite you in the ass, while others knock you on your ass a time or two—literally, as I discovered.

Most of us have stretched the truth to get and keep ahead. I'm not advocating here that you pad your résumé and do or say whatever it takes to impress in a job interview or a pitch meeting, but it's human nature to want to put your best foot forward, even if that *foot* hasn't really earned the step. The problem with this strategy is that the truth can break if you stretch it too far.

That's what happened as I left my interview with the *Hog Wild* director. When the casting director called to officially offer me the part, I had to come clean and admit I'd never been on a motorcycle in my life.

"Shit," I heard through the phone—then silence. For the longest time, there was nothing to say. I was ashamed and certain I'd just cost myself the gig. Finally, the casting director said she would have to call me back and hung up the phone.

A few hours later, the casting director called again to say the director really liked me and wanted to send me to motorcycle school to see if we could make this work. I was thrilled . . . and terrified. I wasn't scared about riding a motorcycle. No, I was scared of failing. I'd already been caught in a lie and given a second chance, and now I was facing the very real prospect of falling short on the merits—or the lack thereof.

We were about a week and a half away from filming, so there wasn't a lot of time for me to earn my chops. Motorcycle school was a full-day affair, from eight in the morning until five in the afternoon. They put me on a Honda 125 to start, and I was able to handle the small bike well enough after just a couple hours. I remember thinking, *I've got this, no problem.* And yet the script called for me ride in a pack, in tandem with the other members of the motorcycle gang, which meant I'd have to ride well enough for camera close-ups.

So after two days of training, they sent me to work with a stunt coordinator. They flew the guy in from Hollywood, and we met at a place they called the stunt ranch, about an hour outside of Montreal. He immediately put me on a Harley-Davidson 1200 with the handlebars up by my ears. If you stood back and squinted, you would have thought I was a total badass. You would have thought wrong. The small bike had been one thing; this bigger bike was something else. It was like going from riding a bicycle to driving a truck. (Also, it was loud . . . *very* loud.) Almost every time I leaned into a sharp turn, I wiped out, and the stunt coordinator would come running, no doubt more worried about the bike than the faux Fonzie dude struggling to ride it.

I was scraped and bruised and humbled.

The next day I got a call from the casting director telling me it wasn't working out. It was a call I should have been expecting, but I was young and arrogant enough to think the world owed me the chance to play this part. Of course, the world owed me no such thing. The casting director said the stunt coordinator had threatened to quit the movie if he had to continue working with me—not because he was frustrated working with a total newbie, but because he was responsible for the safety of the entire production. And so, since I was replaceable and this hotshot Hollywood stunt guy was not, it was the end of the road for me.

I was devastated, crushed. True, I was nearly crushed a bunch of times by that Harley, but it felt to me like I was getting the hang of it.

The silver lining to this *Hog Wild* debacle was that the director liked me enough to offer me a consolation part in the movie, but I didn't grab at it. This surprised the hell out of the casting folks because it was a decent part. Frankly, I surprised the hell out of myself as well, especially with how quickly I stiff-armed the offer. My reasoning? The shooting schedule for this lesser role ran through September, and I was due to start at Ryerson in September. I took it as a sign that this opportunity wasn't meant to be.

In the end, I got a part as a "special business" extra and managed to earn a couple thousand dollars for a few days' work, bringing me full circle to where I was when I started out on this wild adventure that began with that *Pinball Summer* casting call. Obviously, I hated that I'd lost out on one of the lead roles, but the lesson here was that even a disappointment can sometimes land you in the plus column.

Another lesson: it's okay to talk a big game only if you, in fact, have *some* game.

Most significantly, though, this experience taught me that you can reach as much as you want, but at the same time you have to make room for fate. There's a Yiddish phrase that gets close to this concept: *beshert*, which essentially refers to something that is meant to be. Sometimes the universe has a different plan for you than the one you imagine for yourself. Here it worked out that I was able to start school with the rest of my incoming class before this whole teen heartthrob thing had a chance to go to my head. Oh, I wasn't ready to give up on my acting dream just yet, but if it was going to happen for me, it would have to happen on a different timetable. The gift that came with this one dispiriting firing was the chance to remind myself that my education had to be my priority and that there was something *else* coming my way. What that *else* was, I didn't know just yet, but I believed it was out there.

———

I moved to Toronto in September 1979 and focused on finding new ways of extending myself. My wild summer in and around the movie business taught me that when you put yourself out there, good things can happen. The more you try, the luckier you get, so I put myself out there and set off in search of my next piece of luck. I had no idea what form it would take, but I was ready to meet it.

The Ryerson campus was in the heart of downtown Toronto. The first-year students in the RTA program were all there because of our record of high achievement. It was motivating to be surrounded by so many like-minded souls—driven and determined to succeed, just like me. Soon I was deep into it: writing commercials and newscasts, studying the art of announcing, editing film, learning about the business of media and the technical side as well. I even put myself up to be the first-year rep for the RTA Department Council, our version of a student council, and I was honored to get elected. I also tried out for the campus radio station, CKLN—one of the best college radio stations on the planet. It was a professionally run operation, and no freshman had ever earned a regular shift at the station, but I made a push and a pitch and got on the air. (Thanks again, National Institute of Broadcasting!)

With every reach, there was a new opportunity.

One highlight from my radio days was organizing a fifty-hour fund-raising marathon to benefit the Bloorview Children's Hospital. I had this idea that I should try to make a difference with whatever tools I had available to me. I was able to convince the powers that be at CKLN to donate their airwaves to the cause, and I settled in to run my mouth for as long as I could. I corralled some of my friends and some of the other jocks to pop in from time to time, and the pledges rolled in around the clock. About thirty-nine hours into my fifty-hour fundraiser, in the middle of the night, I got a call on the air from a familiar voice—my father, calling from Montreal to pledge one hundred dollars and to thank me for what I was doing.

Another highlight was landing a gig as the color commentator for the Dixie Beehives, a Junior A hockey team that played their home games in Mississauga, about forty-five minutes outside Toronto. I went in on this with my friend Cap Scully, a third-year Ryerson student with a name that left him no choice but to become an announcer. Together we became the voices of *Junior Hockey on Channel 10*, featured on a community channel available across Toronto. Looking back, I have to think Cap pretty much carried me on this gig. He was terrific. I was okay—determined to get better, but just okay.

One of the great benefits to the RTA program was the chance to work with local news organizations on student-run projects. Through my efforts as a director of a documentary series called *Open Portfolio*, produced by the all-news radio station CKO and distributed nationally, I began to think my career path might take me behind the scenes to work as a producer or director. That didn't mean I stopped polishing my broadcasting pipes or working on my delivery, and it certainly didn't mean I was through as an actor.

In fact, that first year in Toronto, I managed to land an agent—a woman named Sandy Newton, who specialized in working with young actors. There was a ton of production going on in and around the city, so it made sense to see what was out there. Sandy sent me out on a bunch of auditions—for beers, computers, and Wrangler jeans—but the first gig I actually booked was for the guest-starring role on a CBC Network sitcom called *Hangin' In*, run by a veteran American sitcom producer named Jack Humphrey. Just like I'd somehow landed *Pinball Summer* in my first film audition, I managed to fool the producers and win the part in my first television show audition.

I don't mean to suggest that this acting thing was all too easy, but these parts seemed to find me when I needed them most. I hated the idea of asking my parents for money, and while my earnings from *Pinball Summer* and *Hog Wild* were enough to pay for my living expenses my freshman year, my funds were now running low, so this guest spot came along at an opportune time. That's how it seemed to work for me on the acting front. A gig would up and happen just when I needed it most, perhaps because in those low-on-cash moments, I was hungry enough to reach just a little bit further . . . to want it just a little bit more.

My mother was the first person I called when I got the part. She was always my first call because she lived for the chance to celebrate the successes of her children. Without my mother's constant and enthusiastic cheerleading, I don't think I would have developed the confidence to make it in the media business. Her belief in me became my belief in myself, and here it was on full display. When the episode aired and my name was listed in the *Montreal Gazette* "TV Times" supplement

I used to read religiously as a kid (and in the "real" *TV Guide* as well!), she was beyond excited.

I've got to be honest here: I think it went to my head a little bit, as these acting jobs seemed to fall so easily into place. Every so often, one of these sitcom gigs would materialize, and I'd reach out to my professors and let them know what was going on, and it was never a problem to juggle my schedule for the shoot. The school was pretty accommodating. After all, they were preparing us for careers in the entertainment industry, and there was nothing like hands-on experience. But at the same time, I made sure to do the work and complete all of my assignments in a timely manner. As for my fellow students . . . well, I sometimes got the feeling that they were jealous of my successes off campus, so I learned to keep my excitement to myself and understood that any slings and arrows and begrudging stares came with the territory. When you put yourself out there and find success, especially *early* success, you're bound to catch some crap from those still on the sidelines.

That part on *Hangin' In* led to a guest spot on another Jack Humphrey sitcom called *Flappers*. When I called home to share the news, I heard a different tone in my mother's voice.

My mother was super excited I was going to be on television again, super proud of me for making these good things happen. Then in the next moment, she became somber and said, "There's more for you, Arthur."

I thought she meant I wasn't doing enough with the gifts I'd been given. "Mom," I said, "this is not enough?"

She hadn't meant to bring me down, of course, so she doubled back and tried to explain herself. "It's not that, Arthur. I just see more for you. I see you headed for even greater things."

As I leaned into my college years, my ritual nightly calls with my mother became more important than ever. My mother was a big believer in me, but she had this way of complimenting me while bringing me down to size. She reminded me that these fleeting successes in film and television were just that: *fleeting*. If I got to where I was counting on them for my future, I could eventually be disappointed. She was able to ground me, to put it out there that it was one thing to set goals and have ambitions, but it was another thing entirely to do these things with grace and intention. Throughout my career, long after I'd left Ryerson and gone on to bigger and better things, Mom would celebrate with me whenever I got a new job or won some industry honor. But she'd always say, "There's more for you." I came to understand she meant it in a good way, in a motivating way.

My mother was right to get me thinking in this way, of course. (She was *always* right!) And so despite my relatively easy successes as an actor, I somehow knew my future would take me behind the camera, and my mother had a hand in shaping that view. It was not so much that she didn't want me to be an actor but that she wanted me to keep reaching across the entertainment industry; she was convinced that my leadership abilities would lead me down a different path.

As it happened, my acting career helped me find that different path—in a sidelong way. During my time on the *Flappers* and *Hangin' In* sets, I spent most of my downtime in the control room with the director, Alan Erlich. I was fascinated by what went on behind the scenes—perhaps because of all the ways it bumped into what I was studying in school—and I found myself running from the sound stage to the control room whenever I was through with my scenes and soaking up what I could at Alan's side.

I got a great education in the control room, but little did I know that all that time in front of the camera as an actor would help me in my work as a producer working with talent—a lesson in taking advantage of every opportunity that presents itself.

—————————

My second year at Ryerson was more hands-on in terms of being allowed to work with all of the television equipment and becoming familiar with the editing room, and the more I worked behind the scenes, the more I believed that this was where I belonged. I really enjoyed producing, writing, directing . . . *developing* ideas for shows we could produce on our nothing budget with the student talent on campus and the equipment on hand.

My days were full and busy and rich with possibilities, but I was determined to grow my game in every possible way, so I started looking for freelance work in the broadcasting field. I was almost always able to hustle or sweet-talk my way into a meeting with someone in a position to hire me, but as soon as that person found out I was a full-time student, I was shown the door. The one exception to this was an executive producer at CBC Radio, Danny Finkleman, who was in charge of a national show called *Variety Tonight*. The guy liked me well enough, so he told me to listen to the show and become familiar with the kinds of stories they did on quirky individuals or trends and to pitch him a couple ideas.

"Find me a story," he said. "If I like it, I'll give you an assignment."

It's likely he thought he'd never see me again, but I was back within a week to pitch him a bunch of stories. He shot them all down. This happened a couple times, but I finally hit pay dirt with an idea for a feature about a sword-swallower in Toronto who could swallow a bunch of swords at a time—an underground novelty act that didn't exactly play on the radio, but I sold the hell out of that story and got the assignment. And then I had to figure out a way to tell a visual story without any visuals, so I came up with this idea of putting a microphone on one of the swords and capturing the sound of the guy's heartbeat from the inside. I had no idea if such a thing was even possible, but I pitched it to the tech guy who was assigned to work with me on the piece, and he thought it could work.

Variety Tonight had a host who conducted all the interviews, so I put together a background piece. Then I did a preinterview with the guest and prepared a bunch of questions for the host. The segment went well enough—but the kicker was the host's stunned reaction to the heartbeat. It would have made a better television segment than a radio segment, but our take was different and creative and *out there*, and the executive producer was pleased enough with my work and my ability to think outside the box that he threw me another few assignments here and there. The money was nothing compared to my occasional acting gigs, but it was good to be working in this professional capacity, to be able to call myself a segment producer on a national radio program. Of course, I don't know that anyone else was calling me a segment producer on a national radio program, but that's what I was, and in this small, incremental way, I was moving the needle on my broadcasting career.

Heading into my last year at Ryerson, I knew there may not be another time in my life when I didn't have the responsibilities of a full-time job, and I wasn't ready to give up on my acting career just yet. So I auditioned for a part in a summer-stock production of Ira Levin's play *Deathtrap*, which was being staged in the Laurentian Mountains about an hour north of Montreal. I don't know what persuaded me to think I was qualified to land a part in a professional play. My acting résumé to this point included a few small parts in movies, a television commercial for the Canada's Wonderland theme park, and guest spots in television shows, but my live-theater experience was limited to camp and school productions. I had no business being on stage with *real* theater actors.

But I didn't let that stop me. It turned out to be one of the most demanding and most rewarding experiences of my life, despite what felt like one of the worst auditions in the history of the theater. I was used to doing television and commercial auditions, where the dialogue was natural, conversational. The scenes were short and sweet. The part I was reading for in *Deathtrap* was one of the leads—a student playwright who writes a play that becomes the envy of his teacher. My character's monologues were particularly long and dense, and I struggled with the material. Shockingly, I got the part, reminding me that I still had a lot to learn and that I wasn't always the best judge of my own performance or abilities.

I had a leading role, and with only five of us in the play, there was no place for me to hide. We rehearsed for a month—ten hours a day, six days a week. It was a totally immersive experience, almost like a boot camp. I was clearly the rookie among this group of professionals, but they made me feel like I belonged. My fellow actors said they were impressed with my television and movie credits, but I was truly in awe of their abilities on stage. Their passion and dedication to the craft was like nothing I had ever seen. The director was a professor from the Banff School of Fine Arts, a real pro, and I learned more about acting from him than I'd learned in all of my other parts combined. I also developed a new appreciation for the craft of acting on stage and for the tremendously talented crew that supported our efforts behind the scenes.

For the run of the play, we lived in a row of cottages in the mountains, not far from the theater. It was a spectacular setting. We ended up doing thirty performances—another huge difference to how I was used to working. In my camp and school productions, we rehearsed for a couple weeks, leading up to a single performance or a group of performances over a single weekend. Here the work continued after opening night. We were constantly tweaking our performances or reimagining the staging, depending on what was or wasn't working. I learned the difference between a Saturday night audience and a matinee audience. I learned that theatergoers who came to see us on a Monday or Tuesday night were much more critical than those who drove up to the mountains on the weekend and decided to take in our show.

One of the great thrills for me that summer was having my family drive up from Montreal one weekend to see the show, and they couldn't have been more encouraging. Really, they were gushing about my performance, which of course I took with a grain of salt because they loved me. Still, it was nice to have this validation from the people who meant the most to me—and to my mother's great credit, she managed not to mix in one of her trademark "There's more for you" assessments along with her praise.

I count this summer run in *Deathtrap* as one of the hardest things I'd ever done, trying to keep pace on that stage and match those talented professionals with a performance that didn't undermine what they were doing. Looking back, I think I met the challenge. There was even a positive review of my performance from the *Montreal Gazette* theater critic, which helped to end my last major acting performance on a sweet note.

There would be other one-off roles here and there, and I even went on to do a substantial amount of voice-over and narration work on our own shows at A. Smith & Co., but after *Deathtrap* I set my acting ambitions aside. There was more for me.

Now all I had to do was find it.

4
FINDING MY WAY

My final year at Ryerson could not have ended soon enough.

I don't mean to suggest that I'd had enough of the school or that I no longer had any use for what my professors or fellow students had to teach me. Not at all. I absolutely loved Ryerson and look back on my time there as one of the most rewarding periods in my life, but I was anxious to get on with my career—like a racehorse penned in at the starting gate, eager to be set loose on the world of broadcasting.

By March 1982, just a few months before graduation, it felt like everyone else had their futures figured out. Some of my friends were headed off to law school or medical school or business school. Some were returning home to work in the family business, and others had landed entry-level dream jobs in their fields. A few of my friends in the RTA program had signed on to become interns or assistants in radio or television. I wasn't there just yet.

In fact, I was nowhere, and this was concerning for someone who was constantly reaching, constantly striving. Out in the real world, it seemed, my successes on campus didn't seem to amount to much. I'd won a bunch of school awards for my productions and announcing, as well as a scholarship, but those successes didn't translate into job opportunities. Another reason I didn't have a job just yet: I hadn't applied anywhere. So I started to focus on potential options.

I thought briefly about full-time acting, but that was no longer the best fit for me—creating and producing had become much more of a passion during my time at Ryerson. I also thought about looking across the border for work in the United States, but I didn't have a green card, and I kept coming back to the fact that Toronto was the epicenter of the entertainment industry in Canada, so I decided to take advantage of what was there.

I applied at CJCL, a sports radio station in town. I was a huge sports fan, I knew my way around a story and a control booth, and I'd excelled in my two college radio experiences. I actually landed an interview at the station and thought it went pretty well, but then I shifted in my thinking and set my sights on a job at CBC Sports. Television was more my thing, I realized. The most creative work I'd done as a student had come when I was telling stories in a visual way, so I scrambled for a way in.

A lot of career counselors might tell young people to flood the market with résumés and hope one lands in the right hands, but I don't buy it. I recommend a less-is-more approach. I tell students to identify one or two prospects and then put all of their efforts into opening doors there. In this way you force yourself to do your homework and be super vigilant and hyperattentive to any opportunities that present themselves. I also tell young people looking to get into broadcasting that once they get a foot in one of those open doors, they should avoid gushing and saying how desperately they want to work there. Don't say you'd be happy sweeping the floors or answering the phones or getting coffee unless you really would be happy doing those things. Think about what you *actually* want to be doing and find the most direct path from where you are to where you want to be.

The more I thought about it, the more I thought CBC Sports was the place for me. I'd been watching sports on television for as long as I could remember, and CBC covered everything. Growing up, I'd sometimes watch the American television networks, which were particularly good at covering big-time sporting events like the Super Bowl and the World Series, but CBC was the home for numerous major events, including the Olympics and *Hockey Night in Canada*, which to a kid from

Montreal was pretty much like the Super Bowl, the World Series, and the Olympics all rolled into one.

I did my homework. I knew the network's sports offerings upside down and inside out. I knew the players, behind the scenes and in front of the camera. When I found out that an executive producer at CBC Sports happened to be a Ryerson graduate, I was all over it. His name was Jim Thompson, the man behind *CBC Sports Weekend*, which was kind of like our version of ABC's *Wide World of Sports*.

The network offices were around the block from the Ryerson campus, so one afternoon I went to his office and waited for him. I now realize how preposterous it was for me to park myself in the reception area outside this man's office and expect to be seen. When I finally saw Jim emerge from his office, I approached him with way more enthusiasm than the moment called for. I introduced myself and told him I was a student at Ryerson and started listing all the different awards and scholarships I'd won and all of the projects I'd worked on. I was talking a mile a minute, cramming in everything there was for Jim Thompson to know about me before he tired of the encounter.

When I stopped for a moment to catch my breath, he looked at me and said, "How long have you been out here waiting for me?"

I shrugged. "I don't know. A couple hours, I guess."

He smiled, perhaps a little reluctantly. "A couple hours, huh? Okay, I guess I can give you five minutes."

He ushered me into his office. Next thing I knew, those five minutes had turned into an hour and a half. We had a very engaging conversation about sports and sports television. I made it clear I knew my stuff, and Jim let me know how much he appreciated that I knew my stuff.

At some point, Jim looked at his watch. "I can't believe I've been talking to you for so long." He had a meeting to get to and suggested we wrap up. In closing, he asked me what I wanted out of this conversation.

I said I wanted to work at CBC Sports.

He said he figured as much but wanted to know what *specifically* I wanted to do at CBC Sports, keeping in mind that he didn't have a job of any kind to offer me at the moment.

"I want to be a producer."

He laughed, almost in a smug way. Jim was an interesting guy, I would find out. Very tough, but fair—a straight-shooter. "A producer, huh?" he said. "Let me tell you how it works." He walked me through the typical career progression at the network. He told me I might be able to get a job as an assistant in the newsroom at a local CBC station somewhere in Canada. If I excelled, I could maybe become a production assistant on the network news side. Once I'd established myself there, if I was lucky, I might be able to move into sports: tons of graduates coming out of schools like Ryerson wanted to work in sports and CBC had the best sports division in the country by far.

"Wow," I said. "Seems like a long road. How long does that take?"

"Fast track? Maybe five years, and that's to be a production assistant in network sports, not a producer."

"Five years! That's not going to work for me."

Jim laughed another smug laugh—only, I wasn't kidding. Once Jim realized I wasn't kidding, he said, "Look, you seem like a smart kid. I appreciate your passion, but that's how it works." He said that if any entry-level jobs opened up, he'd keep me in mind.

And that was that. I thanked Jim for his time, left him with my résumé, and walked back to campus, thinking that a CJCL radio job (perhaps with a side of acting) would be a quicker and far more certain path to meaningful work in sports broadcasting. I still had a couple months to figure out my next move.

About a week later, I drove home to Montreal for Passover. I stopped at my father's office on my way through town. While there, I called my answering machine in Toronto to check my messages and had one that was a bit of a surprise. I'd just greeted my dad after not seeing him for a couple months when I said, "I have to go back to Toronto."

"You just got here."

"I know, but I just got this crazy call about a meeting at CBC Sports."

Someone from the office of Dennis Harvey, the esteemed head of CBC Sports, had left a message that I should come in to meet with him the next morning at ten o'clock. I couldn't imagine why, but I knew from my prep work on Jim Thompson that Dennis was his boss.

My father knew how much I wanted to work at CBC Sports, but he knew my mother would be disappointed if I didn't stop by the house. "Just tell her what's going on," he said.

My mother was happy to see me, of course, and she was disappointed that it was only for a hug, but she understood. In fact, she put on her coaching hat and told me to go for it. "They've called you back for a reason," she said.

The five-hour drive on the 401 Freeway from Montreal to Toronto is one of the most boring stretches of road ever committed to asphalt. With nothing to distract me, my mind was racing. The whole way, I kept imagining myself at CBC Sports. All these years later, I don't even remember driving back to Toronto, except that I was obsessing over this one opportunity, which may or may not have been an opportunity at all. I mean, I'd never even spoken directly to anyone in Dennis Harvey's office—I'd just collected this message off my machine—so my thoughts were all over the place.

I got back to my crappy Toronto apartment on Parliament Street at about nine o'clock that night, and sat down at my typewriter. I wanted to gather my thoughts, and this seemed like the most appropriate way to do so. I began to bang out a bunch of ideas for the network—what I liked about its sports coverage, what I didn't like, what I thought they could do better. As I typed, I told myself I would not go into this meeting the next morning and simply *say* I had some ideas; I would actually *show* Dennis Harvey my ideas. Soon I was deep into a kind of white paper that I intended to share in the meeting the next morning. (Speaking of *white* paper, I used a whole lot of Wite-Out that night because I was such a lousy typist!)

I had no idea what I was doing, really, but I told myself that whatever happened at this meeting, I would be prepared. And I was . . . until the receptionist smiled kindly at me and said, "They're ready for you."

They? I'd thought from the message that this meeting was just with Dennis Harvey, which was stressful enough. As I went in, I was greeted by five or six middle-aged men. One of them introduced himself as Dennis Harvey, and I remembered Jim Thompson. I recognized Bob Moir, who'd gone from an on-air commentator to executive producer of the CBC's Montreal Olympics coverage in 1976. The others I didn't know, but it was clear that this was the heart and soul and brain trust of CBC Sports, all gathered in this one big conference room to meet little old me. Yet I wasn't intimidated or overwhelmed. Why? Because I'd spent all that time on the long drive from Montreal thinking about the current state of the CBC Sports division and all night writing my ideas for the network. I was well and fully prepared to meet this moment. At least I thought I was.

Once introductions were made, it became clear that this wasn't a job interview but rather a chance for this group to see what Jim Thompson had seen in our first meeting. Jim had been impressed, I later learned. He'd gone back and told his boss and his colleagues about this kid from Ryerson who didn't want to pay his dues or work his way up the ranks. They wanted to see if there was anything to see. I think I was more of a curiosity than anything else.

So there I was, twenty-two years old, still in college, facing a group of accomplished executives. I followed my mother's advice and just went for it. Dennis Harvey and his team peppered me with questions about my background, why I wanted to work there, and on and on. I don't remember any talk about a job these executives had in mind for me. It was more about them getting to know me, and me sharing my views. It never occurred to me that this was an unusual situation . . . it just *was*.

Midway through the meeting, I handed out my white paper, which ran six or seven pages. (Luckily, I'd made copies!) I'm sure these men had no idea what to make of me, but I was determined to make the most of this moment. Admittedly, this was a risk, but it was a risk worth taking. I wanted to demonstrate that I had good ideas, and if that meant coming across as brash or aggressive, I was willing to take that chance. When an opening appeared naturally in the conversation, I circulated my document, and if I were British, I would report that the CBC Sports brass was fairly *gobsmacked* by my presentation.

The meeting lasted two hours. I was sweating by the time it was through, but I don't remember feeling nervous or out of my element.

A week later I got a call from Dennis Harvey. "We've got no idea what to do with you," he said. "But give us some time. Maybe we can figure something out."

Another week or so passed, and I got a job offer from CJCL for $12,500—a typical starting salary for an entry-level, on-air, overnight broadcasting job in 1982, even if it looked like nothing next to what I'd made as an actor for just a couple weeks' work on a movie or television set. I was starting to think the unlikely interview with the CBC Sports brass wouldn't amount to much. I was weeks away from graduating, and it looked like I'd wind up at the radio station, which would have been fine.

Then, at the eleventh hour, Dennis Harvey called again to summon me to his office.

I went over to see him that very afternoon, and he put it to me plain. "We want you to work here."

"That's great," I said. "As what?"

He said he was not really sure but that I had made a favorable impression. He and his team had decided the sports division needed new blood, a fresh perspective. They wanted to bring me on as a kind of experiment, to see how they might make room in their hierarchy for aspiring young professionals like myself.

That all sounded too good to be true. "But what's the job?" I asked.

"You'll be a producer."

That was all I needed to hear. I didn't ask questions. I jumped at the offer, the terms of which would be spelled out in a one-year contract.

I immediately called my parents with the news. "I got a job at CBC Sports!"

"That's great," my father said. "Doing what?"

"I've got no idea. I think I'm a producer."

"That's great," my mother said. "What will you be producing?"

"I've got no idea."

"What will they pay you?" my father said.

"I've got no idea."

The CBC contract arrived in the run-up to graduation, while my parents and sisters were in town for the ceremony. I took it with me to their hotel room at the Four Seasons downtown to go over it with my father. The starting salary was $26,000—more than double the radio salary I'd turned down to accept this offer.

I started at CBC on June 14, 1982, the Monday after graduation. I remember walking to the office that first day feeling awkward and thrilled and scared shitless. I had my own office and a production assistant outside my door. You might have thought I was in over my head. I was! I worried that my youth and inexperience would count against me as I met my new colleagues. It was exponentially daunting because I hadn't gotten there in the usual ways. As I fumbled around the office that first day, a thought nagged me: *be careful what you wish for . . .*

It was rough in the beginning. First of all, I didn't know anything. I might have known enough to put my thoughts down on paper and talk intelligently as an outsider, but I had no idea about the inner workings of a network sports division. Plus, the other producers who were meant to be my peers couldn't help but resent me. I'd taken this extreme shortcut to the same job it had taken them years to land. Then there were the production assistants and associate producers, most of whom were in their late twenties and early thirties and still paying their dues. They were pissed at me because I'd somehow leapfrogged over them into a coveted position. I was made to feel at every turn like I didn't belong or like I was taking a spot that rightly belonged to someone else, which was certainly understandable. At lunchtime the producers would all get lunch together and the assistants would all get lunch together, and I'd be the only one left in the office, eating by myself.

I *got* it, but it still sucked.

I had a lot to learn—and a lot of work to do to earn the trust or respect of my peers. I'd been brought in as a kind of apprentice, albeit a fairly high-level apprentice. I hadn't even been in a CBC control room until I started working there, so I had to get from zero to sixty in no time flat.

Happily, I was a quick study. But this didn't help me gain acceptance among my fellow producers or the assistants who were a lot older than me. That would take time.

––––––––––––––

A couple weeks into my new job, I got word from on high that I was expected to produce my first segment. I thought, *Oh, shit, here we go*!

A Canadian high jumper named Milt Ottey was the top-ranked high jumper in the world at the time. Like some of our best track-and-field athletes, he'd been born in Jamaica and moved to Canada in childhood. He'd just taken first place at the Commonwealth Games in Brisbane, Australia, with a jump of 2.31 meters, and my bosses wanted me to do a profile of him to run on our *Sports Weekend* sports anthology show.

To me, this was a huge assignment. To everyone else at CBC, it was just another segment, so it's not like the future of the network hung on my ability to pull it off. There was nobody to help me in any kind of hands-on way. Either they were too busy with their own work or they wanted to see if I could figure it out. So I figured it out. I didn't know how to arrange for a crew or what assistants I could call on to help me with research or what kind of budget I had. Essentially, I was on my own, so I focused on the human side of the story and tried to get to the heart of who Milt Ottey was and what drove him as a competitor—an approach that would become a kind of signature move for me, running all the way through to the work we do now on *American Ninja Warrior* and *The Titan Games*.

Milt Ottey was relatively short for a high jumper, just five foot ten, so I made the leap that he must be an underdog. When I interviewed him for the piece, that's where I placed my focus. I wrote the questions myself, did the interview myself, and directed the shoot with a very talented director of photography I was lucky enough to find and press into service. Normally, the CBC producer would edit the package for air and write the script, and then one of the announcers would add the narration or commentary later on, so that was the model I worked with here. I picked the music to accompany the piece: Survivor's "Eye of the Tiger," from the *Rocky III* soundtrack—a song that has since become a cliché in these types of pieces but back then was relatively fresh.

I'd always loved the beautifully produced, emotion-packed sports features that had become a staple on American network television. The ABC Sports team was especially effective at this, which I'd noted in their Olympic coverage, and NBC and CBS did a great job as well. I didn't just watch this stuff; I paid good and close attention. Now, when it came time for me to craft one of these pieces on my own, I borrowed liberally from the techniques I admired and attached them to new ideas I'd been formulating on my own. In the end, I produced a rich, uplifting, personal piece on this compelling athlete.

It was a pivotal moment for me when the piece went to air. I was twenty-two years old, on the job just a few weeks, so to see my name on network television with a "produced by" credit was a head-spinning and validating experience. Of course, in the grand scheme of things at the network, it was just one eight-minute segment that didn't much matter, but I got some good feedback on it. People noticed. It didn't really change the mood of the room or get me invited out to lunch with my new colleagues, but I got word from Jim Thompson that he was impressed, and Dennis Harvey weighed in with a thumbs-up as well.

(Oh, and in the goes-without-saying department, my parents were thrilled!)

From there, I started doing a ton of pieces and even live events for *Sports Weekend*, producing World Cup skiing, world championship swimming, figure skating events, and on and on. I was into everything, but as soon as I established myself there and got a tiny bit comfortable, I was redeployed by Dennis Harvey and Bill Sheehan, the deputy head of CBC Sports, to the *Hockey Night in Canada* team. Their idea was to train me for a couple months to become a replay director, which I thought was pretty cool.

The *Hockey Night in Canada* unit operated somewhat removed from the rest of CBC Sports, so I had to prove myself all over again. I was foisted on a guy named Wayne Moss, who was tasked with training me. The plan was for me to shadow Wayne, a seasoned director, for a few months and be in the truck with him until I was able to do a game on my own.

It's like I'd died and gone to heaven. *Hockey Night in Canada* was it for me—the pinnacle of the pinnacle. All of a sudden, I was working with hockey icons like Don Cherry, the legendary commentator, and all of these former players who were working with the network as analysts, like Mickey Redmond, who'd won a couple Stanley Cups with my Canadiens, and Gary Dornhoefer, who'd recently won back-to-back Cups with the hated Flyers. I was out of my mind just being in the same room with these guys, and I tried not to let it bother me when they looked at me and said, "Who the hell is this kid?"

Nobody knew what to make of me or how I'd earned my way. All they knew was that I was Dennis Harvey's protégé and training with Wayne Moss, so for the most part, I was left alone to do my thing.

Wayne was a good and patient teacher and an incredibly nice guy. He took his time with me. At the time, there were at least two "mobile" trucks at the venue. One was the live remote truck, and there was a separate iso truck, which was where Wayne and I lived, holed up with three or four tape operators. *Iso* stands for the isolation cameras that captured the action from compelling angles and generated footage for the replay director.

In hockey, as in other sports, there are certain cameras that are meant to cover the run of play and others that are designated for replays. Of course, the live director can cut to any of these cameras at any time, but the job of the replay director, I learned from Wayne, was to communicate with the camera operators about what to focus on, the tape operators to get certain plays or angles ready for playback, and the director about what replays are worthy of integrating into the game.

Each of the tape machines was assigned a color, so you'd be able to tell the director in an instant that you had a goal from three different angles—say, a wide angle on blue, a tight shot on red, an overhead shot on green, and so on. If there's a controversial call or a penalty, a good replay director will be able to tell the live director almost immediately where to find the best replay of the play. You have to be quick, instinctive, and really have an acute awareness of the game and the key players on both teams.

I might have been new to the job, but I'd watched so much hockey on television that the rhythms of the game were ingrained in me. I knew instinctively that each whistle was followed by a fixed point of pause, and that during that brief stoppage in play, there'd be a familiar pattern to the broadcast. After a goal, for example, there's the celebration, then a cut to the wide-angle replay, then perhaps a cut to a slow-motion replay from a different angle, then maybe to a third-angle replay, then a cut to the bench for a shot of the guy who just scored the goal.

Working with Wayne, I learned how quick on your feet you had to be in the truck because there's not a lot of time to find the key play and turn it around. Most of the iso videotape guys I was working with had been on the job for twenty years. They knew their stuff. The guys in the live truck too. They operated as two separate cliques, always making fun of their counterparts in the other truck. Among this group, nobody really gave me a hard time about being young or not paying my dues. They accepted me for the rookie I was and welcomed me into their midst—a refreshing change from my days at CBC Sports headquarters. Of course, *Hockey Night in Canada* was just one day of prep and one night of coverage, so for the rest of the week, I still caught shit from my dubious colleagues, but during these games I was counted on.

About three or four weeks into this setup, Bill Sheehan came to me with the surprising (and jolting!) news that Wayne Moss was leaving to take a job directing *Fraggle Rock* with Jim Henson. That might sound like an unlikely career pivot, but *Fraggle Rock* was shot in Toronto and, at the time, one of the biggest production gigs in town. Many of the guys on hockey worked freelance, like Wayne, so they all had other projects going. It was an opportunity Wayne could not pass up, being the lead director on a Jim Henson franchise.

The *really* unlikely career pivot was that I was asked to take over for

Wayne right away. I didn't think I was ready, but one of my mantras had always been to say yes to everything, ready or not. He would shadow me for just one game, standing behind me in the truck while I manned the controls, but after that I would be on my own.

I couldn't let on that I was panicked, although during my first game in Wayne's seat, my cracking voice gave me away. I felt like a boy in a man's world. The live director, Ronnie Harrison, was in my ear the whole game, calling me "Boy Wonder," chewing me out if I couldn't come up with a replay straightaway. Ronnie was another CBC legend, probably the best hockey director in the business, just a couple years removed from his brilliant work as the director of the "Miracle on Ice" coverage at the 1980 Olympics in Lake Placid. He wasn't *just* on me to bust my chops; he really cared about his broadcasts, so I think he was trying to motivate me and put me to the test.

Wayne hung back for the most part, but midway through the second period, I started worrying how I would get through the next game without him standing behind me in the truck. For now, he literally had my back. This game would be fine, I kept telling myself. This game, I could get through. It was the next game, when I'd be solo, that had me shaking. And the one after that. And the one after that.

As soon as the final whistle blew and we got through the recap, my nerves got the better of me. I'd made it through the game on a double shot of Wayne and adrenaline, but now it was like the air had been let out of me. I raced to a pay phone outside Maple Leaf Gardens to call Montreal. I needed to hear my parents' reassuring voices.

"I don't know if I can do this," I said when they picked up the phone.

"Just do the best you can," my father said.

"Everyone will understand," my mother said.

I wanted to scream and tell them no one would understand. This was not school. This was *Hockey Night in Canada*. It wasn't about *trying* your best; it was about *being* your best.

I don't think I'd ever felt so low, so unsure of myself. I was reaching way beyond my abilities, but I managed to slog my way through work that week. On Friday night, before the game, I couldn't sleep. But then the strangest thing happened. On Saturday, I stepped into the truck and felt a little more comfortable. I wasn't entirely comfortable—that would take time—but it wasn't so overwhelming. I thought I could handle it . . . and I did.

Soon it got to where I was confident enough to make jokes with the other guys. There was a lot of joking in the truck—one of my favorite things about working a live sporting event. Once, early on in my tenure as replay director, I said something funny and everybody was cracking up and then I heard Ronnie Harrison's voice on the intercom, bringing me back down to size. "The jokes come from the big truck, kid," he said.

I thought back to the interview with the CBC Sports brass that won me this job, and I realized that there's a huge difference between getting a job and doing a job. When you're selling yourself, you can tell people what you think they want to hear, but when you're in a live truck directing a broadcast seen by millions, there's no place to hide. The slightest misstep can end your career before it begins, so you had better dig deep and find a way to deliver on your promise.

One reach leads to another, and clearly some are more intense than others.

5
WANTING IT

I could write an entire book about my experiences as a producer on the rise at CBC Sports, but here I'll share just a couple stories where the power of reach came into play—including one that illustrates what can happen when your *reach* and your *grasp* aren't entirely in alignment.

The first of these stories found me after a full season on *Hockey Night in Canada*. All along, I was also producing other sports and gearing up to cover my first Olympic Games in Los Angeles when I was asked to jump in on an unexpected hockey assignment. Ralph Mellanby, the executive producer of *Hockey Night in Canada* at the time, had the idea that we should cover the NHL Entry Draft, which was to be held that year at the Montreal Forum. Live draft coverage has since become a staple on ESPN and regional sports networks, but back in 1984 nobody was airing the draft. In fact, I believe this was a first. I'm pretty sure that one of the reasons Ralph came up with the idea was because his son, Scott Mellanby, was a top NHL prospect that year after shining for the Henry Carr Crusaders of the Ontario Junior B Hockey League. I'd been following Scott's career, because that's what you do when you work at *Hockey Night in Canada* and one of your bosses is the father of a highly touted NHL prospect. Scott was the real deal.

His father was the real deal too—a veteran hand who'd been around the network and the game for just about forever. Ralph was already done with the heavy lifting of coordinating a live event. Some executive producers, I was learning, were very hands on, day to day. Others, not so much. Ralph, at this point in his career, was working at thirty thousand feet and no longer in the trenches, sweating the details, so when he went to the CBC guys to pitch the idea, they agreed to sign off if he could find someone to produce it.

Surprisingly (to *me*, at least), Ralph said, "I have just the guy for this one: Arthur."

Dennis Harvey, for one, was thrilled to hear my name in this context, which I guess he took to mean that his hiring experiment was working. He later shared with me that Ralph had been impressed with my work on the hockey front, and with the ways I enhanced my other sports assignments with music, graphics, and compelling storytelling elements. Mellanby could have tapped any of his veteran hockey guys for this assignment, so I was honored, and a little shocked, that he looked to me.

The Montreal Forum was like a temple to me. Really. When I was a kid, there was the synagogue my family belonged to, Shaar Hashomayim, and there was the Forum—our two houses of worship, as far as I was concerned—so to see the floor set up with tables and a stage and seating areas for the prospective draftees and their families was jarring. Also spectacular. The league really put on a show. There were fans in attendance, the place was rocking, and I felt like we would pull a big number.

Mario Lemieux was slated to be the number-one draft choice, a once-a-generation talent. Mario was French Canadian, and he barely spoke English at that time in his life, so covering him for a national network presented some challenges, but we figured it out. The Mario Lemieux story was national news, even though everybody knew he'd be going to the Penguins with the first pick. The drama really had to do with Mario's reaction once the pick was announced, because the Pittsburgh front office had already presented him with an offer he'd rejected.

We also had our own close-to-home drama built into our broadcast, as we planned to track Scott Mellanby's status throughout the evening, so there was plenty of tension and excitement on the floor, in the truck, and, we hoped, in living rooms across the country.

I finagled a job that night for one of my closest and oldest friends, David Pearl, who was happy to be a runner just so he could have the thrill of being on the floor of the Forum for such a historic moment. We had grown up together, and four years later he would be my best man at my wedding. I wanted to share the excitement with my bud— someone who knew what this day meant. We were just twenty-four years old, fresh out of college and still die-hard fans at heart, so we were like kids in a candy store, being set loose in this magical place. When I had a predraft meeting with one of our hosts—Dick Irvin, the voice of the Montreal Canadiens—I had David sit in and take notes. Not because I needed someone to take notes, but I wanted him to be in on the meeting. My parents were there too. I even arranged for them to come by the truck for a quick peek, so they were able to see me in action for the first time.

Our cameras were set up under the assumption that the athletes would go through a series of predictable motions once their names were announced. They'd hug their friends and family and then run the gauntlet of backslaps and congratulations from people around the league as they made their way to the podium to address the crowd and pose for photos, followed by an interview with one of our commentators. By now, we've all seen this routine acted out a thousand times, but back then it had yet to take hold. And sure enough Mario Lemieux didn't step to the podium to be welcomed by the Penguins representatives. When his name was announced, he stayed in his seat. We might have anticipated this reaction, given the tension between Mario and the Penguins, but for whatever reason we didn't plan on *this*.

Everyone looked to me for direction.

Don Wittman, our announcer on the floor, asked me frantically through his headset, "What do I do?"

"Head to the stands," I said. "Talk to him in his seat and do it now. Ask him why he doesn't want to shake the general manager's hand."

Don sidled up to Mario and asked him the question.

The consensus number-one draft pick, the superstar-in-waiting, the future face of the NHL, simply shrugged and in his broken English with a thick French accent explained that the Penguins didn't want him badly enough.

It was a great live moment—and the whole country was watching.

Apart from this bit of tension from Mario Lemieux, it was a special telecast, filled with historical and emotional moments. There were times during the event when I had to pinch myself to make sure it was all real. That sounds like a cliché, I know, but it's really true. I was so moved, so thrilled, so overcome with emotion, to be taking over the Montreal Forum in this way, producing a live network show.

There were tears in my eyes (*actual* tears!), and I didn't care if anyone saw them. I think I even got a little misty-eyed when the Canadiens announced Petr Svoboda and Shayne Corson with the fifth and eighth picks, because even though I was there as a hotshot television producer, I knew the Habs needed a goal scorer and some help on defense. There were also tears of laughter because my buddy David made his television debut. When the Habs drafted Svoboda, David was in the live shot, applauding wildly with a big smile on his face, as the draftee walked right by him to the stage.

It was an emotional night for Ralph Mellanby too—only, it didn't shake out the way he'd planned. We all thought his son Scott might go late in the first round, but as the night progressed and he remained on the board, we were all a little stressed in the truck. Ralph, true professional that he was, kept his focus on the broadcast, but we could all tell his heart was with his son. Truth be told, the decision of Dennis Harvey and Bill Sheehan to run with this event in the first place was in a lot of ways a giant thank-you to Ralph for his stellar work over the years.

When the twenty-first and final pick of the first round came and went (Selmar Odelein to the Edmonton Oilers) and Scott was still on the board, we scrambled. The plan had been for us to cover the first round live and show highlights from the later rounds on delay, but Ralph made an appeal to the brass to keep the broadcast going into the second round—at least for a while.

Six picks into the second round, Scott was chosen by the Philadelphia Flyers with the twenty-seventh pick overall, and there were hugs and high fives in the booth. Soon after, we cut away to other sched-uled programming. What was so memorable about that night and so significant in my development at CBC was that Ronnie Harrison was directing. Remember, Ronnie was the guy who not-so-gently chided me for cracking a joke from the iso truck when I was just a couple weeks into my stint as replay director and not yet ready for the "big truck." And now here I was, a wise old veteran of twenty-four, working as Ronnie's producer. While I was still not his equal in proficiency, there was something head-spinning about being on this equal footing with him professionally.

––––––––––––

Later that summer I went to Los Angeles to cover the Games of the XXIII Olympiad—a whole other head rush. I was in LA for a couple months, and I absolutely loved my time there. I remember driving around the city, becoming familiar and comfortable in that environment, and thinking I'd find a way to return there for a longer stay—a lifetime even.

Jim Thompson was the executive producer of our Olympic coverage, and he made me the producer of our prime-time show—a big responsibil-ity and kind of cool considering that two years earlier I was the college kid who'd stalked him and pleaded for a few minutes of his time. I organized our nightly coverage, and I also ran our highlight suite, preparing and packaging our features, which was becoming one of my areas of strength. That Milt Ottey piece had hit just the right notes with CBC executives, and now a couple years later they were looking to me to continue to find compelling new ways to tell these human-interest stories, to make the athletes relatable to our viewers.

At one point during our time in Los Angeles, because I couldn't stop telling everyone how much I loved it out there, Jim Thompson started calling me The Coast, and it stuck. Jim was my first mentor at CBC and a tremendous supporter, so to get to the place of familiarity and acceptance where he gave me a nickname was a validation. He might have been ribbing me a bit with that name, but I didn't care. He could have called me Kid or Rookie or anything at all, and I would have felt the same, because when somebody important to you gifts you with a nickname, it's a signal that you've arrived.

I made the most of that opportunity in Los Angeles. The Games helped to establish me at CBC Sports. I stopped being thought of as Dennis Harvey's protégé or "experimental hire" and became someone who'd earned his way as a lead producer. I was steadily climbing the ladder at CBC, always reaching for the next rung, and with each success I moved a little closer to being accepted by my peers. More and more I felt like I was justifying Dennis Harvey's faith in me. Taken together, my work leading up to and during the 1984 Olympics conveyed that I was committed to telling emotional stories and producing content that made our viewers feel something.

Our game coverage was unrivaled. We had the best technicians, the most creative camera angles, the best directors. The live work we were doing was superior to the production values of the big American networks in a lot of cases and every bit the equal in others. That was true before I arrived at the network, and it remained so. What was singular and new and exciting as hell was the emphasis on the stories we wrapped around the game and how we told them. Great music, great writing, great show opens, and great packages—these made our coverage stand out, and I pushed hard for them. Whenever we'd run one of my pieces and the people sitting in the control room were crying or laughing or cheering, that's when I knew we'd nailed a piece. I lived for those moments, when I could shape the narrative in a way that moved even the most hard-hearted viewers to tears of joy, sadness, anger . . . whatever. This was key. And this was where I made my bones as a producer.

When I got back to Toronto after the Olympics, I was increasingly confident in my work, looking to reach and take on bigger and bigger assignments. And this assessment was reinforced by my colleagues and bosses at CBC and by a number of print journalists across the country who covered the sports and entertainment industries. Invariably, I got to thinking of what I might do next.

When you spend a lifetime reaching, you become wired to think of what lies ahead. You meet a goal and immediately start in on the next goal. That was me, and because I was from Canada, I was also wired to think that the most challenging opportunities were waiting for me across the border in the United States. In the entertainment industry especially, there's this mindset in Toronto that leaves a lot of us thinking that we're big fish in a small pond and, if we really want to swim with the sharks, we need to be successful in New York or Los Angeles. I no longer buy into this mindset, but I did at the time. I was twenty-five years old, and a part of me was done with Canada. I wasn't done with sports just yet, but I started to think perhaps I'd outgrown CBC.

Somehow, I managed to convince Terry O'Neil, the executive producer of CBS Sports, to meet with me. He'd go on to write a book called *The Game Behind the Game*, one of the best books I've read about sports on television, but at the time he was this brash, visionary leader in our industry. He was relatively young and hot shit. Because I wasn't just *relatively* young but *actually* young and because I *thought* I was hot shit, I figured we'd get along great. I sent him a letter and told him I was going to be in New York and asked if we could meet. Of course, I didn't mention that the only reason I was going to New York was to meet with him, because I didn't want to seem desperate, but that's how it goes when you're reaching—it's not always a good idea to let others know the true size of your ambition.

It worked out that the day of my trip was July 1, 1985—Canada Day, of all things. It was a relatively quiet day at home because of the holiday, so I booked my ticket on Air Canada and made my way to LaGuardia Airport in New York. I brought a lot of tapes and a résumé with me and figured if the meeting went well, I would leave it all with Terry to review before calling back to offer me a job.

It was just a day trip, but I felt sure it would lead to something. What it led to was an unfortunate, once-removed encounter with Bob Moir, one of the CBC executives who'd been in that first meeting when Dennis Harvey summoned me to his office. Bob had been suspicious of me at the outset and not fully on board with Dennis's decision to place me in such a significant role with no real experience. After my first couple years at the network, we'd overcome this shaky start, and he became a good and trusted ally—definitely one of my most important mentors.

I didn't run into Bob directly that day, but I did run into his wife, Edmae, who was an Air Canada flight attendant. I was flying so often in those days I'd accumulated a ton of miles, so I used my points to upgrade my seat, and there she was, working the business-class section, watching me struggle with my carry-on bag overflowing with three-quarter-inch tapes.

"Arthur!" she said excitedly when she saw me. "I thought that was you."

I'd known in a back-of-my-mind sort of way that Edmae worked as an Air Canada flight attendant, but it never occurred to me she'd be working this flight, on this day. (I mean, c'mon! What are the odds?) I thought, *This is not good.* I was under contract to CBC, and sneaking off to New York on my one day off, hauling a bagful of tapes, could only mean I was headed for a job interview.

We chatted for a bit, and then Edmae asked why I was headed to New York—you know, just making conversation. I said I was going to visit friends. She noticed my bag and said, "And you're bringing all those tapes? To show your friends?"

"I want to show them what I've been up to," I said. "They don't get CBC in New York."

This was true enough, and on the face of it, I thought I might have finessed my way around an awkward encounter, but once we took off, I thought, *She knows. Oh, God . . . I'm so screwed.* After all, it was clear to everyone who worked with me that I was ambitious. Bob Moir had been good to me once we sorted out our distrust of each other, and now his wife was going to mention that she'd run into me on this flight to New York and that I'd had all these three-quarter-inch tapes with me; he'd put two and two together; and we'd be right back where we'd started . . . or worse.

I had a pit in my stomach the whole way to Black Rock, the CBS headquarters building on Fifty-Second Street. I managed to put the encounter out of my mind during my meeting with Terry O'Neil, which went well enough. It wasn't exactly a job interview—he'd already made it clear that there wasn't a job available—but I gave him my résumé and told him what I'd been up to in Toronto. He seemed genuinely intrigued, impressed, engaged . . . all of that. We spoke for about an hour, so I counted it as a good exchange and was glad I'd made the trip. When I left, Terry said we should keep in touch, and that if anything changed regarding his staffing needs, he would let me know.

And that was that . . . except it wasn't. As soon as I got to the elevator, I realized I'd never shown him the tapes I'd brought from Toronto—those incriminating tapes that had likely busted me with one of my bosses. I'd meant to at least leave them with Terry, so I doubled back to his office, thinking I'd poke my head in and hand them off. It had only been about a minute, but Terry was gone by the time I reached his office. His door was open, so I went back inside, planning to leave the tapes in a prominent spot. It occurred to me I should also leave a note, so I looked around for a pen and a piece of paper, and as I scanned the room, I saw my résumé in the garbage pail at the foot of Terry's desk.

It was such a devastating, dispiriting thing—probably the lowest moment of my career. Here I was, risking my job at CBC by flying to New York for an interview for a job that didn't even exist, riding high on my success at the Olympics, thinking the world owed me an exciting new opportunity. The sight of my résumé in the garbage pail hit me like a punch to the stomach. I was sick about it, but at the same time I had the presence of mind to punch back: I took the résumé out of the trash and placed it back on Terry's desk, alongside my tapes—a passive-aggressive *fuck-you* to Terry.

Truth was, I had no power in this situation—none. My résumé in the trash was proof of that. Yet in my own youthful pride, I remember consoling myself with the thought that Terry O'Neil was an arrogant prick, and that his hurtful dismissal was just an example of the ethnocentric, cliquish prejudices I would face as I looked to move into American television. I put it on him, instead of stepping back and recognizing that I might not have been ready—or, at least, that *he'd* thought I wasn't ready.

The one good thing to come out of my meeting with Terry O'Neil was that there was no blowback from Bob Moir. Either Edmae never mentioned our run-in or Bob didn't think anything of it. With more perspective, I started to see that there was a lesson in it as well: Sometimes the opportunities we *think* we're ready to meet are not quite ready to meet us. Sometimes the timing just isn't right and what we're reaching for isn't meant to be ours.

I was reminded of that night at the Montreal Forum the year before, when the great Mario Lemieux snubbed the Penguins on air by saying the organization didn't want him enough. I felt the same way about Terry O'Neil and CBS Sports. They didn't want me enough. (Check that: they didn't want me at all!) So I told myself I would not rise from my seat in the crowd and step to their podium. I would continue to grow my game and reach in my own way and grab at the opportunities that had my name on them.

There's no sugarcoating how demoralizing it was for this twenty-five-year-old kid to be kicked to the curb in this way. However, on reflection, it was a blessing, because if I'd gone off to work in New York, I might never have gone on to produce two more Olympic Games for CBC or been promoted to head of CBC Sports or had the idea to pivot from sports into entertainment when I reached in an unlikely way for a job with Dick Clark Productions in Los Angeles.

But I don't want to get ahead of the story . . .

6

MY YEAR OF REACHING PURPOSEFULLY

In each of our lives, there is a year that stands out as a turning point. For me, 1988 was that year. It was the year I produced two Olympic Games, the year I got engaged, the year I got married, the year I was promoted to head of CBC Sports.

That's quite a lot, don't you think? I was crazy busy and excited about the work I was doing and the life that was unfolding in front of me. At the heart of that future life was my wife, Wendy.

We'd nearly met when I first started at Ryerson. A mutual friend had given me her number and said she thought we'd make a good match, but that number went from my wallet to the back of my drawer, and I forgot about it. Then, a couple years into my time at CBC, I ran into that same friend again, and she asked me if I'd ever called Wendy.

I said, "Wendy?"

She reminded me of the connection she'd tried to make six or seven years earlier, and I felt like an idiot for never calling. In my defense . . . college. That's not much of a defense, I know, but as soon as I got to Ryerson, I was caught in a swirl of classes and work and meeting new people, and time ran away from me.

This time I called. It was right after the World Rowing Championships—when you work in sports television, you start to attach the important moments in your life to whatever event you were covering at the time.

"It's Arthur," I said when Wendy picked up the phone.

When I got nothing back, I scrambled to fill in the blanks. Our mutual friend might have let Wendy know about me back when we were in college, but all these years later Wendy had no reason to know who I was. I went into what I remembered of our six degrees of separation . . . "A friend of Marla's, who's friends with Shari, who's friends with you."

Still nothing.

It was like a cold call. But as long as I had Wendy on the phone, I decided to reach. "So," I said, "do you want to go out?"

I thought I could hear Wendy hesitate on the other end of the line, but finally she said, "Okay."

Naturally, she checked me out with our mutual friends before our date, and I guess I passed the audition because we went out to a nice Italian restaurant and seemed to hit it off. Then we went out again, and on our third date I asked her to join me at an upcoming family wedding in Montreal. Happily, she agreed.

Wendy was working as a paralegal at the time, and I was struck by how sweet she was, how smart, how patient. I really, really liked her, and she didn't seem to mind me too terribly much, so we kept at it. As I leaned into 1988, Wendy and I were very much a couple, and I was firing on all cylinders at work.

It was the final time the Olympic calendar gave us the Summer and Winter Games in the same year. I asked Wendy to marry me after I got back from the Calgary Games. (See what I mean about how I remember those milestone moments?) I'd felt terrible, being away from home for so long and knowing that soon I'd be heading off to Seoul, but even more than that, I missed her—a lot. We both knew by this point that we would get married eventually, but it took being apart for a stretch for me to realize we should start our life together right away.

Once again, happily, Wendy agreed.

While it's possible I wasn't the first person to produce two Olympic

Games and get engaged and married in the same year, I was probably the last.

We've been married for over thirty years, and I always tell people it's a mixed marriage because Wendy is from Toronto and I'm from Montreal, two rival cities—but even more than that, we're cut from different cloth. She's the most patient woman in the world, and she's stuck with a guy who has almost no patience—the most content, most easygoing woman with a restless guy who can't stop reaching. The good news is we come together on the important stuff. We're both big believers in doing the right thing and in the power and strength of family. Our moral compasses point in the same direction. And we have each other's backs.

Around the time we got engaged, there was another big ask coming our way—this one from my bosses at CBC, who decided to make me the head of the sports division. I was floored . . . and uncertain. For the first time in my professional life, I was confronted with a prospect I didn't think I could handle—not yet.

I was twenty-eight years old. What the hell did I know about running a network division? I might have been young and inexperienced when I'd started at CBC as a sports producer, but at least I was working in production, so I was in my element. Running a network division would push me into unfamiliar territory—into the worlds of marketing, public relations, acquisitions, scheduling, and contract and sports rights negotiations. It made my head spin to think about it—but of course I thought about it.

I sat to talk things through with Dennis Harvey, the man who gave me my break at CBC. Now head of the network, he was offering me the job he had when he first interviewed me: head of CBC Sports. Also present was Ivan Fecan, the talented programming head of the network. These two network leaders couldn't have been more encouraging. I accepted the job, and they told me they would announce my appointment the following week, but I wouldn't start for several months because they wanted my full focus on Seoul.

"The Olympics are too important to us," Ivan said.

"We need to know the Games are in good hands," Dennis said.

This was good to hear—and I absolutely took their point, because even though Canadian networks were able to stand on our own, we were often big-footed by the American networks when it came to sports coverage. In 1988 Canada was 90 percent cabled, but we'd had access to US channels for as long as I could remember. This meant that, while NBC had the exclusive rights to broadcast the Olympic Games in the United States, Canadian viewers were free to choose between our homegrown CBC broadcast and the American broadcast. This was especially meaningful in 1988, because NBC had just won the rights from ABC, so the network was putting an abundance of its resources into Seoul.

There was a lot of talk in the press that summer about how the CBC coverage would stand up against NBC with its deep pockets and overreaching commitment, but I felt confident that we could hold our own. I said as much at a press conference in the run-up to the Summer Games, during which I predicted that CBC's "David" would get the better of NBC's "Goliath." It was a brash, hotheaded thing to say, and I regretted it the moment the words came out of my mouth. The next day the *Ottawa Citizen* ran a piece on the developing "battle" between the Canadian and American television networks beneath the headline "CBC's David versus NBC's Goliath." I had put a target on our backs, in biblical terms, and I could only imagine how much worse it would have been if I'd made my remarks as president of the network's sports division instead of as the brash, hotheaded kid in charge of our Seoul coverage.

So that's the buildup and backdrop to what would turn out to be one of the biggest moments of my career—a *reach* moment that found me scrambling to cover one of the most heralded Canadian athletes of all time, while at the same time trying to cover my own ass.

We had about 135 people working for us in Seoul. NBC had about 1,500. Our budget was about one-tenth of NBC's budget. But I never lost sight of my goal: to beat the big boys in the ratings. I'd said at that unfortunate press conference that my strategy in beating NBC was editorial judgment—you know, having our cameras and our crew in the right place at the right time with the right story. A ton of choices fell to me to make in producing the Games: when to go live or play back an event on tape; when to insert a packaged feature or go to the studio for an interview;

when to focus on a marquee event of international significance or cover a smaller, under-the-radar event with a Canadian spin.

An important part of my winning strategy was to beat NBC with our coverage of a marquee event on the track-and-field schedule: the men's hundred-meter sprint. Ben Johnson vs. Carl Lewis—the clash of the titans. Ben Johnson was one of our own and perhaps the biggest star of the Seoul Games. That's how it often goes in the race for the title of world's fastest man, but here the hype was particularly intense because everyone was looking forward to a showdown between Ben Johnson and Carl Lewis, who had been the fastest man at the 1984 Games in Los Angeles, where he captured four gold medals, including the gold in the hundred meters.

In Seoul, Ben Johnson was like a rock star. Even the Koreans were in love with him. His image was on posters all over town, and we played that up wherever possible. In the lead-up to the big race, for example, I instructed my track producer to let me know the moment Ben stepped into the stadium for his warm-ups so we could cover it live. His every movement was a big deal, because I knew that back home there were viewers channel-flipping between our coverage and NBC's coverage and I wanted to keep them glued to CBC. I even tried to burn through our commercials early in our telecast so we wouldn't have to cut away once Ben was on the track doing his thing—that's how significant it was for me to find a way to beat NBC. I had the NBC feed on in our control room the entire time, so I was constantly aware of what they were doing, thinking of ways we could do things a little differently. When NBC was in commercial and we had a live shot of Ben and Carl warming up on the track, I knew we had an edge.

There's something to be said about pushing yourself to meet the level of competition, because our track coverage was tremendous—all the way down to our packaged profiles of the shy, stuttering Canadian, whose star was on the rise on his quest to be christened the undisputed fastest man in the world, set against the companion package we'd produced on Carl Lewis, presenting him as this brassy, ballsy American Olympic hero out to defend his gold medal and hold on to the spotlight a while longer.

By the time NBC came out of commercial, our pregame show was in full swing. Our cameras captured the Seoul Olympic Stadium, electric with seventy thousand people cheering their lungs out for an event that would be over in less than ten seconds. When the place fell silent as the runners stepped into the blocks, we captured that as well.

I was about five miles away in our control room at the International Broadcast Center, but I could *feel* that electricity. I really could. Everyone in our control room was intensely focused on that track, and it was a powerful, gripping thing to be surrounded by so many dedicated professionals with a common rooting interest. As I sat behind my massive intercom panel, which gave me the ability to speak to producers at all the different venues, I felt like a maestro leading a grand orchestra with dozens and dozens of talented people moving to whatever rhythms I meant for us to follow. I'd never worked with a panel so big. But in this moment, I didn't need the panel. There was only this one race with our Canadian superstar sprinter—regarded as the race of the century. Nothing else mattered.

Ben Johnson's big thing was his start. We'd spoken about it in our packaged pieces, and it had been highlighted over and over by our analysts and commentators. Sure enough, he exploded out of the blocks like he'd been shot out of a cannon. For a beat it looked like Carl Lewis was right there with him, but then Ben turned on the afterburners and broke away, on his way to another world record. When he crossed the line, he looked off to the side to see who was coming up in his wake, similar to the way Usain Bolt famously crossed the finish line many years later.

Our control room erupted in cheers and mayhem, everyone jumping up and down and clapping each other on the back. It was glorious—one of those moments in the world of sports where you know you're on the inside of history. The whole time, I kept a dialogue going with our track announcers, Don Wittman and Geoff Gowan, and I remember telling Don what a great job he did on the play-by-play call when he exulted that it was a "September to remember" just after Ben Johnson crossed the finish line.

Our cameras were fixed on Ben as he took his victory lap, draped in the Canadian flag, when I heard a voice in my ear telling me there was a phone call from the prime minister. Brian Mulroney was pretty much the last person I was expecting to hear from in just this moment, but his booming voice was unmistakable.

"What a great moment for Canada," he said.

I could only agree, while at the same time thinking, *This is the prime minister! Talking to me!*

He went on to congratulate me on our coverage of the event and to tell me that everyone back home was so proud of Ben.

I started to wonder why the prime minister was calling. National pride is a stirring and boundless thing, and I supposed it was possible that he was just so damn excited that he wanted to connect with someone on site to share in the thrill of it all. But then he got to the reason for his call.

"I really would like to talk to Ben," he said. "Can you please make that happen?"

I couldn't think what to say in response—I mean, what the hell do you say to the prime minister? Regrettably, I got a little cheeky with him. I said something like, "You're watching, right? You see him down there running around with the flag?"

He laughed—that deep, distinctive laugh—and I thought, *Thank God he's laughing.*

A couple minutes later, we were able to get a headset on Ben Johnson as he stepped into position with our commentators and we patched in the prime minister for a rousing congratulatory exchange. Everyone in the control booth was beaming with excitement.

It was a great night for Canada, a great night for Canadian broadcasting, a great night for CBC Sports . . . just, great. Our coverage that night was the highest-rated program in Canadian television history.

In almost every respect, the night was a triumph, but the story didn't end there.

Three days later, I got a middle-of-the-night call from a source on the Canadian team telling me that one of our athletes had tested positive for steroids. I was groggy, but in my bones, I knew who it was.

"It's Ben, right?" I said, as if the world's fastest man and the entire rest of the world were now on a first-name basis. There had been rumors about steroids, and there was no denying that he was jacked.

My source couldn't confirm my hunch and promised to call me back with additional information as it was available.

I didn't wait. I immediately called our lead anchor, Brian Williams of CBC (not *the* Brian Williams, then of NBC) and told him to get down to our studio because we were going on early. It was about four thirty in the morning, but we mobilized. I got our track-and-field broadcast team out of bed to be available to offer commentary. Then I dispatched crews all around the city, hoping our cameras could catch Ben and we could air some exclusive footage to shed even a small shaft of light on a developing story. We sent a team to the athletes' village, another to the airport, and still another to the hotel where Ben's representatives were staying.

By the time Ben Johnson's name was finally and formally attached to all of this speculation, we were good and ready. There hadn't been time to mourn what we stood to lose as a nation if the story turned out to be true or what it might mean to the sporting world at large. There was a much larger conversation still to be had about what these allegations (and, potentially, these revelations) might mean to these Olympic Games. My sole focus was getting to the heart of the story and making sure we had it covered from every possible angle. And we did. We had Ben at the airport trying to leave the country. We had his agent vehemently denying the charges and claiming that the sample vials had gotten mixed up. We had the leader of the Canadian delegation talking about what a sad day it was for our athletes and for our country.

The spirit of collaboration permeates the International Broadcast Center at the Olympics. Everybody had television monitors showing what the broadcasters from other countries were doing, and we wound up sharing and trading a lot of footage because we weren't really competing with each other; we were all in the trenches together, in pursuit of the same goal. If I needed, say, specific footage of Sergey Bubka, the Ukrainian pole vaulter, I could talk to my Russian friends and see if they had it. As the morning wore on and our colleagues started to notice what we were doing on this Ben Johnson story, the global broadcasting community descended on our stage. Our phones were ringing off the hook, and foreign broadcasters were lining up at our door. We, of course, wanted to accommodate every request, but in those predigital days we had to dub the tapes manually and pass them along one at a time. We were literally throwing the tapes out the door as soon as we made a new copy, just to feed all these broadcasters.

Somewhere in the middle of that madness, I looked up and realized we'd been on this Ben Johnson story for a long time. We'd stopped covering the rest of the Games altogether. I always believed in the maxim that shows *about* sports never do as well in the ratings as the sports themselves. I never wanted to be away from the action for too long.

I wasn't the only one who believed this. Laurence Kimber, one of my early mentors at CBC, came into the control room in a panic. "Arthur, you're making a big mistake with this Ben Johnson thing," he said. "You've done a great job, but enough is enough. You need to get back to the rest of the Games."

It wasn't just Laurence trying to bring me back to our scheduled coverage. There were a lot of folks in our control room and in my headset telling me the same thing, reminding me why we were there, but Laurence's appeal stands out in my memory. He was right—but I had a different take. I respected Laurence a great deal, but this was the biggest story in the country. It was bigger than the Olympics. It could not be ignored or set aside. We had a spirited argument right there in the control room, in front of everybody, but in the end it was my call to make, so I kept at it.

Before I could convince myself that I was doing the right thing, the red phone rang in the control room. The red phone was like our "Batphone"—it connected me directly to the head of the network back home, Dennis Harvey. The guy who took a chance on me and gave me a break at CBC Sports and most recently offered me the job as head of CBC Sports. The red phone almost never rang, so I briefly froze when it sounded, my mind racing to the many decisions and moving parts I'd been making and juggling that morning. Not only had I stopped covering the Games, but I hadn't gone to commercial in ninety minutes. I could only think that I was about to be chewed out for losing sight of our bottom line. Ad buys during the Olympics are among the most expensive in television, and here I had ignored our high-end advertisers. In the flash moment between the first peal of the red phone and the second half peal when I answered it, my heart raced.

"I know, I know," I said before Dennis had a chance to even speak. "I haven't gone to commercial."

"Don't worry about it," Dennis said. "We'll make up the commercials. We love what you're doing. You're making the right call."

I think I actually let out a *phew*! As my sigh of relief at this report from Dennis resonated around our control room, everyone on our Seoul team sighed right along with me.

Eventually, we got to a point where there wasn't much happening on the Ben Johnson front, and we turned our attention back to the Games. But the full day after the story broke was again dominated by news coverage as it became clear that Canada's Olympic hero would be stripped of his gold medal. To this day I can close my eyes and picture a shot we grabbed of an IOC official removing the number one from Canada's tally from the medal leaderboard. It was such a powerful, painful moment presented in such a quiet, somber way, and it stands in memory as a symbol of the highs and lows of those Games, and the artistry we tried to bring to the storytelling.

Our coverage continued into the evening, and I didn't leave my chair the entire time, except for a bathroom break. It was the most draining, wrenching experience of my career—and, in some ways, the most fulfilling. I was so exhausted I passed out in the control room the following day, right around the time Wendy arrived in Seoul to spend a couple days with me and enjoy the Olympic experience. In fact, as soon as she got to the broadcast center, the on-set doctor sent me back to my hotel room to recharge, because I was clearly thrashed. I hated giving up the reins like that, and I hated that Wendy had flown halfway around the world to spend some time with me and I was so completely out of it, but the work had taken its toll.

When we got back to the hotel room that night, Wendy read me a fax from Dennis Harvey and Ivan Fecan: "On Friday, it was the best of times. Last night, it was the worst of times. But through it all, you guys were magnificent."

The Ben Johnson steroid drama gave the lie to that old adage about how no pregame (or *postgame*, in this case) show beats the game itself. In the end more Canadians watched Ben Johnson lose his gold medal than watched him win it—and of those people, more people watched on CBC than anywhere else. In Canada, we ended up beating NBC in the ratings by a ten-to-one margin, the greatest domination of home-grown coverage over US coverage in the history of Canadian television. So on the back of these unfortunate events, I was able to back up my David vs. Goliath boast—not exactly the way I wanted it to happen, but it happened just the same. More than that, our coverage was praised and highlighted in newspapers and magazines across the country—all over the world, even.

Months after the Games, I was invited to the US Olympic Academy in Olympia, Washington, to discuss our methodology in covering the Games and the surprising number of Americans living in border cities who were watching CBC over NBC. And to cap it all, at the end of the year, we were awarded two prestigious Gemini Awards, our Canadian version of the Emmy—one for Best Sports Event for our overall coverage and one for Best News Coverage for "Ben Tests Positive."

Still, I came out of Seoul with mixed emotions. As a sports fan and a Canadian, it was depressing as hell to see Ben Johnson's legacy come apart. Really, it was a killing, dispiriting thing, to see Canada's favorite son diminished in this way. As a producer, however, I thought our team did an outstanding job. Our coverage was without peer, so there was something to celebrate here as well. There was joy and validation in this moment—and an emotional reminder that sometimes you have to jump on the runaway train and hang on for dear life until you figure out where it's going.

The reach here came in throwing away the script and doing what I thought was right, even as those around me were telling me different.

On August 9, 1988, as I watched from my hotel room in Seoul, one of the top stories was the blockbuster NHL trade sending Wayne Gretzky from the Edmonton Oilers to the Los Angeles Kings. It was the biggest trade in hockey history—one of those defining moments that you'll always remember where you were and what you were doing when you heard the news.

The trade sent shock waves across the world of sports. In Edmonton, Oilers owner Peter Pocklington was burned in effigy by fans who felt angered and betrayed by the move. Arguably the greatest hockey player in history, Wayne Gretzky himself was in tears at the press conference announcing the trade, and half a world away I got a little misty as well. I was moved enough to take out my portable computer (which I don't think anyone was calling a laptop just yet) to dial into the hotel's search network (which I don't think anyone was calling the internet just yet). The producer in me wanted to know when Gretzky's new team, the Kings, would face the Oilers during the regular season. I knew that game would be must-see television (even though it would be a while before anyone was using that term either). As I marked the date on the calendar I called Dennis Harvey and Ivan Fecan in Toronto to tell them we should find a way to put that game on our *Hockey Night in Canada* calendar.

Hockey Night in Canada was a national institution. For decades, eight o'clock on Saturday nights was a sacrosanct time, when it felt as if the entire country sat down to watch hockey. The broadcast started out on radio in the 1930s and moved to CBC Television in 1952. In the beginning it was the only way for fans to watch an entire game without going to the arenas themselves. Over time, as teams partnered with local stations, it was possible to watch games throughout the week and follow your favorite teams. However, Saturday night remained *Hockey Night in Canada*, and my predecessors at CBC had done a great job upholding the tradition. Our games featured the best matchups, the best production values, the best commentators. During the playoffs, we'd bring those best elements into play with wall-to-wall game coverage throughout the week, but during the regular season, it was all about Saturday night.

Like a lot of hockey-mad Canadian kids, my entire week had revolved around that broadcast. It was everything to me back then. It was everything to Wayne Gretzky too, as I soon found out.

I got Dennis and Ivan on the phone, and we talked about the Gretzky trade for a few moments, then I went into my pitch. "About that trade," I said. "There's an opportunity for us to get a really big number in October when he comes back to Edmonton for the first time."

Dennis accepted that this was a great idea, and Ivan agreed. Then Ivan looked at the schedule and said, "Damn, that's a Wednesday night."

"So?" It hadn't occurred to me that it would be an issue.

Dennis finished Ivan's thought: "So—*Hockey Night in Canada* is on Saturdays. We're not doing it."

"Why not? There is nothing that we can put on a Wednesday night in October that is going to rate higher. That game is going to be huge."

My bosses weren't feeling it just yet, so I laid it on thick. I talked about the excitement that game was going to generate and how people would want to know how the crowd responded. Would the Great One be booed or welcomed home like a conquering hero? Would he play well or would the moment be too much for him? The hockey season was a couple months away, and we still had the Olympics to get past, but this game could do really well for us, so I pushed for it hard.

"It's up against the World Series," Dennis said after looking at the competition on that night.

"This is Wayne Gretzky coming back to play in Edmonton," I said. "It will do better than a World Series game."

"You're not the head of sports just yet," Ivan said.

"No. But I will be in October."

I think they laughed, but I can no longer be sure. (I *hope* they laughed!)

Finally, they agreed to back me on this because it was clear I felt strongly about it. They reminded me that this would be my first major decision as head of sports, but this just deepened my resolve to broadcast the game.

The game fell on October 19. I'd returned from Korea and started in my new position on October 6, and I was still finding my way in my new role, still dealing with some of the skepticism of the old hands in our sports division who would probably always see me as some upstart kid. One of the people who disagreed with my decision to air the game was the great Don Cherry, the commentator and standard-bearer of *Hockey Night in Canada*. One of the first things I did when I got back to the office was to tell Don we were sending him to Edmonton. I thought he'd be excited.

Instead, he said, "What the fuck for?"

"Gretzky. We're doing the game."

"Why the fuck are we doing the game? *Hockey Night in Canada* is Saturday."

Don Cherry was adamantly opposed to my decision to break from our Saturday night tradition—old school all the way. So was Ron MacLean, his partner on the popular "Coach's Corner" segment of our broadcast. Ron actually wrote about the game in his book, in which he mentioned how pissed Don had been that I broke from tradition and sent them to Edmonton, but I believed that part of my job was to shake things up and inject new life into our established franchises, and this was my first opportunity to do so. I even called Maple Leaf owner Harold Ballard and asked him to move the start time for the Toronto game from 7:30 p.m. to 7:00 p.m., so that when the Kings-Oilers game came on at 9:30 p.m., there wouldn't be much if any overlap. (To my surprise, he agreed. I think he wanted to see the game too!)

I flew out to Edmonton for the game to make sure everything went right and that our reluctant *Hockey Night in Canada* stars would rise to the occasion. Also, I wanted to oversee our packaged pieces on Gretzky and make sure we hit all the right notes.

I booked a room at the Westin Hotel, where the rest of our team was staying. Turned out, it was where the Los Angeles Kings were staying too, and it worked out that I stepped into the same elevator as Wayne Gretzky on the afternoon of the game. (How about *that*?) I held out my hand and introduced myself.

He shook my hand and said, "I know who you are." Then he smiled and shook his head in disbelief. "I can't believe *Hockey Night in Canada* is happening on a Wednesday."

There was something so humble and gracious about Gretzky's demeanor. I loved that the "Great One" didn't think his homecoming was worthy of such a break with tradition. He'd grown up with the broadcast, same as me. He knew what it meant for us to be here, same as me.

"You coming to Edmonton is a big story," I said. "There's no way we could *not* be here."

He shook his head again. "I *get* that, I guess. But come on, it's a *Wednesday* night. It's a regular season game. It just doesn't feel right."

No, I guessed it didn't. But at the same time, to me, it felt exactly right.

Edmonton fans welcomed Gretzky with a long, rousing ovation, and it was truly a thrilling moment. Every time Gretzky stepped back on the ice for a shift, every time he touched the puck, the place went crazy—as if the fans were holding on to what they'd had, grateful for the chance to spend a little more time with the man who had until recently been their franchise player. It was bittersweet, but mostly *sweet*, and I was glad our cameras were there to cover it—and if they were being honest, I think Don Cherry and Ron MacLean would have said the same. (Well . . . maybe not Don.) The game itself was a high-scoring but otherwise ho-hum early season affair. Gretzky notched two assists, the Oilers won 8–6, and we managed to beat the World Series by 10 percent in the ratings, so I put this decision in the plus column and looked ahead to the next one.

———————

Almost as soon as I got the job as head of CBC Sports, I decided to do something special for my dad. We shared a love of the Montreal Canadiens. I think you have to be from Montreal to truly understand the depth of feeling that goes into being a lifelong fan of the Habs. It's a visceral thing. Throughout my childhood, a couple times a year, we'd go to the Forum and cheer on our beloved team. Even when we weren't at the games, the Canadiens were front and center. On game nights, if I went to bed before the third period was over, I could tell who won the next morning by my father's mood.

As a young producer-director at CBC working on *Hockey Night in Canada*, I was able to get us tickets from time to time when I was in town, and I'd even send my parents to a game at the last minute if a pair of seats became available. Now I wanted to ratchet things up a bit and get my father season seats. But getting season tickets to the Canadiens was like finding one of Willy Wonka's golden tickets. Families lucky enough to land season seats treated them like heirlooms. Wills were contested over Canadiens tickets. On rare occasions, the general public could get seats to individual games, but you literally had to be grandfathered in to get season tickets.

The first call I made was to Ronnie Harrison, the executive producer of *Hockey Night in Canada*, who now, strangely, reported to me. I figured if anybody knew how to land a pair of coveted season tickets to the Canadiens, it would be Ronnie.

At first, he couldn't think why I'd want season seats. "You live in Toronto," he said.

I explained that they were for my dad. I didn't have to tell him how much the Canadiens meant to him. He knew.

Ronnie made a couple calls, eventually reaching out to Ron Corey, the team president. "But Arthur lives in Toronto," Ron Corey reportedly said.

I paid for the tickets, of course, but just securing them was a significant hurdle, and the day I was able to present them to my father was one of my very favorite days. At the time, the tickets came in a giant booklet with perforated edges that allowed you to separate the ticket for each game from the rest of the pack. These days, with electronic ticketing and the proliferation of secondary ticket markets, I imagine this would have had less of an impact, but the presentation of this glorious ticket booklet really added to the moment. Wendy and I went back to Montreal for the Jewish holidays, as we would every year, and I found just the right time to present my father with the tickets.

He was floored . . . overjoyed, overwhelmed, overcome.

And I was right there with him. It was one of the great blessings of my life to be able to do this one small but consequential thing for the man who had given so much to me and my sisters. No, it didn't make up for the disappointment I thought I saw in his eyes when I rejected his offer to join him in the fur business, but it got pretty damn close—and it signaled to me in a profoundly personal way that the reaching I was doing in my career was paying off.

7

AN OFFER I COULD NOT REFUSE

It took time to get comfortable with my gig as head of CBC Sports. For all the perks that came my way—bigger corner office, bigger salary, bigger expense account—I started to realize that for everything I'd gained in this new role, I'd given something up. Mostly, I missed the thrill and craziness of being in the midst of a production at a big game. It took stepping away from the control room for me to realize just how much I loved the creativity, the camaraderie, the energy that came with producing a live event, so I found myself looking for ways to replace all of that.

One of those ways turned out to be negotiating, a skill that meant something completely different in my previous roles. Here it came up almost every day, as it now fell to me to negotiate the deals for our on-air talent, make day-to-day decisions regarding the getting and spending across the department, and secure the rights for the major events we would cover. Already, I landed new deals for the National Hockey League, Major League Baseball, the World Figure Skating Championships, IndyCar Racing, and the Albertville Olympics. Also, we'd inaugurated our special edition hockey broadcasts, including doubleheaders on Saturdays, and added prime-time figure skating coverage to our schedule, which required me to roll up my sleeves and do some hard bargaining with outside sports organizations, sponsors, and my bosses.

One of my first tasks as head of sports was to reimagine our *esprit de corps*. To my thinking, then as now, there's nothing more important to the success of a team effort than building morale and knitting people together. It's foundational, fundamental, and I'd stepped into a situation where the sports department had been neglected—in many ways, over many years. We'd been a big moneymaker for the network, but you'd never have known it to look at our shabby offices, so one of my first moves was to give our workplace a face-lift, knowing full well that small touches can yield big dividends. I wanted our people to recognize and celebrate the fact that we were one of the best sports organizations in the world.

If you want to play the part, you need to step up to the role. Over the course of a single weekend, I put some nice couches in our lobby and reception area, along with new carpeting, a sleek reception desk, a 3D display with our CBC Sports logo, and a big-screen monitor running a loop of highlights from our telecasts. When people came in to work Monday morning, it was amazing to see how the attitude of the staff was transformed by these few cosmetic changes. Where the mood of the room had been kind of dismal and dispiriting, now it signaled to all who worked there and to all who worked with us that we meant business.

For the longest time, when I was coming up through the ranks as a producer, people complained about the rundown state of our offices. There was a lot of grousing, and everyone agreed it would be a good idea to spruce the place up, but it had never been a priority for management. Now that I *was* management, I made these renovations a priority, which took me to one of the first learned truths that came to me in this new job:

When it's a good idea, everyone agrees it should get done; when it's a priority, it's going to get done.

Another good idea that needed to be made a priority, I thought, was in the way we dressed our announcers. Like our office space, our on-air look needed a makeover. For as long as I'd been at the network, the talent wore these shockingly ugly orange blazers that looked like they'd been bought in bulk from a Halloween-themed thrift shop. On the plus side, it was easy to spot one of our pumpkin-clad gang in a crowd. On the minus side, it was not a good look—frankly, it was unclear to me that it had *ever* been a good look. The only exception at CBC Sports to this throwback dress code were our NHL guys, who wore baby-blue blazers that were only marginally better in the fashion-forward department. Orange or baby blue, our jackets popped on the screen in a jarring way reminiscent of the 1960s, when our broadcasts went from black-and-white to color and producers must have felt the need to remind viewers of the shift with loud colors.

I understood that it was important for the CBC Sports brand for our announcers to have a uniform look, so I consulted with some designers and determined that we should go with something a bit more classic—a traditional navy-blue blazer. I ran some samples by a couple key on-air personnel, and they all loved the color and the design, but I decided to keep the jacket under wraps because our hockey guys worked as an independent unit with their own management, and I wanted to honor their role at the network by sharing it with them first.

I had a prototype ready ahead of our big NHL kickoff meeting, and I planned to do a kind of blazer reveal as part of my pitch. Ivan Fecan, my boss on the network programming side, would be in attendance, and it was going to be one of my first opportunities to impress him with my leadership style in an in-person setting, so I was excited, heading into the meeting. Remember, I was ridiculously young for a job like this one—by about twenty-five years! I was also still relatively new to my role, and this was a chance for me to make a splash with the network brass and senior staff—some of whom were undoubtedly wondering if I was up to the job.

Before the meeting, I had the prototype blazer tucked away in a box under the table where I would be sitting. I started things off talking about all of our successes the previous season, and then leaned into all the innovations we were planning for the coming season—different camera angles, better storytelling, more dynamic opens, a revamped look and focus for our intermissions . . . all of that. As I was wrapping up, I reached for the box and said there was one more thing I wanted to share. I slipped on the jacket, which just happened to be my size, and said, "I wanted everyone here to be the first to see our new look." I made the announcement with great fanfare—in my head there was a drumroll playing beneath the big reveal.

It sounds almost silly in the retelling, but this was a huge moment for me . . . and very symbolic. There I was, putting it out there that we would no longer be content to do things the way we'd always done them, simply because that was the way we'd always done them. Everything was up for reinvention, even our look. My colleagues around the table applauded, and there was tremendous excitement—and relief— because people had really gotten sick of those baby-blue blazers. I took the response as a great validation because our hockey team was steeped in tradition. They did things a certain way and were grooved into their routines, so for them to be clapping wildly over something as simple as a wardrobe redesign told me I'd tapped into something important. I'd been half expecting some oohs and aahs, but the full-on applause caught me by surprise, and as I looked up, I saw Ivan beaming with what looked to me like pride, clapping right along with the rest of the group.

In the moment, I counted the meeting a great success, but there was some fallout from my presentation—a reminder in the early days of my career as a television executive not to outmaneuver myself when I was looking to make an impact. Ivan called me into his office the next day for a postmortem on the meeting that turned out to be more of a dressing down than a pat on the back. He congratulated me on the plans for the coming hockey season and on my showmanship introducing the new jacket design, but then he set me straight.

"Those guys will be talking about how you revealed the new blazer for years," he said. "But don't you ever do that shit again."

I was thrown by Ivan's comment; he'd been cheering as loudly as anyone. "What, you don't like the jacket?"

"I'm okay with the jacket. It's the surprise that wasn't okay."

During the premeeting I'd walked him through all the relevant talking points, which included some significant changes to one of our core divisions and the biggest revenue generator at the network, but neglected to mention the blazer. In many ways, our hockey group was the lifeblood of our department—a true feather in the network's cap—so of course a guy like Ivan would take a special interest in how it was run. And yet it hadn't even occurred to me to tell him about the new jacket design or that I'd been planning to spring it on everyone. I was wrong.

Ivan was put off—but thankfully not too put off. Mostly, he took my oversight as a chance to remind me that as the head of the network, when he took the time to hold a prep meeting with the head of sports, he expected to be *fully* prepped on what to expect. It was an object lesson, but an important one. Even though Ivan liked the new jackets, I hated that I'd let him down—or, at least, that I'd disappointed him in a way he didn't expect to see again.

A few months after the sports jacket incident, in July 1989, I somehow put myself in a position to blindside my boss all over again. I got a call from someone claiming to be Marlon Brando's publicist. On the face of it, there was no reason for Marlon Brando to be reaching out to the likes of me, but his representative was calling for a very specific reason. True to my own internal marching orders to think big and reach and make an immediate impact, I'd been able to secure the broadcast rights to Mike Tyson's upcoming fight with Carl "The Truth" Williams, one of the most talked-about sporting events of the season. This would be the first time the network would carry a Tyson fight with only a one-day delay, following the exclusive live coverage on pay-per-view.

We'd been promoting our broadcast, and Brando, who was in Toronto filming a movie called *The Freshman*, had apparently seen our ads and instructed his publicist to reach out. I'd never heard of the publicist and had no idea if he *really* represented Marlon Brando, but Toronto had become a hot location for many Hollywood productions, and I was dimly aware that the iconic actor was in town shooting a movie. It was an odd call, but enough of the pieces fit that I figured I'd hear the guy out.

"Marlon's a huge fight fan," the publicist said. "He was wondering if he could come by the CBC studios and maybe watch the fight on the live feed. Could that work on your end?"

This had to be some kind of joke. I mean, Marlon Brando? One of our greatest living actors? Surely, there were other ways for him to see the fight.

"You're kidding, right?" I said.

The man on the phone assured me this was a legit call, and he was knowledgeable enough about the industry to know that if we had the next-day broadcast rights, the live feed would be coming into our post-production facility, so I told him we could work something out. In fact, I started to get excited about the idea of having the live feed piped into my office and inviting the great Marlon Brando to watch the fight. I could order in some food, mix up some drinks, and we could hang out—a good and appropriate use for my spacious new office, and one of the sweet side benefits of leading the top sports television department in the country.

After just a couple minutes, it was all arranged. "Mr. Brando," as his publicist kept calling him, would stop by my office at around nine o'clock that evening, perhaps with a friend or costar or two, and we would watch the fight together. I let my imagination run away from me, thinking we'd bond and become great friends. (Yeah, right . . .)

About an hour after I got off the phone with the publicist, I got a call from Ivan Fecan, checking in on some other matter. We chatted for a bit. One of the things we talked about was the fight. He was thrilled we were finally broadcasting a Tyson bout, and I ended up mentioning that Marlon Brando was coming by the offices later that evening to watch the fight. I suppose I was trying to impress my boss with this casual mention, but in the moment I made it sound like no big thing. As I might have expected if I'd stopped to think about it long enough, Ivan was all over this bit of news. Before I could tell him what I had planned, I could hear him through the phone yelling to his assistant to arrange for a catering crew to come to his office.

"We'll do it here," he said. "There's a lot more room."

This was true enough, but I didn't see that we needed any more room for our small group. My understanding from the publicist was that I was meant to keep our little gathering under wraps, so I told Ivan to be cool about it. The last thing I wanted was for Marlon Brando to show up and be bombarded by a room full of people. Ivan assured me that he'd keep our plans mostly to himself. I told him I would probably bring my wife because I knew she'd get a kick out of it, but that would be it.

I called the publicist to tell him of the slight change in plans and then went home for a quick dinner and to change into more casual attire. On the drive home, I picked up my state-of-the-art mobile phone to call Wendy and fill her in on what was going on. I've got to be honest here: I liked everything about the scene that was taking shape. There I was, twenty-nine years old, the youngest head of CBC Sports in network history, calling home on a newfangled mobile phone the size of a brick to tell my wife I was going to be hanging out with Marlon Brando. As moments go, this was pretty damn grand—impressive as hell, although Wendy was the last person I needed to impress.

"I've got some good news and bad news," I said when she picked up. "Which do you want first?"

I couldn't tell from Wendy's groan if she was more annoyed by my question or my teasingly playful tone and the picture she must have known I was carrying around in my head—me, driving around town, talking on my mobile phone like some high roller.

"Might as well get the bad news out of the way," she said.

"The bad news is I have to go back to work after dinner."

Another groan—this time of the more familiar variety that told me Wendy was annoyed at the way CBC Sports was constantly pulling me away from our personal time.

"And what's the good news?" she said—ever the good sport, still playing along.

"The good news is you're coming with me," I announced with the same tone and fanfare I'd brought to my ill-fated jacket reveal. "We're going to watch the Mike Tyson fight."

There was a silence for a beat. "I'm still waiting for the good news. That can't be it!"

Even through our crude mobile phone connection, I knew my good news had landed with a thud, as planned, so I played it up a bit. "You're right. There's more. We're going to be watching the fight with an Oscar-winning actor, probably the most distinguished, most iconic actor of our time." Then, to tease out the moment, I hummed *The Godfather* theme.

"Al Pacino?" Wendy blurted out, unable to contain her excitement.

I was mildly disappointed in her response—I really thought she'd get it right out of the gate. I swallowed a laugh. "Guess again."

"Not Marlon Brando?" she said, as if such a thing was beyond possible.

"Bingo!"

I knew Wendy would be as excited about our evening plans as I was—and, sure enough, by the time I got home, she'd gone through a couple outfits, sorting through her wardrobe for just the right thing to wear to a fight night with a man who was arguably the greatest living actor and only a couple decades removed from a time when he was one of Hollywood's great heartthrobs.

Cut to nine o'clock or so that night. Ivan had laid out an incredible catered spread. True to his word, he kept the gathering quiet—way over the top, but quiet. When Wendy and I arrived, there was only Ivan and his assistant, and we all got comfortable. The feed was already on, the undercard playing on the large-screen television that dominated Ivan's office.

At 9:15, Ivan wandered over to me and casually asked what time Marlon Brando was due to arrive, and I said I'd told him to come at nine.

At 9:45, with no movie star in sight, Ivan wandered over again, wondering what the hell was going on.

It was around this time that I started to feel like the moment had gotten away from me—that I had once again overreached in a way that left my boss second-guessing my motives . . . and perhaps my grip on reality. Think about it: Marlon Brando? The two-time Academy Award winner? Coming up to the office to watch the Mike Tyson fight? It was such a wild, absurd scenario, and yet I'd somehow brought Ivan into it.

I'd been on such a roll since taking the job, and I didn't want anything, even the *slightest* thing, to slow that roll. A part of me worried what would happen if this evening turned out to be a bust.

At 10:15, Ivan seemed pretty pissed. Presumably, he'd canceled whatever Friday night plans he'd had and was now thinking he could have been someplace else doing something better. Ivan was one of those larger-than-life types who cared very much about appearances. He'd gone to all this trouble, brought in all this food, and here it was looking like we'd been set up or pranked.

By 10:45, things were so awkward in Ivan's office I started thinking Wendy and I should just leave. This was beyond embarrassing . . . this was humiliating, ridiculous. Ivan was beyond pissed. The folks around CBC were all a little afraid of him, careful not to set him off, and here I'd made him look foolish.

Finally, just before 11:00 p.m., Brando walked in with a small entourage—the cast and creative team of *The Freshman*: Matthew Broderick, Penelope Ann Miller, and Bruno Kirby, as well as Mike Lobell and Andrew Bergman, the famed producer and the writer/director. They were loud, loose, determined to have a good time.

I could not have been more relieved. If it had just been me, waiting on Brando in my own office, I wouldn't have been stressed over whether or not he'd show, but once I'd brought my boss into it, the waiting was super stressful.

The first thing I noticed about Brando was that he was huge—both in body and personality. He wore a big, flamboyant straw hat. He was especially warm and attentive to Wendy, like the way an uncle would look after a favorite niece, and I looked on with a secret thrill at the peculiar career path and the unique set of circumstances that had made this close encounter possible.

Brando's colleagues made themselves at home. They helped themselves to Ivan's spread. There was alcohol, but I don't think too many of them were drinking. A couple of them grabbed the plush, expensive pillows from Ivan's couch and tossed them on the floor. They completely took over the place. Matthew Broderick and Bruno Kirby splayed out on the carpet in

front of the television, propped up on pillows. Marlon Brando commandeered Ivan's office chair, his feet on Ivan's desk, looking like he owned
the place. This last bit took some getting used to, I'll admit. No one sat
at Ivan's desk—other than Ivan, that is. He had such an intimidating air
about him, such a commanding presence, no one at the network would
have dared. Yet here was the two-time Academy Award–winning actor
with complete disregard for the carefully cultivated stature of his host.

Ivan, to his credit, was a good and gracious host. If he minded at
all about the feet on his desk or the pillows on the floor, he didn't let
on. He seemed more put out by Brando's focus on Wendy instead of
him. He was used to being the center of attention, especially around
the office, but he was a world-class schmoozer, as slick and charming
as anyone I'd go on to meet in the entertainment industry, and he
seemed very much in his element, hosting this grand, unlikely party.

Everyone in that office was an alpha personality in their own way, but
Brando sucked the air out of the room. I'd hung around actors enough
to know that you don't rise to the level of these stars without a forceful
personality, and you don't get to write or direct or produce a big-budget
movie unless you tick some of the same boxes. Ivan, too, had risen to
become head of the network because he did as well, and yet even among
this group of high-achieving, high-octane personalities, Marlon Brando
was the alpha among alphas. When he spoke, everyone listened, like he
was holding court. When he laughed, everyone laughed. And when he
had an idea, everyone went along with it.

"We should have some money on this fight," he said in his unmistakable voice.

And so it was agreed—we would all bet on the fight. This was prob-
lematic, however, because everyone wanted to bet on Tyson, so Brando
came up with a solution. We could all bet on the champ, he said, but
the actual wagering would be on how long the fight would go. This,
too, was a problem because everyone wanted to pick one of the early
rounds, convinced "Iron Mike" would make quick work of "The Truth."

"Ah," Brando said with a mischievous smile, "but we're not going
to have a choice."

He took a piece of paper from Ivan's desk and tore it into pieces. Then he wrote a number on each piece and crumpled it up. Matthew Broderick stood up from his spot on the floor to help him, and the two actors tossed the crumpled pieces of paper into Brando's big hat. It was like a scene from a movie, the way they set up the betting—although I suppose I was helped along in this thinking by the fact that they just happened to be big-time movie stars. Then we each picked a number and tossed twenty dollars into the pool.

I kicked in forty dollars for me and Wendy. I drew the eighth round. Wendy drew the third round. Brando, of course, drew the first round, and I've always wondered if he somehow palmed the number or fixed the passing of the hat to ensure that he wound up with the first round, which of course was what everyone would have picked because the champ was so heavily favored.

Sure enough, Tyson came out of his corner like he had someplace else to be. He knocked Williams to the canvas with a left hook about a minute into the round, and even though Williams managed to get back up, he was clearly rattled and the ref called the fight after ninety-three seconds. (For the record, it was the second-quickest title fight of Tyson's career—just a year or so after his ninety-one second victory over Michael Spinks.)

Brando gleefully collected his winnings—around two hundred dollars by my math—and no one seemed to begrudge him the money. In fact, it's like the outcome had been preordained, and all these years later I still carry this vivid image of the great Marlon Brando lustily counting out his twenties and pocketing all that cash.

And then, less than ninety-three seconds after the fight was called, Brando and his entourage were gone. He kissed Wendy on both cheeks on the way out the door, and as our Hollywood interlopers left, Ivan and I looked at each other like we couldn't believe what had just happened. All told, Brando and company were there for less than an hour, and there was something surreal about the whirlwind visit.

As you might imagine, the story of the night an iconic actor came by to watch the Tyson fight became one of my favorites, and yet each time

I tell it, I'm taken back to the tentative ways I moved about my boss's office as we waited on Brando's arrival. I hated how those moments left me feeling—uncertain, vulnerable—and I've come to recognize that I was so caught up in the excitement and possibility of this visit that I'd somehow put myself in a position to show up my boss, just like I'd done a couple months earlier with our hockey guys and my sports jacket reveal.

Yes, it always pays to reach—that's the message at the heart of this book. But it also pays to be mindful of the situation and not *overreach* because you just might put yourself in a tough spot. Here it worked out that I was able to recover and wind up with a couple good stories to share, but in each case things could have gone another way.

That's how it goes when you extend yourself. If you play it safe and only grab at what's within reach, you'll never lift yourself up and onto the next thing. Basically, you have to stick your neck out—and thankfully, my neck remained intact.

8

THE GREAT 18

Growth—big or small, personal or professional—is essential to one's happiness.

Sometimes growth up and happens on its own. But then there are other times, like when you're reaching, that you're able to take matters into your own hands and achieve *greater* growth and *greater* success on an accelerated timetable. At least, that's how it's tended to work out for me. I've never been one of those people who waits for the next opportunity to present itself. I'm always out there looking for it, reaching for it, doing everything I can to make it a part of my reality.

I believe we make our good fortune. Landing that first part in a feature film, being awarded a scholarship at Ryerson, catching my big break at CBC, becoming head of CBC Sports—all of those opportunities came about because I put myself out there . . . because I *reached*.

Naturally, reaching alone doesn't always get it done. It's not enough to simply set your sights on a goal. You have to earn your way to it. Sometimes there's a hurdle you can't seem to get past, or maybe a hoped-for opportunity doesn't have your name on it. Even when you're on a roll, you'll occasionally need to slow that roll to match your reality. That's how I came to see my disappointing trip to CBS Sports in New York. I told myself it just wasn't meant to be. But I picked myself up and vowed to become one of the leading producers of sports programming in the country, and I did enough to impress my bosses that they made me the youngest head of sports in the history of the network.

With that, I achieved a certain amount of notoriety and the confidence to reach again, and when it came time to consider some kind of next move, I sat down and wrote a letter to Dick Clark—a letter I would have never written if Terry O'Neil at CBS hadn't been so quick to write me off. In it, I shared the story of my career, going back to the grand CBC "experiment" that brought me to the network right out of college. I expressed my desire to expand beyond sports and get back in the trenches, developing and producing entertainment programming, a genre his company was the leader in. I took a risk and closed the letter with the following bold strokes: "Thank you for taking the time to read this letter because I can appreciate how busy you are, but reading this letter is not a waste of your time and meeting me will not be either."

One week later, I received a letter inviting me to Los Angeles for that interview I wrote about earlier—you know, the one where my mother accompanied me and waited for me in the lobby of the Sheraton Universal while I went off in search of my next career move. Even though I had spent a few months in Los Angeles when I produced the Olympics five years earlier, I drove past Dick Clark's unusual building a couple times before I realized this was indeed his office. His company was headquartered in Burbank on Olive Avenue, nestled among all these great studios and office complexes, but the building itself looked like a private home—a mansion, really, covered in ivy.

Inside it looked like a memorabilia museum had exploded all over the place. In his conference room, Dick displayed Elvis Presley's cape, a pair of Michael Jackson's shoes, and a light fixture from *The Sonny & Cher Show*. There were gold records on every wall and music memorabilia in every nook and cranny—pretty much what you'd expect from the guy who hosted and produced *American Bandstand* all those years.

The office was disarmingly casual. Two big dogs had the run of the place. Coming from the very corporate, very buttoned-down environment of our CBC offices back home, this struck me as kind of interesting—at any rate, it was certainly *different.*

And then I heard his voice: "Arthur!"

That unmistakable voice. Calling my name. It was a real *pinch-me!* moment.

Just as I had done on that first meeting with CBC when I was just a kid, I'd come prepared with a bunch of ideas. I was good and ready. And so was Dick. We got right into it, going through every single one of those ideas once we got past our introductions and the requisite small talk. Right away we had an easy, professional rapport, almost like we were already working together. It was an unbelievable exchange. On one level, he was interviewing me, but on another, I was interviewing him, and we went back and forth in this very collaborative way for a couple hours.

One of my ideas was for a show I called *America's Funniest Home Movies*—the premise is right there in the title. This was 1989, and camcorders or home video cameras had replaced the bulky and expensive film cameras and were now all the rage.

Dick smiled when we got to this one and said, "This is just brilliant, Arthur."

I thanked him.

"But there's just one problem," he said. "ABC just bought it. They're calling it *America's Funniest Home Videos*. But I like the way you're thinking."

(Not for nothing, but this is *still* on ABC, more than thirty years later!)

The meeting couldn't have gone any better, and it ended in much the same way that first CBC meeting had ended all those years earlier.

Dick said, "I really enjoyed meeting you. You're an impressive young man, but I'm not sure what to do with you."

And that was that. When I got back to the hotel, my mother pumped me with questions. She wanted to know everything about the meeting, what Dick Clark was like, what the job would be like . . . all of that. I couldn't really tell her anything because I had no idea what the job would be like or even if there was a job to be had. Similar to my targeted approach with CBC, I had researched and focused my attention on this one man and his production company. It's not like I was out there casting a wide net and hoping to catch a break. This was my one net. And the one I was ready to leave my head of CBC Sports job for.

The next morning at 7:30 a.m., the phone rang. "Arthur," that unmistakable voice said on the other line. "It's Dick Clark. I hope I didn't wake you."

"Not at all," I lied. "I'm always up early."

"Listen, Arthur. I really enjoyed our conversation yesterday. I'm going to call you back in three weeks, and maybe in that time I'll figure out a way to keep that conversation going."

Sure enough, three weeks later *to the day*, Dick called and offered me a job. He moved me to Los Angeles, became a huge mentor, and helped me to set my career on a whole new course. Finding my résumé in the trash was one of the luckiest breaks of my career.

I'd made my bones in television working at CBC Sports, so this shift from sports programming in Canada to entertainment programming in the United States was a reach and a departure for me, but I was determined to grow my game and push myself in a new direction. I was still young enough to double back and regroup and continue on in sports if this reach didn't work out, but I had to give it a try. I'd gotten to where I needed a new challenge, and although I loved working in sports and would always be a die-hard sports fan, television itself was my first love, and I wanted to see if I could make my mark in the industry.

My role with Dick Clark included some tending to the care and feeding of many of the great franchises he'd developed over the years, including the *American Music Awards*, *TV's Bloopers and Practical Jokes*, and *Dick Clark's New Year's Rockin' Eve*. But I was primarily there to build on that list with new franchises of my own. I delivered new shows like the *USA Music Challenge* and *Battle of the Bands* for ABC; *Caught in the Act* and *When Stars Were Kids* for NBC; and a show honoring the best in cable TV, the *CableACE Awards*—all solid performers and contributors to our bottom line.

At the same time, I was looking to adapt to my new California lifestyle. Wendy and I didn't know many people in Los Angeles, and as a result I found myself playing a lot of golf.

People say golf runs in families, but in my case it looked like it might skip a generation. My dad was an avid golfer, and I'd join him on the course whenever I could, although for me it was more about the company than the sport. However, once I moved to Los Angeles to work with Dick in 1990, I started to play more and more. It was a great way to meet people and decompress from some of the stresses of my new job. Plus, in a city like LA, it was one of the all-time great bargains. There were a ton of terrific public courses, so there were always interesting places to play and, just as important, interesting people to round out your foursomes. Soon, I was playing all the time. My father got a great kick out of the fact that I'd taken up the sport so quickly. It became common ground for us.

Because of my background at CBC Sports, opportunities that crossed Dick's threshold that had anything even remotely to do with sports tended to flow to me. For example, when we produced the *Jim Thorpe Pro Sports Awards* for ABC—a sort of precursor to ESPN's Espy Awards—that was a natural fit for me and a great way to tie my old world of sports to my new world of entertainment.

Dick was great about making time to hear people out. He'd take a meeting with an old friend as a show of respect, even if he knew there was nothing in it for him. Since he couldn't be in two places at once, he had his associates take some of these meetings on his behalf—a part of the job I welcomed because it helped me to gain my footing and connect with interesting and influential people in and around the entertainment business. So when he asked me to meet with a well-known television game show host and announcer named Bob Hilton and a freelance producer named Bert Rhine, I thought it could be about a project at the crosshairs of sports and entertainment. It turned out to be one of the most meaningful and, for a time, maddening projects of my career, which gifted me with the most enduring and enriching moments I ever shared with my father.

Bob Hilton had the primary connection to Dick Clark because

they'd worked together on *The $25,000 Pyramid*. (Go ahead and google him and you'll see that Bob was the voice of some of the biggest game shows on television.) But this was really Bert's idea, and it was clear to me right away that he had a passion for it, a passion I happened to share.

You see, Bert wanted to talk to me about golf—specifically, about iconic courses all over the world. He had an idea for a show that would be part travelogue, part history of these spectacular playgrounds, part excuse to play a couple epic rounds on someone else's dime and pass it off as work. He explained how golf was the only sport where every playing field was unique. I'd never really thought about it in that way, but there was no arguing the point. The sport was not only known for its great, historical courses, but also for its iconic holes—like the island green on the seventeenth hole at Sawgrass in Ponte Vedra Beach, Florida, or the tenth hole at Winged Foot in Scarsdale, New York.

When you work in development, you're always thinking in terms of what might make a good show. It becomes a part of your mindset, one of the ways you look at the world. Every book you read, every newspaper or magazine you subscribe to, every movie or television show you watch— you're always on the lookout for the spark of a new idea. When you talk to someone knowledgeable or fanatical about a certain subject, you lean in and listen just a little closer. When you're on a never-ending quest for a new idea for a show, a single question runs through every waking moment.

What would happen if . . . ?

So I turned to Bert and said, "What would happen if we did a tournament?"

"Sure, why not?" Bert was there to pitch a specific show, but he'd been around enough to know that if his idea sparked a related idea, it was worth discussing.

"What would happen if we played one hole at eighteen of the greatest golf courses?"

Bert landed immediately on the same page, and soon we were spit-balling a concept that we called the *American Great 18 Golf Championship*—a made-for-television tournament that would pit four top golfers against a stitched-together course composed of eighteen signature holes at eighteen of America's most famous golf courses. The tournament was built on a simple conceit, but pulling it off was extremely complicated with a lot of moving parts. From a production standpoint, it would turn out to be a logistical Rubik's Cube—a puzzle I thought I might never solve.

Our first order of business was coming up with our list of eighteen legendary courses. Some of the courses on our wish list were public, some were private, but each had its own rules, its own beauty, and its own idiosyncrasies. Naturally, we had to pay attention to golf math—meaning, there had to be the right amount of par threes, par fours, and par fives to create the most unique par seventy-two golf round ever played. Then we had to get out a map and figure out a way to accomplish this odyssey on a four-day shooting schedule, which seemed to us a workable timetable.

Within those parameters, we came up with a technical plan to give viewers state-of-the-art coverage of the golf itself, along with a behind-the-scenes chronicle of the journey. In practical terms, we had to assemble an all-star golf crew to travel with us from hole to hole, as well as production coordinators at each location who would be charged with hiring local support staff. Once we had that part figured out, we had to convince four of the best golfers in the world to throw in with us on this crazy adventure.

For Bert, this was the biggest reach of his professional life to date, and he worked his tail off to make it happen, but before we could even get going full tilt we had to tee things up in such a way that I could take it to Dick Clark for his approval. I needed to convince myself that the show we had in mind was doable, but the *real* reason I did so much prep was that I'd been around Dick long enough to know I'd have one shot to make my case. I was helped along by my assistant, Deana Delshad, and some friendly consultants like Greg McLaughlin, the PGA tournament director for the LA Open, although most of the heavy-lifting fell to me and my new partner, Bert Rhine.

We drew up a wish list of all the legendary courses we wanted to consider—Medinah Country Club in Illinois; Harbour Town in Hilton Head, South Carolina; Merion Golf Club in Ardmore, Pennsylvania—in consultation with tournament directors and golf journalists and the people we knew who were passionate about golf. Right from the beginning, we decided to call our tournament the *Great 18*, because of course there was no such thing as the *Greatest 18*. There were too many storied championship holes for us to consider that any list would ultimately be subjective, and we didn't want to leave ourselves open to criticism later on.

At certain courses, there were standout holes that had to be in the mix, like the sixteenth hole at Oakland Hills in Michigan or the fourteenth hole at Olympia Fields in Chicago, but once we got out a map and a box of pushpins to help us chart the likely progress of our tournament, the one certainty was that we would close our storybook round on the eighteenth hole at Pebble Beach in California. The greatest finishing hole in the game would have to be *our* finishing hole.

We ended up working on this thing for months—on our own and every so often as a group huddled around a big table with a giant map of the United States, lining up all these moving parts. When the big picture finally became clear and I had enough verbal agreements to put together a reasonable pitch, I set up a time with Dick.

Dick Clark had seen everything there was to see in the television business. He'd been around so long that it seemed like he'd heard every pitch a dozen times over. As often as not, he'd cut me off and say, "Did it" or "Heard it" or "Alan Landsburg's company is doing it."

Another thing: Dick didn't care about sports. He had a general knowledge, but he wasn't a passionate fan, didn't know the names of the players beyond the top superstars of each sport, and he certainly didn't play golf. (Dick's hobby was work.) Moreover, in Dick's mind there was always a good reason *not* to develop a show, so I knew I'd have to make a compelling case in favor of this one wild idea.

I gave him the whole presentation: the only sport where the playing field is different from course to course . . . eighteen magical holes on the most revered and famous golf courses . . . four top golfers traveling together on an epic adventure . . . each champion out for bragging rights on the mother of all courses. I had my map and my pushpins. I had the names of several players who were prepared to throw in with us. I let my obsession for this idea take over. I was totally sold on what Bert and I had put together.

When I was finally through with my pitch, Dick looked at me and said, "That's the stupidest idea I've ever heard."

Some people might have heard that as a resounding no, but when you're reaching, when you believe in something so deeply that you put your all into it, you're not about to be dismissed—even when the person doing the dismissing is your boss and a television legend.

I doubled down and pushed back. "I'm telling you, Dick. This is special. If you play golf, if you're a sports fan, you'll love it. Nobody's ever done anything like this before."

To be a successful producer, you need to be endlessly curious with an open mind big enough to accommodate the next big idea. Dick's initial reaction might have been to stiff-arm the pitch—and perhaps to test my resolve—but he trusted me enough to know that if I believed so strongly in a project, there might just be something to it. The fact that no producer or golf promoter had ever attempted to pull off such an ambitious project wasn't necessarily an argument in my favor, but it was one of the motivating factors for me. It appealed to my creative side. My thinking, then as now, was to look for new ways to tell compelling stories. The impulse to cover new ground, to stand apart, had always been my driver when I was producing sporting events for CBC, and I wanted to bring that spirit of innovation to the work I was now doing on the entertainment side of the business.

Dick had a flurry of follow-up questions: "Can we get the courses? Can we get the players? How much is this going to cost?" And most important, "Can we make money?"

I reminded Dick that golf had been a weekend staple on the networks for decades and that our concept came with a strong opportunity for title sponsorship. I also explained that over eighteen holes there were eighteen additional opportunities to sell meaningful sponsorships on a local or regional basis, complete with on-site hospitality and other incentive packages to help build out our deal.

Most of Dick's programming of late had been prime-time network fare, but he was certainly aware that there was money to be made in the weekend daytime landscape—that's where he'd gotten his start with *American Bandstand*. It was the golf piece he didn't fully grasp just yet, so I tried to sell him on that. After a while, he put up his hands and said, "I get it, Arthur. If you think this is something that can work for us, you can go ahead and play. Let's see if someone will actually buy it."

It wasn't exactly resounding enthusiasm, but it was enough for us to continue. And in the end, the tournament and the show would not have come together without his support. His imprimatur and the weight of his production company was enough for us to move the project forward.

———————————

All along, I was working a dozen other projects in various stages of development or production, but I started spending more and more time on this one crazy idea, finding some time nearly every day to consult with Bert and smooth over some detail or other.

For every major step forward, there was a significant step back. We secured most of the golf courses on our list, and once it was clear we'd be able to get the rest, I flew to New York to pitch the show to the networks. FOX Sports didn't exist just yet, so I was only dealing with ABC, CBS, and NBC. All three had a long history of golf programming, but even though the networks knew the market and understood the singular appeal of our concept, none of them were willing to take the risk that everything would come together the right way or that they could sell the idea to sponsors. This meant we'd have to buy our way onto their airwaves—Dick Clark Productions would purchase the airtime, and in exchange the network would allow us to sell the majority of the advertising inventory on our own and keep most of the proceeds. Basically, Dick would have to take the risk, while the networks would provide commentators and graphics and promotional support, so that it would look like a show that belonged on their airwaves.

All of the network executives I pitched in New York told me that I'd have to get waivers from the PGA Tour, allowing our four golfers to participate in a non-PGA tour event. As it happened, I knew John Evenson, the director of broadcasting at the PGA, from back when he was working at IndyCar and I was at CBC producing the Toronto Indy. So I called him up, reintroduced myself, and made my pitch.

When I was through, there was a long moment of silence.

"You'll never pull this off," he finally said, adding that before he could even think about signing off on a project like this, we'd have to get agreements from the individual golf courses.

I told him we already had letters of intent from a number of them.

He said we'd need to get the players.

I told him I'd spoken to a bunch of player agents and that there was a lot of interest.

He said we'd need a deal with the broadcast network.

I told him we'd have one of the networks on board soon enough.

With all of these roadblocks, I got the feeling this was something the PGA didn't really want to deal with, but John could hear that I'd done my homework.

"Come back to me with signed agreements from the network, the courses, and the players, and I'll give you the waivers you need," he said.

I decided to pursue a deal with ABC because the logical time for us to take this special event to air was in the fall and they had some openings. Golf had become almost a year-round sport, but the Tour Champion-ship in the fall typically marked the end of the big-time tournament season. To be sure, we couldn't compete against a traditional golf tour-nament—the PGA would never give us our waiver. NBC and CBS had committed most of their fall Sunday afternoons to football—I would have loved to position our tournament as the second half of an NFL doubleheader, but there were no time slots available—so in the end we made a deal with ABC.

David Downs, ABC's vice president of programming, agreed to hold two Sundays for us in October, and when I went back to Dick Clark to report, we turned our attention to a working budget. Basically, he wanted to know what this thing was going to cost us. Without a fee from ABC for broadcast rights, all he could see was a whole lot of money going out and not a whole lot of money coming in. I gave him my back-of-the-envelope math: about $1 million for the airtime on ABC, $1 million in player guarantees and prize money, $1 million in projected production costs.

"So how are we going to make money, Arthur?" he asked again—this time facing the prospect of roughly $3 million in expenses.

"We'll get a title sponsor, hopefully in the multimillion-dollar range. And then we'll have the commercial inventory and all those sponsorship packages to sell."

I'd learned at CBC that sports programming tended to be over-indexed with advertisers because sports offered the best opportunity for advertisers to target men. Advertisers wanted their brands to be associated with major, talked-about sporting events. Golf in particular appealed to advertisers looking to reach upscale men, such as financial companies, luxury car brands, and credit card companies. To sweeten the deal, we offered tournament packages to go along with their ad buys: event signage, hospitality on the course, VIP tickets, and more. These sweeteners had long been a great selling tool for the Super Bowl or the Olympics or the Masters, and here we offered potential sponsors an embedded experience with four of the game's greats and an all-access pass to one of the most unusual (and hopefully memorable) golf tournaments ever conceived.

When I mentioned that golf broadcasts typically featured ads and title sponsorships for cars, Dick's ears pricked up. "I know a guy," he said.

(Dick Clark *always* knew a guy.)

In this case, the guy was Ken Laurence, the national director of marketing for Chrysler, a bear of a man who happened to love golf. Before I knew it, I was on a plane to Detroit to meet with Ken to pitch the show. The great thing about meeting with the client directly was that we could bypass their ad agency, so Dick's introduction was invaluable.

The more I thought about it, the more I thought a car company would be a perfect fit. There were eighteen photo ops built into our concept, which would allow us to drive the golfers to each course in a Chrysler vehicle, as well as eighteen opportunities to host hospitality events for their local dealers, so I built that into my pitch. Chrysler was already a major golf sponsor, and my hope was to appeal to Ken as a golfer and to get him to see the synergy in partnering with us on this unique event.

Ken was a big guy—about six foot three, maybe 250 pounds. When I pitched him the idea, he practically jumped up and down with excitement. His interest filled the room, so I kept adding all these sweeteners to the mix. He loved the concept right away, but he liked all these add-ons even more—the product placement; the hospitality; the chance to associate the Chrysler brand with a new, high-profile event; and, maybe best of all, the chance for him and his team to ride the private jet with these great players and soak up the action in an up-close-and-personal way.

"This is amazing," he said after I'd laid it all out for him. "Let me think about it."

We didn't have a deal just yet, but the meeting couldn't have gone any better. As I boarded the plane for the trip home, I realized we'd never discussed a price for the title sponsorship package. This wasn't a strategy so much as an oversight. Ken had been so caught up in the excitement that I'd gotten caught up in it too.

Ken called me the next morning and said, "We're in."

"But I never told you the price."

"So tell me the price."

I leaned on the best guesses I'd laid out for Dick Clark and said, "Three million."

We quickly landed on a number close enough to our projected costs to take a lot of the risks out of doing the show. Alongside the title sponsorship, there would still be approximately 75 percent of the ad inventory for us to sell, so there was an opportunity for Dick Clark Productions to do well. However, there were also plenty of opportunities for things to fall a different way. I wanted to be sure we could absorb any unexpected turns.

We were met with one soon enough. After a couple weeks, I went back to the PGA with my contracts and letters of agreement in hand, having been led to believe that the promised waiver would just be a formality. But PGA's John Evenson threw us another curve by taking an entirely different position than the one he'd taken in our previous conversation.

"You'll need to pay us a rights fee," he said.

"What?" I wasn't sure I'd heard him correctly.

"For the media rights to show our players on television, playing golf."

"You're kidding, right? You're a union. I'm paying your union members guaranteed money. I'm putting up prize money. And now you're stepping on their ability to earn all that money by insisting on a rights fee you didn't think to mention in the first place?"

The rights fee, as I recall, was $350,000, which of course didn't fit in our already tight budget, so I went back to Dick Clark and told him where we now stood.

"Fuck 'em," Dick said in his inimitable way of cutting straight to the point. He asked why we even needed the PGA waiver. I explained that ABC had a long-term relationship with the organization and wasn't about to go against them on this, and that even if we could get the players to go against them, we'd almost certainly be sued.

Dick considered this latest predicament for about ten seconds and said, "Well, then I guess we're not doing it."

This was an easy decision for Dick, but it was not at all easy for me. I understood Dick's thinking, of course. It was his money on the line, not mine. Moreover, we had so many balls in the air at Dick Clark Productions, we didn't really have the time to chase one errant toss. He was inclined to let *any of them* drop when things started to bounce the wrong way. I was cut another way, especially when I was this deep into it.

Dick explained that he felt like the PGA was holding our project hostage with this late demand and that he wasn't about to be black-mailed, but I thought there might be some way to push back. There was no denying that the additional $350,000 put our company at risk, so I told the players and the courses the tournament was off. Everyone was disappointed—upset, even. Me especially. I'd just spent eight months on this project, thinking I was playing by one set of rules, while on the other side of the table we were being jerked around.

I called John Evenson to tell him we were out. I was pissed. "You never said anything about a fee," I reminded him.

"Of course there's a fee," he said. "There's always a fee."

From his tone, it was clear he thought I'd been naive to think otherwise.

From mine, it was clear I thought his position was unethical and unprofessional.

Dick had a scheduled trip to Florida coming up on his calendar, and I suggested he stop in to see John's boss, PGA tour commissioner Deane Beman. Dick was game. He would not be blackmailed, but at the same time he would not be pushed from a project that had this much time invested in it. The meeting was cordial, and Dick was able to get the PGA to take a reduced rights fee, but by this point our window had started to close. I couldn't get ABC to hold the time, and it wasn't clear Chrysler would still be on board. Ken Laurence had room in his budget when we'd shaken hands on a deal, but now that we'd hit the pause button, I couldn't be sure those monies were still in place.

When you reach for something meaningful and it eludes your grasp, keep reaching. I put it out there to Bert Rhine and everyone else who'd been on this journey with us that we'd find a way to stage the event the following year. It was a promise I made to myself as much as to everyone else. There were no guarantees that I could find a way to realign all these moving parts at a later date, but the only person I'd told that our project was now in jeopardy was my father. He'd been so excited about the tournament and understood my frustration. To everyone else—the folks at the network, at Chrysler, the players and their agents—I kept putting a positive spin on things, telling them the tournament was going to happen. I was like a broken record with all of my positivity.

It's going to happen.

It became a mantra, like I was talking myself into believing it, manifesting the outcome I hadn't realized I so desperately wanted, and I'm happy to report that we pulled it off the following year. The golf gods smiled, and we were able to tap back into whatever reservoirs of momentum and good faith we'd left behind. After another round of pitching and arm-twisting, Chrysler was back on board, and ABC agreed to put us on the schedule for back-to-back Sundays in the fall. All that reaching finally paid off.

Our playing field looked a little different than what we'd originally planned. Fred Couples and Craig Stadler had to drop out because of scheduling conflicts, but I was able to replace them with Tom Kite and Davis Love III—a fortuitous turn because Kite had just won the US Open in 1992 and Love had won the Players Championship that same year. That duo joined two of the most popular players on tour—John Daly, who won the 1991 PGA Championship, and Fuzzy Zoeller, a Masters and US Open winner—giving us a fearsome foursome that was truly at the top of its game.

The Chrysler American Great 18 Golf Championship aired on ABC in October 1993. By almost every measure, the tournament was a success. We got positive media attention from national outlets like ESPN and *USA Today*, as well as in local markets at every stop along the way. The one area where we came up short was in the moneymaking, which as far as Dick Clark was concerned had been the point of the whole enterprise. To be clear, we made a small profit on the project, but we didn't exactly get rich on it. In golf terms, you could say we made par—but, hey, some of my most memorable rounds have ended with me shooting par.

(I wish!)

All of the reaching and reaching again and reaching yet again brought us to the sixteenth tee at Oakland Hills, in Birmingham, Michigan—our first hole! The golfers were giddy with the thought of playing all these tremendous holes. I stood with them in the tee box at Oakland Hills, and as they were getting ready to tee off, I overheard Fuzzy Zoeller lean into John Daly and whisper, "You ever play this course before?"

John Daly smiled and said, "Never sober."

In that one exchange, I realized I had somehow made a place for myself on the inside of something special.

We had a documentary-style crew filming behind-the-scenes footage during the entire run of the tournament: on the plane, on the course, at the meals we managed to scarf down on the fly. We were planning to include the footage in our broadcast—an accent to the tournament itself— so I wanted to make sure we captured the ordinary moments inside this extraordinary adventure.

We had a beautiful charter plane at our disposal with about one hundred first-class, luxury seats—plenty of room for our key camera and tech people, our four golfers and their caddies, reporters from *Golf Digest* and *Entertainment Tonight* who would publish and report major behind-the-scenes pieces ahead of our broadcast, Ken Laurence from Chrysler, those of us on the production side . . . and one more important person.

For months, I'd planned on surprising my father with an invitation to join me on this trip, but I waited until everything was all set. The last thing I wanted was for him to have his heart set on this, only for it to fall apart over some last-minute snag—like, say, the PGA holding the project hostage again.

When I told him we were back on and good to go, he was delighted.

"It's finally happening," I said.

"I'm so proud of you, Arthur," he said. "You never gave up."

"You're coming with us."

"What?"

"I have a job for you. You're going to be the head marshal."

"No joke?" he said.

"No joke. Just get yourself to Detroit and I'll have someone pick you up and take you to our first tee. I'll take care of everything else from there."

I knew my father. There's no way he would agree to join me on this trip of a lifetime if he felt like some kind of hanger-on. But since I wrapped the invitation inside a job offer, he jumped at the idea. His primary responsibility would be to work with local volunteers to maintain crowd control—a big deal, as it turned out, because thousands and thousands of people turned up at each course to take in the spectacle and watch these great players play one hole of golf.

In all, we traveled about ten thousand miles, so one of the great lines that surfaced among our group was that the course played "ten thousand miles from the back tees." Another great line: "It was two years of killing ourselves for four days of fun."

My father and I shared a room at the Riviera Country Club in Pacific Palisades one night. The course was only twenty minutes from my house in LA, but we needed to get an early start for our jam-packed final day of shooting, so I'd commandeered one of the guest rooms at the club and made the best of it. I hadn't shared a room with my father since I was seven or eight years old on a father-son fishing trip to La Vérendrye, a wildlife reserve in Quebec, during which I'd washed down a disproportionate number of cheese sandwiches with a disproportionate number of Cokes, all before eight in the morning. As we relived the events of the day before we drifted off, I asked my father if he remembered those cheese sandwiches.

"I remember," he said.

"That was something, right?" I said.

"This is something, Arthur. This trip is something."

And it was . . . it truly was.

The tournament itself was a nail-biter. A nasty hurricane battered the North Carolina coast in August 1993, forcing us to cancel play at Pinehurst Resort and the Country Club of North Carolina, but we were able to juggle our schedule and add the storied sixteenth hole at Colleton River Plantation on Hilton Head Island in South Carolina and the 516-yard fifteenth hole at La Quinta's famous Mountain Course in California.

Our four golfers brought their A games. You don't get to be a champion without being wired to win, so even though it was a made-for-television tournament and there was tremendous camaraderie as we vagabonded from hole to hole, the competitive juices were flowing among this group. (The $250,000 first prize surely helped!) Everyone involved also brought their A games, in fact—all the way down to the host groundskeepers at each of these legendary courses, who made sure their greens all featured their most precarious Sunday pin placements, that the rough was high and the greens were fast . . . basically, that their courses were at their most difficult and showcased in the best possible light.

Fuzzy had been leading most of the way until we reached the thirteenth hole at PGA West in La Quinta, California, a 215-yard par three that was serving as our sixteenth hole. I'd played that course a bunch of times, and like a lot of amateurs I always froze at the thirteenth—a diabolical hole rimmed on one side by water. Regrettably, Fuzzy froze as well, putting two balls into the drink, which dropped him into a tie with Davis Love III going into the seventeenth—a 365-yard par four at Spyglass Hill in Pebble Beach.

Under normal circumstances, a tie headed to the final two holes would be a dream for a tournament director—a surefire way to keep viewers glued to their sets straight up to the closing credits. For us, it was more of a nightmare. I hadn't counted on a tie, and here it was already midafternoon as we were finishing up in La Quinta. We were only three holes into the day's shooting schedule. We still had to get to Pebble Beach to our final two courses, and the sun wasn't going to stay out forever. This was a concern . . . a *big* concern.

We couldn't end a tournament for the ages in a tie, but there was no contingency in our plans for the tournament to spill over onto a fifth day if we needed to stage some type of shoot-out. I was only able to contract with these golfers for four days of play, and our all-star crew had other assignments lined up all over the country. There wasn't room in our budget to bring back these golfers or our production team for what could potentially be another few holes of playoff golf. I caught myself thinking in worst-case scenarios.

Oh, man . . . that final day of shooting in California was wild. We piled onto the luxury tour bus I'd arranged to ferry our golfers to the next course, and John Daly noticed a fast-food restaurant by the side of the road and insisted we stop for burgers. He was starving, he said. He wanted to get burgers and fries and shakes for the entire crew. I didn't think there was enough cushion in our itinerary to absorb an unscheduled rest stop, but two things I'd learned over our four-day shoot was that there was no denying Big John when he wanted to stop for burgers . . . and that his largesse was as large as the man himself. I remember the sight of these four famous golfers spilling out of this luxurious ride into a fast-food joint on the outskirts of one of the golf capitals of the world, and the look on the face of the kid at the counter as John Daly ordered fifty burgers for our entire entourage—a story I could only assume the kid would dine out on for years.

Mercifully, Davis sank a long birdie putt on our seventeenth hole at Spyglass to take a one-stroke lead, and I breathed a sigh of relief, even though I knew deep down that this single stroke hadn't put us in the clear just yet. Fuzzy could easily have found a way to reclaim that stroke on the next hole, but I wouldn't even let myself go there in my thinking. Not just yet.

We hit the course at Pebble Beach the same way we'd hit the seventeen previous courses. The camera operators in our traveling party ran to their camera positions, which had already been set up by a local crew. The assistant pro at the host club then went out and played the hole so everyone could make sure we had the cameras positioned just right, because we'd only have one crack at it, while our four golfers splintered off to warm-up and try for the last time to find their swings and the rhythm that might have left them on the plane or drive.

Before the golfers teed off, we always conducted a little ceremony. Our tournament director would introduce the players to the gallery, and then I'd step up on behalf of Chrysler and Dick Clark Productions and present the general manager of the club, or perhaps the head pro, with a commemorative plaque to thank them for being a part of our Great 18 tournament.

For years, my parents kept a beautifully framed picture from one of those presentations by my father's bedside—a shot of me with my dad, the honorary head marshal, beaming in the background. I'd forgotten all about the picture until I went to my father's apartment to clean out his things after he passed. Of course I took it home with me and gave it a place of honor in my home office, where my father continues to watch over me.

It was quite a scene that day at Pebble Beach along the rocky shore above the Pacific. All of the Chrysler bigwigs were there. The network brass. The local dignitaries. There was pomp and circumstance and majesty . . . all that good stuff.

Dick Clark had been on hand to kick off the tournament in Michigan but was away on vacation for most of our shoot. However, he was able to fly in for the eighteenth hole at Pebble Beach. He later told me he was blown away by the excitement we'd created for our silly little tournament—"the stupidest idea I've ever heard!"—but I don't think he was fully aware of the stress we were under as we played golf's greatest finishing hole. The sun was fading fast. In an *Entertainment Tonight* piece to promote the show, it almost looked like we were playing in darkness. We had to turn up the iris on our cameras as we were losing the light so our broadcast viewers wouldn't notice.

There were some great highlights. When John Daly, who'd been struggling for most of the round, sent a ball sailing into the ocean, Fuzzy asked to see his club, which he then promptly hurled into the water. Of course a bunch of spectators scrambled down those rocks to retrieve the souvenir. When John finally reached the green, well out of it by this point, he handed his golf bag to a kid in the crowd and said, "Maybe you'll have better luck with these clubs than me." Then he pulled his putter from the bag and went to see about his putt while the crowd cheered and the kid beamed at *his* souvenir.

Davis's one-stroke lead held, and we managed to avert the disaster of a tie.

For me, the greatest highlight of all was walking the fairway with my father in twilight, approaching the eighteenth green on this legendary finishing hole in the footsteps of these legendary golfers. My father threw his arm around me, like he used to do when I was a kid, and even in the dim light I could see that he was smiling.

He said, "Can you believe this, Arthur? Can you believe this?"

It really was unbelievable.

One of the great side benefits to this incredible adventure with my dad was the way it lifted him in the eyes of his buddies. For a time, right after the shoot, they all thought he was exaggerating—a teller of tall tales. He'd come back to Elm Ridge Country Club, his home course in Montreal, and couldn't stop talking about our tournament. Naturally, all these guys liked to brag on their children, and for years he'd been telling them about his son the television producer. I suspect he was already losing his audience by this point, but now everything was Fuzzy this or Davis that. Pebble Beach this or Winged Foot that. The routine at Elm

Ridge, as elsewhere, was to have lunch in the grill room after a round or hang around the locker room *kibbutzing* with the guys, watching a tournament on the big screen, and my father would go on and on, and these poor guys on the listening end would say, "Yeah, yeah, Solly, we get it" or "You told us that one already" or "Stop bullshitting us, Solly."

The show was on a tape delay, so it was months before the tournament aired, and when it finally showed up on the screen one Sunday afternoon at Elm Ridge, my father's golf buddies were floored. They saw him on television, getting almost as much screen time as the pros, having the time of his life, and they looked over at him in astonishment.

I was happy for my father that he had this moment in the sun with his friends, but even more so for what we'd shared. What a blessing to make a sweet memory for a man I so loved and admired. For the rest of his life, we'd swap stories from that trip. I'll always be grateful for the precious gift of this time with my father, crisscrossing the country in a private plane with his favorite golfers, visiting all these iconic golf courses, and most especially for the chance to invite him into my world in this up-close-and-personal way. In a lot of ways, it's the *only* thing that mattered in the end.

As I set these memories to paper, I reflect on what it means to work after all. Why do we roll up our sleeves and chase the arbitrary goals we set for ourselves? Why do we reach just a little further, push ourselves just a little harder, give just a little more than everybody else who might be out there reaching, pushing, and giving in service of those same goals? Do we do it to feel recognized or validated in some way? Do we do it for the money or job security that might come to us as a result? Do we do it to leave a mark or change the world in some way? Do we do it to lift ourselves onto some higher pedestal, from which to climb even higher? Or do we do it to carve out the luxury to spend time with the people we love, doing the things we love?

The answer, for me, falls somewhere in that great line we shared within our ranks. *Two years of killing ourselves for four days of fun?* That's a trade I'd make all over again.

9

"START ROOTING FOR THE PACERS!"

When I moved to Los Angeles to work with Dick Clark, I thought I was done with sports. I worked on a number of sports and entertainment projects, like the *Jim Thorpe Pro Sports Awards* and *The Chrysler American Great 18 Golf Championship*, but those were specials—part of a well-rounded suite of shows that really covered the television waterfront. Most of our programming was centered around entertainment, about as far away from a stadium or arena as you could imagine, although from time to time I'd catch myself looking at a new project through the eyes of a veteran sports television producer. In a lot of ways, the energy and excitement of an awards show, complete with backstage interviews and prepared packages on the stars or nominees, was like the drama of a big game, complete with pregame and postgame interviews, analyses, and sidebar features on the athletes. It was all of a piece.

Still, sports was in my blood . . . and in my bones. Even though I was out of the game on a day-to-day basis, I was still attuned to the ways the games were covered on American television. As a newly minted Angeleno, for example, I watched the Lakers games with both a rooting interest and a professional eye. When the Olympics came around on the calendar, I was glued to my set, cheering for the athletes who were introduced to me through the packaged profiles I had helped to popularize when I was just starting out.

Perhaps it was inevitable that I wound up working in sports, but after moving to LA, I never thought I'd wind up back on that same path. I started hearing from industry headhunters, looking to recruit me for some executive position or other. At first I rejected these entreaties—none of them felt like my next *reach*—but after a while I felt restless and wondered if it was time to consider a move.

I was in my early thirties and had only been in LA for a few years when Steve Unger, a well-known Hollywood headhunter, called to see if I'd be interested in running the USA Network. It gave me pause. I thought about it, long and hard, and finally decided it would be pretty cool. Steve was in no position to actually offer me the job, but he said my name was on the list. After a series of interviews with the chairperson of USA, Kay Koplovitz, it was down to me and one other person. At the time USA was 50 percent owned by Paramount and 50 percent owned by MCA Universal, so Kay of course wanted the owners to weigh in and sent me to meet with the most senior executives at both studios.

In the end, I didn't get the job. It stung to come so close to such a big job, and I'd allowed myself to think that it would work out, just like it had for my reaches with CBC and Dick Clark. I wondered why it hadn't worked out. I thought back to that low, low moment at CBS in New York when I found my résumé in the trash—a disappointment that turned out to be one of the best things that ever happened to me. I wasn't ready to make that kind of move, back then. Apparently, there were still some amazing assignments I needed to see through at CBC. I leaned on the lesson of that earlier disappointment as I tried to understand this one, and I consoled myself with the idea that it just wasn't meant to be, that perhaps I was meant to do something else.

On the heels of that USA Network disappointment, I was offered jobs at both Universal and Paramount, but I turned them both down because they were purely senior executive positions that didn't appeal to me. And yet Universal kept calling, determined to find some kind of fit.

Finally, the chairman of the television group, Tom Wertheimer, called with what seemed like a dream position. He wanted me to become the senior vice president of the entire television group, a new position he would create with me in mind. He said that I'd be tasked with developing programming, that I could pursue any projects that appealed to me, and that I would work with all four of the studio's division presidents to see where that programming might fit—network, syndication, cable, or home video.

It all sounded too good to be true, and as if *that* wasn't enough, I heard from two of the most powerful people in the history of show business, telling me how much they wanted me on board. One of those people was Lew Wasserman, the chairman of Universal and widely considered "the godfather of Hollywood" at the time; the other was Sid Sheinberg, the CEO and the man who discovered Steven Spielberg.

I told myself that this was the reason why I didn't get that USA job, but in the end it really wasn't. My time at Universal was the shortest stint of my career, although it was not without a measure of success. I developed shows that made it onto every one of the major networks, but I missed working hands-on. This feeling was awfully familiar, and it took me back to a few years earlier when I was adjusting to my role as head of CBC Sports.

I'm at my happiest *making* television, not just developing it. Dick Clark and I had an agreement that whatever I developed, I would produce as well. Frankly, it's what I do best, but at Universal there was no room in the studio model for an executive to do both. In this corporate environment, my primary job was to make money, and so once one of our projects got sold, it was on me to develop and sell something else.

Deep down, I knew this going in, but the chance to work at a studio in such a top-level way was too good to turn down. Sometimes when you reach, you realize the thing you're chasing is not the thing you really want. I discovered I didn't like being a senior studio executive, despite the money, the power, the prestige.

Before I could act on that discovery, I was derailed by a corporate shake-up: Universal was sold to Seagram's, and all of a sudden I had a new boss, Greg Meidel, who came over from FOX and encouraged me to stay on in this executive position despite my misgivings, with the assurance that he would set me up with my own little production company under the Universal umbrella at some unspecified date in the future. I signed a new deal with Greg and agreed to soldier on for the next while, in hopes of bigger, more creative things to come. However, the next while didn't last too terribly long.

Just two weeks into this new arrangement, I was gifted an opportunity to return to sports television . . . at FOX. I wasn't interested at first—FOX was primarily a football-only outlet at the time and I thought I was done being the sports guy. During my time at Dick Clark Productions and at Universal, I had worked hard to shed that narrow image and was now thought of as an entertainment guy. Still, I was persuaded to at least take the meeting with David Hill, the head of FOX Sports—a charismatic Aussie who was boisterous, charming, and funny. He had Rupert Murdoch's complete trust to run FOX's sports division, which was about to be transformed. David told me about the master plan for FOX Sports, and as he laid it out for me, it was clear that football was just the beginning. I was impressed . . . excited, even.

David offered me the job of executive vice president of programming, production, and news for FOX Sports Net. I grabbed at it, but with one caveat: I wanted David's assurance that I could work in a hands-on way on certain projects.

He smiled and said, "It's your network. Do what you want to do. Fair warning, though. We're going to be getting very big, very fast."

So there it was: the reason I didn't get the USA job, spread out before me like a glorious opportunity . . . and another big reach.

After just eighteen months, I was out of Universal and back in sports. My thing, always, was to set the bar high and then work like crazy to meet it, to beat my own expectations and surpass the expectations of others. We were able to turn FOX Sports Net from a small, up-and-coming enterprise with just a handful of employees to a multibillion-dollar organization with a massive reach and a staff of thousands.

Perhaps our most notable accomplishment at FOX Sports during my tenure was the development and launch of twenty-two regional sports networks, which were instrumental in helping us establish the network as a viable competitor to ESPN, which had been recognized by many as the leader in sports programming when I signed on. For whatever reason, it bugged the hell out of me that ESPN had claimed this distinction for the network, because in reality ESPN was no such thing. There might have been a time when they were the lead dog in the hunt for wall-to-wall sports coverage, but there was a lot of innovative, game-changing work being done in sports television by a number of networks—and now, especially, at FOX Sports.

Once I got to FOX Sports, I was determined to push back on this notion in whatever ways I could. Indeed, I got a tremendous kick looking for ways to tweak or needle or otherwise annoy the competition—really, I went out of my way to drive ESPN crazy, partly because I had it in my head that we were in a kind of tug-of-war with them for the mantle of industry leader, but mostly because it was a whole lot of fun. (For *me*, anyway.)

Perhaps the best example of this came toward the end of the 1998 baseball season, when Mark McGwire and Sammy Sosa were duking it out to beat the storied single-season home run marks established by Babe Ruth and Roger Maris and become the game's new single-season home run king. At the time, FOX Sports covered the baseball waterfront—we carried over two thousand games because we had the rights to almost every Major League Baseball team through our local packages and regional networks, in addition to our national broadcasts. Chances were, if you were watching a baseball game in 1998, it was one of ours, and we were enormously proud of our coverage.

Trouble was, ESPN had previously negotiated a "cut-in" deal with MLB, allowing them to cover a milestone moment as it was taking place. The live cut-in could happen in the middle of *SportsCenter* or *Baseball Tonight* or some other game or sporting event they were covering. To be clear, they couldn't join our coverage for an entire game—just long enough for that moment to unfold, like a single at bat or half inning. Invariably, the games they were cutting into, live, during this legendary home run chase tended to be one of ours—which I saw as a singular opportunity to promote our network on our rival's platform.

With this in mind, I instructed our production team to make sure the FOX Sports logo was displayed fairly prominently (and unavoidably!)

in the corner of the screen, in such a way that ESPN couldn't squeeze the picture and keep it off their air. I'd be watching the games in my office, where I had a wall of monitors displaying the games we were covering live, so whenever McGwire or Sosa were at bat, I'd call the remote producer at each game and tell them to do a FOX Sports promo, either as a simple voice-over or in combination with a graphic supered underneath the action. I had a hotline to the truck, and it got to where everyone knew that if a call was coming in from me, it would probably have something to do with this one-sided battle with ESPN I was playing out in my head.

McGwire would step to the plate and our announcer would say, "Coming up on FOX Sports Net, the leader in sports television . . ." Or we'd promote one of our upcoming national games or a car race or our FOX Sports National News with Keith Olbermann and Kevin Frazier—whatever we were prioritizing in our marketing at the time. Basically, we would find some way to drop the name of FOX Sports Net in the middle of our coverage when ESPN switched over to us.

Once, when Dallas Cowboys wide receiver Michael Irvin was about to announce his retirement, and I learned ESPN was planning to cover the press conference live, I reached out to Michael with a special ask. We'd signed Michael to be an NFL studio analyst, and we'd already started training him and looking ahead to the work he'd do as part of our football broadcast team, so he was happy to take the call and do whatever I needed him to do, within reason of course.

"Someone's gonna ask you at that press conference what you plan to do in retirement," I said, when I got Michael on the phone. "Just tell them you're going to work for FOX Sports, the leader in sports television."

"You got it, Arthur," he said.

"But say it just like that," I said. "'FOX Sports. The leader in sports television.' It's super important."

Of course, it wasn't *super* important, but it was important to me. It gave our team a lift and demonstrated that our footprint in this space was every bit the equal of ESPN's.

Plus, it made me happy.

Years later, I ran into some of the key executives at ESPN who had been at the network during this time, and one of them turned to me and said, "You were like public enemy number one back in those days."

This, too, made me happy—and illustrates how sometimes we reach to feel better about ourselves or to help those around us feel better about themselves. If, in the reaching, you put the competition on notice . . . well, so much the better.

———————

One of my most satisfying initiatives at FOX Sports was the development of our documentary division. Our stated mission was to seek compelling, out-of-the-way stories behind familiar headlines and to provide an outlet for top-tier journalists and filmmakers looking to shine meaningful light on the human side of sports—a genre that by now has become a staple but back in 1998 was relatively new. Years later, ESPN would get a lot of well-deserved attention for the success of its *30 for 30* documentary series, which continues to deliver tremendous content. Various streaming services have subsequently entered this arena and produced some excellent sports-themed films, but we were out in front on this.

Our first production was a look back at the life of Baseball Hall of Famer and legendary humanitarian Roberto Clemente, which featured one of my favorite quotes from an ex-ballplayer assessing the impact of a great rival: "He didn't play right field. He performed in right field." The line was from Hall of Famer Frank Robinson, whose Baltimore Orioles had been famously drubbed by Clemente and the Pittsburgh Pirates in the 1971 World Series.

We also produced a fine documentary on the controversial UNLV basketball coach Jerry Tarkanian called *Between the Madness* that ended up generating a lot of positive attention and attracting a number of prominent filmmakers to our space.

Another of the stories we explored for our first slate of films was the enduring rivalry between Larry Bird and Earvin "Magic" Johnson, which dated back to the 1979 NCAA Championship game that pitted Bird's

Indiana State Sycamores against Johnson's Michigan State Spartans. The 1979 tournament was a turning point in the growth in popularity of college basketball, a moment in time just before March Madness came to occupy such a prominent place on our annual sports calendar. Just to give you an idea of the impact of that one game, the Nielsen ratings for the finals that year were the highest ever for *any* basketball game in the United States, college or pro, and it would remain the highest for nearly forty years. As Larry Bird and Magic Johnson ascended to the NBA, their great rivalry continued and helped to build the league into the global brand it is today.

Since we were looking ahead to the twentieth anniversary of that game, it made sense for us to revisit it. We surrounded the game and its aftermath with insightful commentary from players and coaches and combined both familiar game footage and sound bites with never-before-seen images and fresh interviews. Clearly, no reappraisal of Magic Johnson's championship run or Larry Bird's emergence on the national stage would have been complete without hearing from those two superstars, who by this point had stepped away from their legendary professional playing careers, so our top priority was to secure their participation.

I'd already had the unique privilege of seeing these two greats on the same basketball court in a behind-the-scenes way in 1992—one of the most memorable celebrity encounters of my career. I was working for Dick Clark in Los Angeles, producing *The Jim Thorpe Pro Sports Awards*, which was a kind of precursor to ESPN's ESPY Awards. That year, Michael Jordan was scheduled to receive our Player of the Year Award in basketball, and we'd tapped Magic Johnson to present it to him. Our writer was an up-and-coming comedian, actor, writer, and producer named Larry Wilmore, who'd go on to create *The Bernie Mac Show*, executive produce *Black-ish*, and star in his own late-night talk show. As this was during the run-up to the Summer Olympics in Barcelona, where each would play a prominent role on the so-called "Dream Team"—the first American Olympic team to feature active professional players from the NBA—Magic and Michael couldn't be at the show live. So we arranged to tape the presentation following the US team's practice session at a facility in Portland.

I got to the gym with Larry Wilmore and our camera crew just as the Dream Team was finishing one of its final practices before heading to Spain for the Olympics. Of course, we knew we'd be arriving on the heels of the practice, but it was a heady thing to see all these great players gathered on the same court, preparing to set off in pursuit of their shared goal: a gold medal. There was Michael Jordan, Charles Barkley, Patrick Ewing, Clyde Drexler, Karl Malone—the very best of the very best.

We'd arranged for a spot in the dressing room to film the presentation, so we hung back and waited for the players to disperse—and sure enough, most of them moved to meet with their agents or their wives or girlfriends and went their separate ways. Very quickly, the area around the court emptied, but then I noticed two of the players hanging back, still working on their games. Those two players? Magic and Bird . . . at opposite ends of the court, shooting, grabbing their own rebounds, squeezing every last drop from this workout even though the clock had run out on their formal practice and their teammates had all left the court.

I couldn't interrupt Magic Johnson while he was still in his "office," so I walked over to my cameraman and quietly told him to roll tape.

"Why?" he said. "What am I taping?"

I shrugged. "I've got no idea. Just roll tape."

Honestly, I had no plans on how or when or if I'd ever use the footage, but I knew that we'd been let in on something special—the chance to see these two greats lost in the rhythms of the game, doing their thing as if no one was watching. Since I was a producer and had a cameraman on hand, I tried to capture this scene.

This is what greatness looks like, I thought. This was what it means to put in the work, to be prepared. These two professionals were at the tail end of their brilliant careers, locked in a decades-long rivalry, momentarily joined as teammates for these Olympic Games but committed to perfecting their craft and pursuing excellence in their own solitary ways.

In the end, I never used that footage, but the moment has stayed with me over the years. It reminds me of the power of living in the present. I don't believe in living in the past, and I'm careful not to let my dreams run too far into the future, where they might be just out of reach. If I could talk to my younger self, I would tell him to enjoy and appreciate the *now*. It took seeing these two all-time greats, quietly going about their business, for me to see this clearly. There was nothing left for them to prove, and yet here they were—the two oldest players on the Dream Team working on their games like nothing else mattered.

Cut to 1998, we were prepping our documentary, which we were calling *Magic Versus Bird: The Game That Changed the Game*. Magic was a (reasonably) easy ask. I knew his manager, Lon Rosen, and Magic and I would occasionally run into each other in and around Los Angeles, so we had him come by the office one day to discuss the project. This was around the time Magic was building his postcareer business portfolio, investing in movie theaters and Starbucks franchises, so he was open to exploring anything that smelled like an opportunity. It was unclear just yet that this documentary would be a moneymaking proposition for him, but he was immediately engaged. He asked meaningful, insightful questions, and by the end of our meeting he wanted to be on board—not just as an interview subject, but as a producer.

Just like that, the great Earvin "Magic" Johnson was one of my producing partners. I would have let him call himself the director if that's what it took to enlist his support and enthusiasm. Keep in mind, producer credits are tossed around like candy in Hollywood. They're not always indicative of a person's role or contribution to a project. Here, though, I understood that Magic wanted to be involved, so I put his interest back on him and said, "You can have a producer credit, but your first job is to get Larry."

He laughed and flashed his trademark smile. "The only way we get Larry," he said, "is to go talk to him in person."

Magic explained that even though the two had been great rivals, they'd become great friends, and he knew his friend's mind. He knew Larry didn't trust the media and that he'd be leery about granting us an interview or participating in any way. Magic was almost the complete opposite—he never met a microphone or a camera he didn't like.

"Trust me on this," Magic said. "Him and me, we're different."

So I trusted him—after all, we were now partners, right?

Larry Bird was coaching the Indiana Pacers at the time, so we pulled out a schedule and compared calendars, thinking we would travel to Indianapolis to take in a game and meet up afterward with Larry to discuss the project.

Let me tell you, going to a basketball game with Magic was a treat— and a revelation. For a lifelong sports fan like myself, who'd been to more playoff games and championship fights and World Series and Super Bowls and Olympic Games than I could possibly remember, there was nothing quite like sitting with one of the all-time greats as he watched one of his all-time rivals coach his team to victory. The way he was able to break down the game was astonishing to me—and I'd had the plea- sure of sitting in the booth with some of the best sports broadcasters in the business. But this was more personal, more intimate. He'd lean in and share a specific observation about a specific player that would never be meant for public consumption or his eyes would light up and he'd break into a giant *hey-I-told-you-so!* grin when something he'd told me was about to happen on the court actually up and happened right on cue. It was like having my own private play-by-play commentator, complete with a boisterous laugh track and inside banter.

Mostly, I was impressed with the way Magic moved about in public. This couldn't have been easy, especially at a basketball game. Fans kept coming up to him, asking for an autograph or a picture, and he kept deflecting them with graciousness and good cheer. He'd say, "Hey man, I'm here to watch the game with my friend. Hit me back at the end of the quarter." He couldn't have been nicer about it, but he was clear that he valued his private time and these Pacers fans should value it as well.

The game was what sportswriters used to call a seesaw affair. The Pacers were up for a stretch, and then they trailed for a stretch. The two teams kept trading the lead. It was edge-of-your-seat stuff, and Magic was into it. The only thing that would have made the game more enjoy- able was if I'd had a rooting interest in the outcome. Finally, with about three minutes left in the game, I learned that I did. The Pacers were down by a basket, and Magic leaned over to me and said, "You know, if the Pacers lose, we can't talk to Larry."

I wasn't sure I'd heard him correctly. "What do you mean?"

"I mean exactly that," Magic said. "If they lose, Larry's gonna be in no mood to talk."

This was news to me. "You're kidding me, right?" I said.

"I wish," Magic said. "You don't want to be the fool who asks Larry Bird for something after a loss."

No, I didn't. But at the same time, I didn't want to be the fool who flew to Indiana for no good reason. We were booked to fly out in the morning, and we each had demands on our time back in Los Angeles. It's not like we had the luxury of waiting around for the Pacers to put one in the win column.

"So what do we do?" I said, starting to think we'd set out on a wild-goose chase—or in pursuit of an even more elusive Bird.

"They lose, we'll just have to come back," Magic said matter-of-factly.

What's interesting here, as I look back, was the casual way Magic approached the situation, alongside my own panicked approach. To my mind, just then, coming back simply wasn't an option. We had a schedule to meet if we had any hope of getting the documentary ready in time for the twentieth anniversary of the Indiana State–Michigan State game.

"That doesn't really work for me, Earvin," I said—calling him by his given name to let him know this was serious. "There's got to be another option."

Magic seemed to give this serious thought as the seesaw tipped once again against the Pacers. "Well then," he said. "There's only one thing left for us to do."

"What's that?"

He flashed another one of his trademark smiles and said, "Start rooting for the Pacers!"

Something about Magic's smile and his deadpan delivery hit me in just the right way, at just the right moment. I laughed. Long and hard. And Magic was right there with me, laughing as well. For the rest of the game, the two of us cheered like kids, jumping up and down and high-fiving every time the Pacers made a basket or a stop, having ourselves a grand old time. We were totally into it, and if any of those fans who'd approached Magic earlier in the game had been looking on, they might have wondered why the hell the two of us were rooting like crazy for the Pacers in the waning moments of an apparently meaning-less regular season game.

The Pacers won the game on the final possession. I couldn't remem-ber the last time I'd had so much fun at a basketball game—or when there had been so much on the line. After the game (and after Magic had made good on all those pending requests for pictures and auto-graphs), we went down to the Pacers' locker room. Magic went in first, and then he brought me in to talk to Larry, who was in a good mood after the Pacers' come-from-behind win. He agreed to participate in the documentary, so the trip to Indianapolis was a success and Magic had made good on his first order of business as producer.

Sometimes it's not enough to simply reach and expect to grab what-ever you need to move ahead. Sometimes you need to sprinkle a little pixie dust on your goal, to root, root, root for the home team, and hope like crazy that the gods are smiling on your affairs . . . in just the right way, at just the right time.

10

HANGING OUT MY OWN SHINGLE

I'd worked with some pretty interesting, mercurial, creative, fearless bosses in my career to this point, but no one embodied *all* of these qualities with the flair and force of Rupert Murdoch, the billionaire media tycoon and chairman and CEO of News Corporation, the parent company of FOX Sports.

To cite just one example of Rupert's business acumen, in December 1993 he decided to "wildly overpay" for the broadcast rights to NFL games, which had traditionally been the domain of the Big Three American networks (ABC, CBS, NBC). Some years earlier, when I was at CBC Sports, it had fallen to me to negotiate the rights with major sports organizations, so I knew this territory. I knew a lot of the players and I certainly understood the stakes, so I looked on with real interest and genuine understanding. What I don't think anyone in sports television appreciated at the time, other than Rupert Murdoch and his team, was the *vision* behind this extraordinary play.

Rupert himself put it best in a Monday Morning Quarterback–type interview he gave not long after the deal was announced. "Like no other sport will do, the NFL will make us into a real network," he said. "In the future there will be four hundred or five hundred channels on cable, and ratings will be fragmented. But football on Sunday will have the same ratings, regardless of the number of channels. Football will not fragment."

Pretty damn prescient, huh?

This move changed the sports landscape and lifted FOX from an upstart, also-ran among the broadcast networks into a major player. The other networks (and industry analysts) failed to realize at first that Rupert was working with different money, different math. He was building an asset, and he knew the incremental value of what he was adding—not just to the FOX network but to his FOX stations—would more than make up for what he'd supposedly overpaid for football.

On top of that, the NFL provided this tremendous promotional platform for FOX's overall slate of programming: almost overnight, ad buyers stopped referring to the Big Three broadcast networks and started adding FOX into the mix as part of the newly minted Big Four . . . all on the back of this NFL deal. It was a reach among reaches.

At the time FOX caught a lot of ridiculous criticism for the move—in part because the network had upended the usual order of things. But that's how it goes when you shake things up—the conventional ways of doing business don't always apply.

Rupert could be hard to figure. There was one exchange with him that perfectly captured the way his mind worked. I wasn't in the room for this one, but it was shared with me afterward by one of my colleagues who, like me, couldn't help but marvel at what the moment revealed about our boss. Rupert was meeting with a group of FOX Sports executives when the discussion turned to a dip in our NFL ratings. Rupert wasn't a football fan—he just knew the game and the league as a commodity and as FOX's greatest asset.

"Why are the ratings down?" he asked the room.

One of Rupert's deputies suggested that the viewers weren't watching the games so fervently because the Dallas Cowboys were having a bad year. After all, the Cowboys were "America's team," and when the Cowboys were lousy, the ratings were lousy. Rupert must have known the Cowboys were a huge draw, but this was the first he was hearing that one weak team on the field could so directly correlate to a weak season in the ratings.

"What's wrong with the Cowboys?" he wanted to know.

Another colleague responded that the team's star quarterback that year was injured, which could perhaps explain the team's underperformance. (By the way, that star quarterback was Troy Aikman, who went on to become the top analyst at FOX Sports, where he was paired with legendary sports broadcaster Joe Buck for nearly twenty years. The two are still working in the booth together, but they've taken their act to ESPN's *Monday Night Football*.)

"How much are we losing in advertising?" Rupert asked. "How much are we making good?"

Making good, in television adspeak, meant reimbursing the sponsors according to a set formula if the ratings fell short of a certain target.

The answer came back at an estimated $25–$30 million.

"How much does a top quarterback cost?" Rupert asked. At the time, top salaries around the league put those numbers at about $12 million. Rupert did the math in his head and came at the problem in a disarming (and *charming*!) way. "What if we took that money and gave it to the Cowboys?" he said. "They could buy themselves a new quarterback, and we'd still come out ahead."

He was joking, of course—or, at least, the other executives believed he was joking. Surely, there would have been some interesting antitrust exposure if we put this idea into play. Still, it was an indication of Rupert Murdoch's approach to business. He had this uncanny way of dissecting a complex problem and addressing it in the simplest way. He looked beyond the numbers for clues or patterns that would allow him and his team to come out on top. During my time at FOX Sports, that mindset trickled down through the ranks. We were all encouraged to think outside the proverbial box and find creative ways to shore up our bottom line.

At first, I was thrilled with the move back to sports, which was where I'd made my bones. In my first tour of duty in television sports at CBC, I was too young and too focused on proving myself to really enjoy the work. On this second tour of duty, I drank it all in: the Super Bowls, the World Series . . . pretty much every major sporting event. The work was hard but exhilarating—and a whole lot of fun. I loved the freedom the network initially afforded me to evolve the FOX Sports brand, and we came up with some cool innovations. I was constantly on the move, and our growth was transformative—just as David Hill had promised. But then, as our footprint got bigger and bigger, I found I was spending less and less time in the production control room, and more and more time navigating the tricky waters of office politics. When I started at FOX, there were only a handful of us, and I was pretty much left alone to do my thing. Then, very quickly, our ranks grew exponentially: there were thousands of us, and the entity was valued at over $4 billion.

I was no longer being left alone to do my thing.

I never minded when there were show-related issues that needed to be hashed out, because those battles were always purposeful and never personal. But some of our interoffice battles had more to do with office politics than with what we were putting on the air. In my fourth year at the company, a programming decision of mine was nixed—for reasons I couldn't understand. I had never been overruled before. The decision was a wake-up call, telling me it was time to think about my next move.

Again, I desperately missed being in the trenches, producing. Every time I ascended to another senior level—as head of Sports at CBC, as senior VP of the television group at Universal, and now as head of programming and production at FOX Sports Net—I'd look up one day and realize I'd moved myself further and further from the trenches. It was frustrating. As corny as it sounds, I realized that producing was (and is) my calling, and I vowed never to make this mistake again—no regrets though, because all of these experiences prepared me for the biggest reach of my career.

For the longest time, I'd had the idea of starting my own production company. In fact, the notion first hit when I was at Universal. As I noted earlier, the studio approached me about starting a company on the lot, but that idea went onto the back burner when I moved to FOX Sports.

As soon as the idea of starting my own production company switched back on in my head, I was all over it. I wanted to return to a broad base of programming that wasn't limited to sports, and I wanted to be back to actual producing on a more regular basis. Also, I wanted to work in an environment where I would once again be left alone to do my thing.

Starting my own company felt to me like the best way to accomplish all of these objectives all at once.

I didn't have a business plan just yet. I didn't have a plan at all, in fact. But I knew I couldn't work any longer in a corporate environment, so I set out to create a company where the focus would simply be on making great television—where we could develop a wide variety of projects in the nonfiction and entertainment event space; where our employees would be treated with respect and given the freedom they'd need to do their best work; where our clients and partners would get great service and know at all times that they were in good, capable hands.

Tall orders, all—but hey, size matters when you're dreaming big.

During my time at FOX and Universal, I often hired production companies and individual freelance producers, and I was almost always disappointed in some way by the quality of the outside work. I wanted to create a company that allowed the network executives who hired us to sleep at night without headaches or hassles. They would never have to worry about their shows or the millions of dollars they'd invest in those shows, which in turn meant they wouldn't have to worry about their jobs.

I was thirty-nine years old and excited about going out on my own, especially because I had a broad range of contacts and experiences, and I knew there'd be plenty of work. (Or, at least, I *hoped* there'd be plenty of work.) Of course, I was also terrified because I was leaving a great job with a healthy paycheck. Wendy and I had two young daughters—Rachel was seven and Leah was five—and even though there was the possibility of success, there were no guarantees, so I absolutely worried about the security I'd be giving up at FOX. I had another year and a half to go on my FOX deal and they'd just come to me to talk about an extension, so I also worried if the timing was right for me to go out on my own.

When I sat down with Wendy to talk it through, she didn't indicate that she was at all concerned. She wanted me to be happy—that was her bottom line.

I also ran the idea of my own production company past my role model and my coach. My dad had some real concerns, beyond the fact that he *loved* telling everyone he knew that his son was a big shot at FOX Sports, but he didn't try to talk me down from the idea. My mother had some of the same concerns, but she did her cheerleading thing and talked me up. At one point during the conversation with my parents, my father quite reasonably asked how much money I expected to make in my new venture.

"I've got no idea," I quite unreasonably responded.

I could only imagine that my answer was not all that reassuring.

In my mind, I was hoping I would make half of what I was making at FOX. As it turned out, in year one, I would be making double. But I didn't make the move for money. My *reaches* have always been based on my passion to create, to produce. I tell myself that either the money will come . . . or it won't. Fortunately, I work in a business that rewards success in a big way, so my focus as we started out was on making hits and not just shows.

Aside from Wendy, there was one other person who didn't waver at all in support of this decision and that was my older sister, Marylin. As a talented special ed teacher and freelance writer, she was wired to be both nurturing and observant—two qualities I needed to call on here. Even though she knew little about the inner workings of the entertainment business industry, she was savvy about people. Plus, she knew her little brother.

"Arthur," she said when I reached out to get her take, "producing is what you are meant to do. You don't need to chase titles or fancy positions anymore. You've done that. Chase the work you love to do."

Marylin's words sealed the deal for me.

As I thought more and more about the company I wanted to start, I found myself thinking about working with a partner. It would be good to have a sounding board, a collaborator, an ally, someone to share in the heavy lifting. I thought about all the people I'd worked with over the years whose skills complemented mine, and one name came immediately to mind: Kent Weed, a young director I'd hired when I was working with Dick Clark.

I'd brought Kent in to direct a show I'd created for NBC called *When Stars Were Kids*, and we'd worked really well together. He was an enormously talented director, and we were about the same age. Like me, he always pushed for a fresh approach. I'd continued to hire Kent from time to time over the years, at Universal and FOX, and had been impressed with his instincts and his work ethic.

I figured Kent could handle the directing and technical side of the business, leaving me to focus on the producing and writing side. But, of course, I couldn't start a partnership in my head. I had to see if the idea of starting a company together appealed to Kent. For all I knew, he was perfectly happy working freelance and had no interest being saddled with a company. So I asked him to join me for lunch one afternoon at my gym in West LA to kick things around.

I cut right to it. "I'm thinking of leaving FOX to start my own company," I said, "and was hoping you'd want to partner with me."

Kent was shocked—more about my decision to leave FOX than the proposal I'd offered him. "You have the best job in the world, Arthur," he said, incredulous. "And you're good at it! Why would you give that up?"

I told him about my frustrations at FOX and my desire to get back to producing all types of programming in a more hands-on way. Once I explained my thinking, his mood shifted from concerned to excited.

"I'm in," he said.

He didn't need to think about it or talk it over with his wife. He said he'd be honored to be my partner, that he believed in me and what we could build together, and that was that.

"Have you said anything to FOX?" he asked after we'd shaken hands on our "deal." Kent knew how much I'd invested in the growth of FOX Sports and how attached I was to the brand, so I'm sure he thought it would be tough for me to walk away.

"Not yet," I said. "They're actually on me to extend, so it'll be an interesting conversation."

The *interesting conversation* came about the very next day. Actually, it was three interesting conversations in three separate meetings. One was with David Hill, the chairman. One was with Jeff Shell, president of FOX Cable. And one was with Tracy Dolgin, the COO. The *interesting* part was that none of them were interested in letting me out of my contract. Separately—and then together—they determined that I was too much of an asset for them to let slip away, but as I kept pressing and they understood that I wasn't jumping ship to work for a competitor but to start my own production company, they softened and agreed to let me out of my contract . . . eventually.

After some back-and-forth, they asked me to stay on for another six months. We were about to launch FOX Sports Regional News, which we were rolling out over the FOX Sports Net regional networks, and they wanted me to oversee the launch and stick around long enough to ensure a smooth transition. Since I was responsible for programming, production, and news, this seemed like a reasonable ask, so I got with Kent to talk it over, and together we agreed that I was getting off easy. I mean, I *did* have another year and a half to go on my deal, so it could have been worse.

I was disappointed that Kent and I would have to wait half a year to roll up our sleeves and get our company off the ground, but I wanted to do the right thing by FOX. I've always believed that the way you leave a position is a reflection of your character, and since I was leaving to start my own company, I knew it would serve me in the long run to leave on good terms. Plus, I wanted this rollout to go well, so I swallowed hard and agreed to stay on. I ended up working harder in those six months than I'd ever worked in my life. No one at FOX outside of that executive trio knew I was leaving, and none would have guessed it from the long hours and the genuine enthusiasm I brought to work with me every day.

We finally announced my departure at a huge staff meeting about a month before I was due to leave, and I was struck by the warmth and graciousness of my colleagues when they heard the news. It was bittersweet—but I knew in my heart that it was time to move on and go for the biggest reach of my life.

Soon after that meeting, Tracy Dolgin called me to his office. He almost never summoned me to his office for a closed-door conversation, and I couldn't think what was on his agenda. My mind raced immediately to worst-case scenarios. *Do they want me to stay on for another six months? Are they not going to let me out of my contract after all?* Kent had been so patient, waiting out this term with me and putting the next phase of his career on hold—the last thing I wanted was to ask him to wait any longer.

Tracy looked serious when I sat down to meet with him. He said he'd been talking to Jeff and David and the three of them were enormously appreciative of all that I had done in building FOX Sports and of the hard work and dedication I'd shown over these past months.

"I wish you'd reconsider, Arthur," he said, "but we still want to work with you."

As a token of their enormous appreciation, they'd decided to offer me a kind of parting gift—an enormously generous parting gift, it turned out.

"We want to order the first show from your production company," Tracy said.

"Wow," I said. "That's great. But what's the show? We haven't started developing anything."

Tracy explained that they wanted me to produce sixty episodes of *You Gotta See This*, a show I'd created and piloted at FOX that was ready to go into production. *You Gotta See This* was a fast-paced clip show, featuring some of the craziest, wildest videos, with background footage, interviews, and amusing commentary highlighting the stories behind those videos.

"You're kidding me, right?" I said, not wanting to overplay my hand and show how excited I was at the thought of landing our first show order before we were even officially in business. I couldn't believe it. Sixty episodes!

Tracy shook his head. "We know you'll do a great job," he said. "You've already done a great job on the pilot. It's your show, Arthur. You created it. You should make it for us."

I called Kent to tell him we had a sixty-episode order. He screamed with joy when he heard the number. Then he dropped the phone, he was so excited. Like me, he couldn't believe it.

He went immediately into preproduction mode. "We'll need an office," he announced, like he was reading off a list. "No, we'll need a building. And a business plan. And a staff."

He was on it.

I still had another few weeks to go at FOX, but in that time we leased a small building in Santa Monica and purchased three edit bays. We were suddenly and absolutely in business . . . all on the back of this initial order. We didn't have to take out a loan to start the company or worry how we'd keep the lights on, because there was this gift of cash flow from the very beginning, and we would go on to produce roughly two hundred episodes of *You Gotta See This*.

I made an extra effort to leave FOX on good terms. It wasn't a strategy so much as a philosophy—to treat people decently, to do the right thing, to honor my working relationships. It was no different than when I left CBC, Universal, or Dick Clark, and after leaving every one of those venerable organizations, I continued to do business with each of them. I didn't leave on good terms just to pave the way for future work: it was always about doing the right thing—it was the Saul Smith way.

It's a philosophy Kent and I took with us to the opening of A. Smith & Co., where we continue to place an emphasis on integrity, commitment, and loyalty. After all, there's no point in reaching for the next big thing if you burn your bridges along the way. In a relationship business—like the fur business or the television business—those bridges are an all-important link from the work you've done in the past to the work you hope to do in the future.

11
WHAT THE HELL IS A CHARETTE?

I didn't want to meet with Paul Allen the first time he reached out. For the life of me, I couldn't imagine why the billionaire investor and philanthropist and cofounder of Microsoft would want to meet with me. I mean, this was the *third richest man* in the world! I couldn't imagine what we would have to discuss.

Kent Weed and I had just launched A. Smith & Co., and I was laser-focused on making it as an independent production company. We had our tentpole compilation show *You Gotta See This* up and running on FOX Sports, which was helping to fund our early stages of oper-ation, and on top of that, we had a number of promising projects in development, so I couldn't see the benefit in pulling myself away to take a meeting in Seattle with a guy who seemed to have no need for the services of our fledgling production company.

But then Brad Marks, the influential headhunter, pointed out to me that this was Paul Allen, one of the brightest minds on the planet and by all accounts a good person to know. Brad put it in terms I'd under-stand: "*Schmuck!* Take the meeting!"

Turned out Paul wanted to offer me a job. I didn't know this just yet, but I found out soon enough. In addition to his various businesses and philanthropic efforts, he'd recently launched a company called Vulcan Media. He had a vision of building a suite of digital cable channels and was looking for someone to head up that effort. Because of my experience at FOX Sports launching twenty or so regional networks, Brad convinced the people at Vulcan that I might be a good fit. And so I was brought in on this by a guy named Jerry Maglio, who worked with Paul as a consultant. Jerry set up a meeting, and Paul and I immediately hit it off.

I ended up spending more time with Paul Allen in this two-hour introductory meeting than I did in any subsequent meeting. This is how it often goes when you're dealing with super successful people. Things had gone in much the same way in my first meeting with Dick Clark and with the heads of the CBC and FOX. Accomplished individuals have a way of drilling down and sizing up potential partners at the outset, and they know to devote as much time as necessary to getting the best possible read on someone they hope to work with. They clear their schedules to make this first meeting a priority. After that, when you're on the team and down to business, you develop a shorthand, checking in with each other to make sure your targets are being met, but for the most part you're left alone to do your thing.

It was, I've learned, an admirable approach, and I've gone at it the same way when considering a new hire or meeting a potential producing partner for the first time—but then there was a lot to admire about Paul Allen. What I admired most of all was how passionate he was about the things that were important to him. Yes, he was brilliant and clever and shrewd, but his best quality was that he cared so deeply about people and places and causes and put that care into action. For example, he bought the Seattle Seahawks—not because he was a football fan but because he was a loyal and devoted citizen of Seattle and he wanted to make sure another owner didn't come in and move the franchise, as had been widely speculated. He purchased the Portland Trailblazers because he was passionate about basketball and wanted to immerse himself in that world and elevate the appeal of the game in the Pacific Northwest. He built Seattle's Jimi Hendrix Experience Museum, now known as the Museum of Pop Culture, because he was a die-hard music fan and wanted to honor one of his city's favorite sons and celebrate the music that meant so much to him.

Paul was a tremendous champion of new technology, though he

didn't always look for a return on his investments right out of the gate. He put a lot of seed money into start-ups, backing entrepreneurs and innovators he believed in, without worrying too much about making his money back on any kind of predictable timetable.

It was great to be in a room with someone who was so excited about things and had the wherewithal to act on that excitement. At another time in my life, I might have jumped at the opportunity to work for Paul, but I'd just left FOX Sports and made this big bet on myself. I was determined to see it through, so I thanked him for his interest, and that was that.

Only it wasn't *that* . . . not just yet.

A couple days after the meeting, I got a follow-up call from Jerry. He said, "Paul really wants you to work with us on this."

I thanked Jerry for the interest and reminded him that the timing just wasn't right for me. I already had a full-time job building a company, but he would not be put off. He said, "Maybe there's a way we could make this work."

After some back-and-forth, I agreed to sign on as a consultant and to give about 25 percent of my time to Paul's media efforts. My idea was to put my consultant's fee right back into the company, and to treat the assignment like any other gig or partnership that would come our way at A. Smith & Co. I didn't go into the relationship planning to keep a clock on my work. I figured some months it would work out to be a bigger chunk of my time, and some months it would work out to be less—just like juggling a new show. If something needed doing, I'd do it. If it could wait, I'd turn my attention to another something that needed doing and get back to it.

Consulting for Paul allowed for another adrenaline shot of cash into the company Kent and I were trying to get off the ground. It also gave me an opportunity to make some key connections and take full advantage of the intersection of Paul's interests and the interests of A. Smith & Co. One week, I could be examining the business plan for the Oxygen Network and advising Paul on whether to increase his investment, and the next week I could be pitching a show to Oxygen executives.

Paul's investments in and around the media business were varied and huge. He owned more of DreamWorks than Steven Spielberg, Jeffrey Katzenberg, and David Geffen, DreamWorks's founding partners. Hardly a week went by that I didn't make an important new connection while working on Paul's behalf or that one of Paul's partners or potential partners had to come by my quaint start-up offices in Santa Monica for a consult. The crossover benefits to our little enterprise were enormous.

I was accustomed to having powerful and demanding bosses, but now that I'd gotten used to being my own boss, it was nice to be able to work my own schedule, in my own way. Paul put an immediate end to that feeling of freedom, however. Once, early on in our relationship, I got a call first thing in the morning from Jerry Maglio, who acted as a kind of mediator in my relationship with Paul—better, like a consigliere.

"Why aren't you answering Paul's emails?" he asked, a little agitated.

"Jerry," I said, "I just got to the office. It's nine o'clock in the morning. I'll open his email first thing and respond right away."

"That's not good enough, Arthur," he said. "Get a BlackBerry."

"What's a BlackBerry?"

This was 2000, so it's not like I was a Luddite on the technology front. I had a really heavy laptop computer back in the '80s. I had a cell phone back when there was nobody to call on *their* cell phone. But this BlackBerry thing was new to me.

Jerry explained what it was and said, "If Paul emails you at midnight, you need to answer him."

So I got a BlackBerry, and within the first week Paul sent a late-night email. The device pinged, and I remember turning to Wendy and saying, "How cool is that? I just got an email from the guy who invented email."

Of course, this was not entirely true, but he'd certainly had a hand in bringing it to the masses. Anyway, Wendy took my point and agreed that it was certainly cool in a *meta* sort of way.

My role with Paul was to build a support team to execute the big-picture ideas that developed out of my consultancy, so one of my first tasks was to make a few strategic hires. The most significant of these turned out to be a young man named Sean Atkins, who would go on to become the president of MTV and a lifelong friend. Sean had worked at Disney and knew his way around media and business.

One of the first projects I worked on with Sean was a deep dive into the world of Japanese anime—an area we had identified as a potential opportunity. We went to Japan, along with a blond, Bay Area investment banker who spoke perfect Japanese, and we spent the better part of a week learning the lay of the land. We wound up taking twenty-one meetings in just five days, so it was a grueling trip—also illuminating. One of the key takeaways was learning that the animation business in Japan was controlled by a ton of smaller companies, which was in sharp contrast to how things worked in the United States, where there were four or five major studios controlling most of the production. In and around Tokyo, you had all these little mom-and-pop shops doing important, innovative work with an indie-like freedom and sensibility. It was exciting as hell.

In Japan, I learned, the business card is everything, and that it should be given with two hands and accepted with two hands. Also, it is customary to take a few moments to read or consider the card when you receive it. If you're at a meeting, seated around a conference table or a dinner table, it is expected that you keep the cards you've collected on the surface in front of you during the meeting or the meal—and, of course, make sure to take them with you when you leave. You should never ask for someone's card twice because it's an indication of carelessness and a show of disrespect. Another show of disrespect: putting a card in your back pocket.

I came back from that whirlwind tour of Japan's animation studios and meetings with the senior executives at Sony with the idea that Paul should launch an anime cable channel. He had relationships in place at Sony and I knew we could partner with them in some way, so Sean and I came up with an elaborate proposal in support of this idea. We mapped out a plan for the channel, which included a research phase, a full-on development phase, and a launch phase, with anticipated staffing needs along the way.

We also pitched two additional channel ideas to accompany our pitch for the anime channel: a channel called DOX, which we hoped would become the definitive documentary network, and one called FEAR, which would feature suspense and horror content. I encouraged the idea of launching a suite of channels instead of just one, because we would be able to amortize the staff and facilities across three channels and be profitable in a significantly shorter period of time, even though the initial investment would be bigger. We outlined all of the reasons why it made sense to get into the anime business in such a dedicated way, as well as the arguments in favor of DOX and FEAR, and all of the opportunities for future growth. On the anime front alone, we calculated that the global fan base was sizable enough and reasoned that, with our partnership with Sony and others, we could become the default destination for this type of programming. We also saw similar opportunities with DOX and FEAR.

As we developed these ideas, I looked to match my expertise with Paul's expressed desire to launch new channels and penetrate new markets. In so doing, I shared my thoughts with him on what I thought he needed to build a new media platform:

1. He needed to have control of a clearly defined space.
2. He needed to develop and establish a definitive brand within that space.
3. He needed to become *the* destination for a sizable and passionate audience.

I pointed out to him that many successful cable channels, including HGTV, MTV, CNN, the History Channel, and ESPN, had become multibillion-dollar businesses based on these principles.

Over several months, we put together a killer proposal, and when it came time to present it to Paul, I got an interesting phone call from Jerry Maglio.

He said, "When you go to see Paul tonight, maybe think about wearing a proper shirt."

I usually showed up for meetings in a T-shirt and jeans. I liked to be comfortable, and I'd worked my entire career in an industry that didn't much care how I dressed. "Really?" I said. "You don't like the way I dress?" (Note: I already knew Jerry didn't care for the way I dressed.)

"Really," he said. "Maybe even a jacket."

"Okay, if you say so. But why?"

He followed with a good piece of advice. "When you're asking someone to invest hundreds of millions of dollars in your idea, it's a good idea to wear a proper shirt."

Noted.

I took Jerry's advice and wore a nice shirt, as I've since tried to do at every consequential meeting I've taken when someone else's checkbook was involved. For most everything else, I've stuck to my jeans and T-shirt.

The pitch meeting with Paul could not have gone any better. I laid it all out for him, walked him through the costs and our projections, and when I was through, he turned to me and said, "This is freakin' genius, Arthur. I love it. This makes complete sense."

I was thrilled. It's always nice to have your ideas validated with such enthusiasm by such a savvy investor and innovator. "So what would you like me to do next?"

"Nothing. It's a great idea, and you've done a terrific job laying it out for me, but I'm not going to pursue it."

I couldn't believe it. There was a real opportunity here—Paul himself could see it.

"What do you mean?" I finally said.

"I'm not into it." That's all. *I'm not into it.*

That was Paul Allen in a snapshot. It wasn't about making money for him. It wasn't about seizing an opportunity. If a deal didn't excite him, if it didn't light something in him, he wasn't interested, no matter how much sense it made.

I ended up working with Paul for about a year and a half, consulting on all things media, beyond the launching of these cable channels, including the selling of his TechTV channel, the Portland Trailblazers television rights, his investment in the Sporting News, and a number of other initiatives and proposals. It turned out to be a very profitable relationship. Of course, it helped that my fees as a consultant represented more money to me on an hourly basis than I'd ever earned in my life. However, the huge added benefit came in the collection of people

I met as Paul's eyes and ears in media and the insights I gathered from the brightest minds in tech and entertainment and sports.

Every day on the clock for Paul was an education waiting to happen, like the time he invited me to attend what he called a *charette* on the San Juan Islands in northwest Washington, one of which Paul happened to own. He explained that it would be a gathering of top minds from media and tech and business—a combination think tank and salon and retreat. He rattled off a list of names of folks who'd attended in the past, including his principal money manager, Bill Savoy, who referred to himself as "the guardian of the vault," and Carl Vogel, the president and CEO of Charter Communications. The leaders and visionaries who were slated to attend his upcoming event included Geraldine Laybourne, the former president of Nickelodeon and current CEO of the Oxygen Network, which she'd cofounded with Oprah Winfrey. I was impressed . . . and excited. The thought of being in the same room with all of these industry leaders had an enormous appeal because I loved talking shop with people who knew their stuff.

I had one question for Paul, though: "What the hell is a charette?"

The word sounded French, but I'd grown up in Montreal, spoke a fair amount of French, and never come across it before.

"It's a charette," Paul said, not really explaining much of anything. "Just come. You'll see."

So I put it on my calendar and looked forward to it.

Three weeks later I got a call from someone in Paul's office wanting to know the agenda for the upcoming charette.

"I don't know," I said. "What is it?"

"You're coming, yes?"

"Yes," I confirmed. "Paul invited me."

"Great. So when do you think you'll have it ready?"

"Me?" I shot back. "An agenda? I'm just a guest."

"No, no, no. You're running the charette."

There followed a frustrating back-and-forth, in which I explained that Paul had only invited me to *attend* the charette, while this person in Paul's office insisted that I had been invited to *lead* it. Paul had never said any such thing. In fact, his tone had been welcoming, suggesting only that I should come and meet some interesting people.

But there was no arguing the point. I had no idea what went on at one of these charette thingies—*do I bring a toga?*—but now it appeared I would be running it. Oh, and Paul Allen wanted my agenda on his desk by noon. I immediately called Sean Atkins, who was by now on the full-time payroll and planning to accompany me to the seminar.

"Sean," I announced, "we're fucked. We're running the charette."

"What are you talking about?" Sean said. "Remind me again. What the hell is a charette?"

I told him what little I knew, and he agreed: we were well and truly fucked.

The two of us scrambled to come up with a topic. We studied Paul's guest list to see if we could tailor our agenda to the particular interests of this group—on the theory that if we were hoping to engage some of the world's top minds, we should at least know their areas of expertise. Very quickly, we decided to focus on *my* area of expertise and address the cable television marketplace—where it had been, where it was at present, where it was headed.

Back in the early 2000s, cable was a hot topic. This was before the rise of streaming services and the rush of content that followed, but we were at an inflection point, where some major players in cable were starting to beat their broadcast counterparts at their own game. There was a lot to discuss, but we didn't have a whole lot of time to circle the wagons and set up a world-class presentation befitting Paul's world-class guest list. We were in turbo-reach mode, trying to create an agenda in just a couple hours.

We focused on top-line stuff: trends and developments I'd already been following and predictions for the future. I had no idea if it would be insightful or new or interesting to these people—but we were scrambling. I'd had a fair amount of experience giving seminars at FOX, CBC, and various conventions and universities, but those typically lasted an hour or two and included a question-and-answer period. The charette was scheduled to run for two days!

I managed to get the agenda to Paul by the deadline, and a short while later I got a one-word response: "Great."

Sean and I scrambled over the next couple weeks, growing our agenda into an actual presentation, until we had what we thought was the spine of a productive two-day seminar. Sean drafted everyone on our team to pitch in, and we managed to produce what we all thought was a viable deck. I worried if we had enough material to fill two day-long sessions.

"Arthur, you don't have two days here," Sean assured me. "You have a whole week."

The trip to San Juan Island was . . . well, *trippy*. We took one of Paul's sea planes, and when we touched down, we were met by a very serious group of men wearing sunglasses and dressed all in black. It felt like I had been dropped onto the set of the *Men in Black* sequel. Paul occupied the main house on the island, while his guests were assigned private bunk houses—only, the "bunk house" designation didn't really do our quarters justice. Mine was outfitted like the finest room in the finest hotel I'd ever visited. Because we were guests of Paul Allen, each unit was wired with state-of-the-art everything. I'd never seen such a high-end touch screen remote control pad, with access to every channel in the world and every movie ever made. Ten-year-old me could have holed up in there for months—and forty-one-year-old me, still a TV-mad kid at heart, could have happily done the same.

We were surrounded by every imaginable luxury—and by some unimaginable ones. The place was immaculate, but I never once saw a cleaning or maintenance person. Every time I left the room, even for a short walk or to meet with Sean for a quick meeting, it would be tidied before I got back. Each room was outfitted with an assortment of high-quality, expensive pens, and when I grabbed one and took it with me to our first session on the morning after I'd arrived (because I thought it was kind of nice and that I just might have to keep it), it had been swiftly replaced in the pen quiver by the time I got back to my bunk house.

The first night, following an absolutely fabulous and yet somehow casual dinner at the main house, somebody asked how we all planned to spend the rest of the evening. I said it would be great if we had a foosball table. It was just something to say. (Also, I'm pretty good at foosball.) The next night, the nicest foosball table I'd ever seen appeared in one of the main rooms, flown in by chopper!

The presentation went well, extremely well. I spoke in great detail about the key factors a successful cable channel needed to have and presented a ton of research to back up my ideas and insights. Next, I led the group through a series of case studies, examining the development histories of existing channels. In each case, I tried to identify what had gone right in the launch of that channel, what had gone wrong, and why. Then we talked about the opportunities and pitfalls going forward.

It really was quite a thrill and an honor to lead the charge on this and to confirm Paul's faith in me in taking on the assignment—especially since I *still* didn't really know what a charette was.

As it played out, there was one major problem with our presentation: we shot through our prepared material in the first day. (So much for filling a week!) Paul was a quick study and wanted to keep things moving. As I spoke, I'd catch his eyes across the room, and he'd be flashing me this look that said, *Move on, Arthur!* or *We get it!*

During one of our first breaks, I turned to Sean and said, "At this rate, we're not gonna have anything left to talk about tomorrow."

In a panic, I called an audible and made the second day of our presentation a participation exercise. We drafted a summary document outlining opportunities in the world of cable, and then created a questionnaire asking our participants to prioritize those opportunities.

At the end of the first day's session, I vamped and mentioned that people were probably wondering what we would talk about on the following day. This was a real pivot because our deck ended with a conclusion page that might as well have been headed *The End*. I threw out a line that we'd raced through our agenda with intention because we wanted to have the full day tomorrow to discuss the results of our questionnaire and look at future courses of action as they related to our specific businesses. It was, I'm afraid, a line of bullshit, but it was polished bullshit of the first order. And of course it helped that I believed wholeheartedly that there was real value in the open-ended, free-flowing session I was now planning for the next day. We would fill the time meaningfully, I felt certain, even if it wouldn't be in quite the same ways we had initially imagined.

Sean and I worried briefly if we'd have time to print and bind the questionnaire and document on such short notice, but then we remembered we were at Paul Allen's place, where anything was possible—especially anything tech-related. He had a full-time support staff, wired and ready to handle this type of request, and we were able to have the questionnaires distributed and the responses tabulated in the time it took Sean and I to shake our heads in wonder.

Bottom line: Paul was thrilled with the charette and said it was one of the best he'd ever held. Most of the attendees weighed in afterward to thank Sean and me for our time and insights. Having the second day open for everyone to jump in and discuss what we had covered, along with the enthusiastic debate on the results from the questionnaire, turned out to be the perfect combination of presentation and participation. (No one had to know we'd hit upon this balance not by design but out of necessity!)

I don't share this story to pat ourselves on the back and crow about how we managed to pull ourselves out of a tough spot. The reason this story has stayed with me all these years is because it reminds me that we don't always get to pick our reach moments. Sometimes you've got no choice but to throw a Hail Mary pass and hope it lands in the arms of one of your receivers. Desperation can be a good and useful operating mode, if you find a way to rise to the challenge.

12

FOOD, GLORIOUS FOOD

We were on a roll at A. Smith & Co. We'd had a major hit on FOX with *Paradise Hotel*—the number-one-rated show of the summer in the coveted 18–34 demo. It was our first big prime-time hit, a pioneering show in the relationship genre that continues to echo across today's "reality" landscape in shows like *Love Island* and *Bachelor in Paradise*. It also went on to become an international sensation, with local versions of the show in fifteen countries and close to four thousand episodes produced worldwide. We followed that up only months later with the controversial makeover show *The Swan*, the second-highest rated show on FOX at the time.

It's something to notice when a production company comes out with two hit shows on the same network back-to-back, and my great friend Mike Darnell at FOX was a major reason for our successful streak. Mike was (and remains) a legend in what I guess I'll have to refer to here as *reality* television. He was the biggest risk-taker in the genre—creative, bold, but careful about where and how he stuck his neck out. He was always pushing his conservative network colleagues to take risks and pursue comparatively bold projects. I liked him enormously and wanted to keep our good thing going.

The shows we'd worked on together were certainly successful, but Mike was also known for producing other noisy, attention-getting shows like *Temptation Island* and *Joe Millionaire*, as well as for overseeing the network's *American Idol* franchise. He lived for ratings and went out of his way to make sure his shows got noticed, so from a producer's standpoint, he was a great guy to have as an advocate on the network side. It's a rare thing for a network executive to promise you the moon and then deliver on that promise, so as an independent producer, I looked forward to a long, mutually beneficial relationship with Mike. He trusted me, and I trusted him.

I told myself I'd be open to any idea he brought to me, just as I knew he'd be open to any shows I pitched to FOX. One day in 2004, I was at The Grove Shopping Mall in Los Angeles when Mike called.

"Arthur, I want to send you some tape on a chef. His name's Gordon Ramsay. I'm telling you, there's something there. He's great television."

"Wait, you're not thinking of doing a *food* show?" I spat the word from my mouth like it had gone bad.

"No, I'm asking you to watch the tape and then call me," he said—clearly not in the mood for my second-guessing.

Creating a long-running prime-time network hit is always a reach, but when you're reaching in an area that's never had any real or lasting success, the challenge is even greater. There had never been a successful food show on network television—and it's not like nobody had tried. Mark Burnett had come out with a show called *The Restaurant* with celebrity chef Rocco DiSpirito, and it didn't draw. Back in the prefoodie dark ages of 2004, food in America was nothing like what it is today, when every major city can boast high-end restaurants fronted by star chefs and gushed over by foodies and reviewers. Food on television at that point had been relegated to cable, where cooking shows were sometimes able to capture enough of an audience to justify their existence.

So I wasn't too excited to watch this tape of a chef I'd never heard of. But if Mike had asked me to watch tape of a burning yule log and give him my thoughts, I would have done so. I took the tape home so I wouldn't interrupt my day at the office and popped it into my VCR that night.

The show was a UK production called *Hell's Kitchen*, and it wasn't great. Gordon Ramsay, however, was mesmerizing—fresh and smart, sharp-tongued and sharp-witted, and basically unlike any television personality I'd ever seen. The show featured a number of British celebrities working in a kitchen, where Chef Ramsay would lay into them for some reason or other. It was clear he was a perfectionist—only, the setup didn't provide him with a real opportunity to let his full personality shine through as he struggled to teach these B-level celebrities a thing or two about cooking.

When Mike called the next day, I gave it to him straight: "Love Gordon. Love the title. Don't love the show."

A part of me thought the conversation would end there, but Mike pressed me for details. "What, specifically, don't you like about the show?"

"It's slow. It's basically a show for foodies. Even with American celebrities, it will never work for a broad audience here in the States."

"Arthur," he said, stopping me before I went any deeper on the ways the show wasn't working. "There's something about this Gordon Ramsay guy. He's a star waiting to happen. I just know it. Let's figure something out."

I understood straightaway what had Mike so excited. Gordon was different—a singular personality. He could be abrasive and acid-tongued, but at the same time he could be thoughtful and encouraging when one of his wannabe chefs showed some promise. He didn't suffer fools, and that was part of his special appeal. People loved to watch a drill sergeant rip into someone for not doing their job or for being an idiot, but they especially loved it when that drill sergeant also had a soft spot for raw talent or a good human-interest story.

"If you don't want in on this, let me know," Mike said. "But I'd love to make another show with you."

"Give me some time and I'll get back to you," I said. "I really don't know where to go with this, but wherever we go, we have to find a way to make it broad."

Mike agreed.

I was about the furthest thing from a foodie, so at first I couldn't think what to do with this explosive, talented chef. I kicked around a couple ideas on my own, and another couple ideas with Kent and our team, and I didn't love any of them. During this time, I went out to dinner one night with my wife, Wendy, at Il Fornaio in Beverly Hills. We happened to be seated right next to the huge open kitchen, and I was fascinated. My poor wife was trying to have a conversation with me, but I was distracted by the noise and energy of the chef barking out orders, pots and pans clanging, the servers grabbing the plates and hurrying out with them as soon as they were ready. It was like a window into a whole other world—for me anyway. I'd never worked in a restaurant or known anyone who did, so this was unfamiliar territory. I was drawn to it. I started to think that our dinner service was like a game, and out of that I got the idea for a competition show where every player had an important role, where there was the pressure of a clock ticking and demanding customers waiting to be served.

It hit me: *Hey, it's like sports!* Sports, I knew. Restaurants, not so much.

I had a vision: we could develop a show with two teams of aspiring chefs, working in two kitchens, competing with each other to impress *real* diners—and, most importantly, Chef Ramsay. There would be pregame footage, where we'd observe the chefs and get inside their heads as they were preparing for the meal; the meal itself, which would be like the big game; and then a postgame section, where we'd watch the chefs and witness the fallout from dinner service as they either praised or pointed the finger at each other. Throughout, we'd be blown away by the brilliance and the temper of the master, Chef Ramsay, who would essentially be running a culinary boot camp, overseeing these two massive kitchens, and presiding over the entire operation. American audiences would get to see Gordon Ramsay for the first time, in his element, as this tough, talented, and ultimately fair-minded arbiter of fine dining—a *chef whisperer* who wouldn't hesitate to throw someone out of his kitchen if they screwed up.

As the concept for the show came together in my head, I thought, *I'd watch that.*

I called Mike the next morning and pitched him the idea. He loved it—and, as always, added some really good ideas to enhance what we had proposed.

"What's next?" I said.

"Next is you need to make a deal with ITV."

ITV was the British television studio behind the UK production of *Hell's Kitchen*, and even though the show I had in mind was completely different than the show they had on the air, they controlled the title and the rights to Gordon at the time.

As soon as I formed a partnership with ITV, FOX ordered ten episodes—something that rarely happened. It was our first tangible indication that the show we were about to grow would be unlike any other production we'd seen.

Our first order of business was to bring in Gordon Ramsay for a meeting, which we set up at FOX. Trouble was, for all his charms and his many gifts as a network executive, Mike was notorious for running late. Always. And this meeting with the star of our show, a couple ITV executives, and me and my partner Kent Weed was no exception. The group of us sat awkwardly for a good long while in the FOX cafeteria, waiting to be called up to Mike's office. Gordon wasn't feeling it. This was our first meeting, and he wasn't quite sure what to make of me. He wasn't angry or anything, the way he could be in the kitchen, but he certainly wasn't warm. He still seemed a little pissed off and put out when we got up to Mike's office, so I figured the thing to do was pile on the charm and put on a kind of full-court press until Mike and I could win him over.

One of our big tasks was introducing Gordon to an American audience. He was already very well-known in the UK, but the US market was a whole other landscape, so our conversation turned to how to promote the show and build out the *Hell's Kitchen* and "Gordon Ramsay" brands.

After the meeting, I convinced Gordon to come back with me to our offices just down the street, where we continued the conversation. I went into more detail about the concept I had for the show, shared my thoughts on what the dinner service would be like, what some of the challenges would be, but I could tell from Gordon's dubious expression that I was digging myself into a deeper and deeper hole.

At one point he turned to me and said, "You really don't know much about food, do you?"

I gulped—and thought, *So this isn't going well.* But I quickly recovered and shot back, "No, but I do know a lot about making television."

There was a long pause, but then Gordon laughed—and this finally broke the tension.

I made Gordon a promise. I told him that everything we did on *Hell's Kitchen* would honor and support his vision for what a world-class restaurant should be. Every challenge would be purposeful, testing the qualities he believed were necessary to be considered a great chef.

Gordon smiled and said, "Fuck yes!"

For the first time, I felt a connection—and the seeds of a friendship that would be one of the most rewarding of my career. I think Gordon felt it too.

I asked him—you know, since I didn't know much about food and all—if he could tell me what qualities he was looking for in a great chef. He ran off a list: palate, leadership, creativity, imagination, technical skills, memory, discipline.

I said, "In every challenge, we'll find a way to test at least one of those qualities. The mission will be clear. But you'll have to trust me to put some showmanship into the mix."

"Of course, mate," he said.

After a bit of a rocky start, our first day "working" together was going great . . . until it came time for lunch. We had agreed to work through lunch and order in. There weren't exactly any gourmet restaurants that delivered, but Gordon assured me he didn't mind. He said, "Hey, mate. I eat everything."

I ended up ordering in from California Pizza Kitchen, and it worked out well enough. By that I mean Gordon cleaned his plate and didn't spit anything out—but I wondered what the hell he must have been thinking, throwing in on an American show with this Canadian producer who didn't know a thing about food and could only think to feed him a fast-casual pizza with a bunch of weird toppings.

Gordon went back to the UK after our daylong session, while Kent and I rolled up our sleeves and went to work. Job one was finding a location. We scouted restaurants in and around Los Angeles but couldn't locate any that would work—none of them had two kitchens, and none were big enough to house the production we had in mind. So we ended up building our own restaurant on La Brea Avenue on an abandoned studio lot. It was a massive build, art-directed by the abundantly talented John Janavs, who would eventually be nominated for an Emmy for his design.

The set had two state-of-the-art kitchens, a beautiful and spacious restaurant, and an amazing set of dorms that sat on top of the structure, where we would house our two teams of aspiring, competing chefs. To make sure our coverage was as unobtrusive and as authentic as possible, we installed eighty robotic cameras across the facility, allowing us to capture the action over every square foot of interior space from every conceivable angle—our version of *The Truman Show*, where everything was fair game and nothing would go unnoticed.

Everyone involved in the show was excited as the buildout neared completion because none of us had ever seen a setup like this for a television show of this kind. Hell, there had never really *been* a show of this kind, not at the network level and not built to this scale, so that added to the excitement. Behind the scenes, we built two massive control rooms, offices, an art department, a test kitchen, and a workstation to house our food team.

We were actually running a restaurant, so our food team ordered our food, organized our waitstaff, and oversaw the food requirements of our challenge department. There was a ton of work done behind the scenes that allowed us to test our chefs constantly with a variety of challenges in addition to our *hellish* dinner services.

The restaurant portion of the set was designed to be a full-functioning establishment, complete with valet parking, professional servers and hosts, and all the flourishes you'd expect to see in a high-end restaurant.

By every outward measure, our show looked different than anything else on television. Still, it was a reach. "Reality" television had burst onto the prime-time scene in the early 2000s in a big way. The various formats that fit beneath that broad term were turning out to be ratings gold—especially the season-long, elimination-type competition shows. This was around the time *Survivor* and *American Idol* found their footing as durable smash hits, around the time the *Bachelor* franchise took hold. If you looked at the production-to-hit ratio at play in this space, it was much higher than you'd find in television's scripted counterparts. But by 2004 and into 2005, the conversation in a lot of network programming offices was centered on whether or not "reality television" was a fad. As hard as it might be to believe now, there was a school of thought that suggested this genre might have run its course. I thought the *school of thought* needed to update its curriculum.

Before *Hell's Kitchen*, reality-competition show contestants tended to be actors, personal trainers, models, aspiring "influencers"—people looking to deposit a little bit of limelight into their fifteen-minutes-of-fame accounts. That wasn't the case here. Our competitors were chefs from all over the country, from various backgrounds. They were real people working in real kitchens, looking to jump-start their careers and learn from Chef Ramsay—and, in success, hopefully establish themselves on the next rung of the kitchen ladder.

On our first day of shooting, I gathered the production team and told them we were all in on the ground floor of something special . . . and different. I relished these moments with our team just before kickoff. "We're pioneers," I said without overstatement. "We're trying to be the first food show to work on network television, and with our incredible setup and our incredible Gordon Ramsay, we have a unique opportunity to show America what life is like on the front lines in top-rated restaurants and the admirable, often invisible work chefs perform night after night."

My partner Kent did a masterful job leading the directorial part of the show: how it looked . . . how it was shot . . . how it was paced. He made sure to put camera-blinds in the kitchens and dorms, and hide our camera crew behind a bunch of one-way mirrors, which was instrumental in establishing the show's authentic feel.

One of the most valuable "hidden" pieces of equipment we used on the set was the IFB device Gordon wore in his ear. IFB is short for "interruptible foldback," and it was basically a one-way communication device that allowed me to offer Gordon some lines, stage directions, and other instructions as he was on the set—a standard tool in a live production. Gordon had worked with an IFB in the UK, but I never imagined he would respond to my cues with such facility. For a while, I thought he might not respond at all.

I'd been warned not to talk to him during the dinner service. I understood it to be akin to interrupting a surgeon during a gastric bypass—something to be avoided except in an emergency. This directive didn't come from Gordon, but from his longtime UK producers. On the face of it, their warning made sense: what the hell could I have told Gordon Ramsay about cooking or running a kitchen? But I had different ideas on how to help guide Gordon through his paces as we established a template for the show—differences that would soon lead to my first dustup with our star chef.

There was a lot to track, a lot going on. We had eight chefs in the "red" kitchen, eight chefs in the "blue" kitchen, along with one hundred diners and a whole bunch of story lines we needed to follow—not to mention Gordon himself, my main focus. It was exhilarating (and busy!) as hell, and it felt like covering a major sporting event, the way we'd set things up.

That's how it goes sometimes, don't you think? Over the course of a long career, you can't help but pick up on things in one aspect of your work that will invariably inform some other aspect of your work, which is why I always tell young people there is a lesson to be found in every experience. Here, without really thinking about it, I drew on my experiences in one arena and attached them to this new experience, and the reason I was able to do so *without really thinking it* was because I'd given that first moment so much thought at the time. Be fully present in your work, while fully expecting to reach back into your past to inform (and enrich!) the work at hand.

Our first days of shooting could not have started out any better. We set up zone coverage, and producers were assigned different parts of the kitchen and the dining room. Our first dinner service got off to a tremendous start, but halfway in, a fight broke out among our chefs in the blue kitchen. Gordon was in the red kitchen at the time. I needed to let him know what was going on and redirect him into the blue kitchen, so I whispered something in his ear through the IFB.

The next thing I knew Gordon was heading off the set. At first, I assumed he was headed to the blue kitchen to put out the fire that had started there, but he'd pivoted in the opposite direction, headed straight for the control room.

This can't be good, I thought.

I left my spot at the controls and stepped out into the hallway to meet him, thinking I could intercept him and defuse the situation.

"What's happening?" he said as soon as he saw me. "Didn't they tell you not to talk to me during the dinner service?"

I wasn't about to get caught up in any kind of power struggle with our mercurial master chef. I just wanted to smooth things over between us and get back to work.

"They did," I said. "But on the UK show, you're only working with one kitchen. Here, we've got two kitchens. There's a lot going on. I'm able to see things on our eighty-plus cameras you're unable to see on the set. In this case, you've got some hot tempers flaring in the blue kitchen. You need to know about it in real-time."

Gordon stood there for a moment, not saying anything. I could see that he was thinking this through. For all his hotheadedness when his buttons were pushed the wrong way, he was thoughtful, smart, and shrewd. He knew he had something special with his on-camera persona, and during our work in preproduction, I think he'd come to recognize me as someone who would honor and nurture that persona. In other words, I think he'd begun to trust me and know that I only wanted what was best for the show, which in turn would be what was best for him.

"I see what's right in front of me," he finally said. "I react to what's right in front of me. That's the essence of show, mate."

"Yes and no," I said, trying to agree while at the same time pushing him to see the bigger picture. "I'm sure you can appreciate the benefit in having another set of eyes in the back of your head. I got your back."

There was another pause as Gordon looked me over. After a long while, he said, "Fuckin' hell." Then he held his hand up for a high five, which I took to mean things were good between us.

And they were. From that moment on day one, Gordon and I have been in sync on set. For close to five hundred episodes, I've been in his ear, suggesting lines, giving him cues—and got to say, he's as good as anyone I've ever worked with in terms of being able to respond to a suggestion on the fly. I'd put him up against any of the top play-by-play men in sports or news commentators who can deftly handle the twists and turns of a breaking story. We've developed a practiced shorthand, and it's worked out great, but it might never have come about if I hadn't pushed him that first day on set . . . if I hadn't *reached* and asked him to reach right along with me.

Just as Mike and I expected, Gordon Ramsay was a phenomenon. There was nothing like *Hell's Kitchen* and there was nothing like its breakout star. Audiences loved him. He was brash, bold, opinionated, and even occasionally charming, and in addition to being a master chef who really knew his way around a kitchen, he was a master television personality. It's like he was born to the medium—and specifically to this role. We had all the tears, all the laughs, all the high drama you could hope for in an inspirational, authentic competition show—and you didn't have to be a foodie to enjoy it.

But before *Hell's Kitchen* had a chance to become a first-season success, we had to get the show on the air, and we had some trouble getting on the schedule once our initial episodes were in the can. This was a surprising turn. I would have thought that if a network gave you a ten-episode commitment they'd be anxious to get the show on the air and start to see a return on their investment.

What slowed our progress here was a change in personnel—business as usual in network television. We'd gone through a bunch of rough cuts for our first episode, trying to get the tone and pacing just right, but every time we took our latest edit to Gail Berman, the head of the network, she pushed back in some way. She wanted more of *this* . . . less of *that* . . . and on and on. Mike, for maybe the first time in his career, had recently launched a number of shows that hadn't quite worked, and Gail was concerned that this might be because people were tired of reality television.

One of her first notes was that the show seemed overproduced, so we stripped out all the music and trimmed our opening tease. Then she wanted us to "soften" Gordon—meaning to cut the footage in such a way that he wasn't ripping into these hopeful chefs quite as much. She wanted him to appear more relatable to viewers, which she thought would make him more likable. To me, these fixes siphoned off the elements of the show that made it special. Gordon Ramsay was a different breed of talent. There had never been a front man quite like him on television. But with each round of edits and comments, we lost a little bit of his essence, and I fought and pushed back on all these changes.

And yet Gail Berman was the one paying the bills, so we jumped through her hoops and made some of the repairs. The compromises we made still maintained the integrity of the show. It wasn't *exactly* what I wanted, but what we had was solid. Still, we couldn't get an air date for the show.

We completed the edit at the beginning of 2005. Then our episodes sat on the shelf for months until Gail left as chairman of FOX in March 2005. She was replaced by Peter Liguori, who came over from being the head of FX. As it happened, I knew Peter quite well. We'd worked together at FOX Sports in the late '90s, when he was head of marketing and I was head of programming and production. We had a good relationship, and when news of his hiring filtered into our offices, I thought this shift at the top might help us to get *Hell's Kitchen* on the air at long last.

Mike Darnell and I lobbied hard for the show, which, despite being sanitized with all those edits, still managed to retain some of its teeth, reflecting just enough of Gordon's distinct personality for it to stand out in a meaningful way. Trouble was, as often happens in a changing of the guard, Peter Liguori had his own agenda in his new role, so his focus was on the shows he wanted to develop.

Finally, Peter realized he had a potential hit on his hands—or Mike and I had just worn him down!—and the show was scheduled to air on Monday, May 30, 2005. We were thrilled to have an air date, but May 30 was Memorial Day, so we were somewhat less than thrilled to be launching on a holiday Monday. But when you reach, sometimes you're only able to grab a piece of what you wanted. It's the grown-up version of that line we teach our kids in preschool: *You get what you get and you don't get upset.* In the moment, I wasn't so sure I agreed with the sentiment, but I allowed myself to think that, despite the network's tweaking and taming of our show and despite my fear that we had been relegated to scheduling Siberia, *Hell's Kitchen* would find its way to an audience.

Two weeks before the show was set to air, I was headed to a meeting when I ran into a FOX executive on Mike Darnell's team named Sabrina Ishak in the parking lot. We chatted for a bit, and then she asked, "Are you okay with the changes to *Hell's Kitchen*?"

I had no idea what she was talking about.

"What changes?" I asked. "The show has been in the can for six months. We air in two weeks."

"I'm sorry," she said in a way that confirmed she'd let the proverbial cat out of the bag. "I guess Mike hasn't talked to you yet. You should probably talk to him."

Yes, I thought. *I probably should.* I ran up the four flights of stairs to Mike's office, too impatient to wait for the elevator. The whole time, my mind was racing through every worst-case scenario. The show had been delivered. We no longer had any *Hell's Kitchen* postproduction staff on the payroll. I couldn't see how we'd be able to make any changes at this late date.

I'd taken the steps two at a time and was a bit out of breath when I reached Mike's office.

"Talk to me," I said. "I just ran into Sabrina in the parking lot, and she gave me a heads-up. You know I have no *Hell's* editors. You know I have no post staff. What's going on with these changes?"

"Calm down, Arthur," Mike said. "What makes you think these changes are a bad thing? I think they're a good thing." He told me to take a deep breath so he could walk me through what he had in mind.

"I can't calm down, Mike. Not until I know what's going on."

"I know we drove you crazy with the cut of the first episode," he explained. "We had to make all those concessions because Gail wanted the show to be less produced, and Gordon to be less . . . *Gordon*."

"Yeah, so . . ." I started, not entirely sure where Mike was going but pretty sure I wouldn't like what was being asked of me.

"So, since Gail's no longer here and Peter wasn't involved in the edit and doesn't feel strongly about it one way or the other, I thought we could get closer to your original cut for the show."

My head was spinning. Even though I really appreciated that Mike wanted to give me the opportunity to cut the show the way we'd originally envisioned, I couldn't see how we'd get there in just two weeks with no budget and no staff. Normally, you'd have months to work on an edit like this, with multiple editors.

Before I could say anything, Mike threw me another curve. "Just so you know," he said, "there's no money here to pay for the reedit."

"So what am I supposed to do?" I shot back.

"Are you telling me you don't want to air the show the way you put it together in the first place?"

I was frustrated by the tight turnaround time, and yet I was impressed by Mike and how much he cared about the product. This was Mike

Darnell in a nutshell. He always wanted what was best for the show, no matter how painful it might be at the time.

"Not at all," I said. "I want to do it. But Gail left months ago. Why didn't you come to me with this when we had a little more time? I don't have any of the tapes or the staff."

"You can get the money from ITV," Mike quite reasonably suggested. "They're going to sell this show all over the world. They've got a lot riding on this too."

I called ITV, but they immediately pushed back and said they were good with the show in its current form. In the end, I sat with Kent and an editor, and we figured out how to recut the show and pay for it and deliver it ourselves . . . one day before we were set to air. I was obsessed with making the best show possible, no matter what it took. I really thought we had a shot with this one, and so did Mike Darnell, which was why he wanted to honor our original instincts and present our first version of the show.

The show was a success right out of the gate, winning its time period in its first week, and everyone involved was thrilled. It went on to win its time period every week and became one of the highest-rated and most talked-about shows on television that summer.

In our second season, we continued the string, winning our time period each time out, and in our third season, we were even the number-one show on all of television for a number of weeks. Gordon Ramsay was becoming a huge star—to where both he and the show were being parodied on sketch shows, in magazines, and on late-night talk shows.

By almost every conceivable measure—and even by some inconceivable ones!—*Hell's Kitchen* was a runaway hit, and soon it was inevitable that I sat with Gordon, Mike, and ITV to join forces on another format based on a UK show. That's television, right? When you have a good thing going, you look to keep a good thing going however you can— like with a spin-off or a brand-extension or some other way to build out a franchise.

Unlike *Hell's Kitchen*, we leaned heavily on the UK template, which was centered in and around the restaurant industry. *Kitchen Nightmares* featured Gordon not only serving as a *chef whisperer* but also as a kind of *restaurateur whisperer*—and a very loud one at that. We liked the UK show but knew we would have to ramp up the pacing and the drama for the American audiences. The focus would still be on food and food service, playing to Gordon's strengths, but there was an emphasis on the owners and families who were running these struggling restaurants, as Gordon did whatever it took to help them revive their business. The often painful process made for very compelling television.

Like *Hell's Kitchen*, *Kitchen Nightmares* was an immediate hit—so not only did we launch the first successful food show on network television, but we were also responsible for the second. Indeed, I could write a whole other chapter on our follow-up effort, and I'm sure there are another few chapters I could pull from the many twists and turns and triumphs we've experienced at *Hell's Kitchen* over our first twenty seasons. But that's for another book.

For this one, I'll just say that *Kitchen Nightmares* ran for seven seasons, and just as I'd promised Gordon when we first got together on *Hell's Kitchen*, I was on the set with him for every one of our nearly one hundred episodes, providing him with insights and commentary and little things I wanted him to try—and he was always game to try, cementing what has proven to be one of the most enjoyable collaborations of my career.

By far the greatest benefit of my long association with Gordon Ramsay has been the amazing friendship we've developed over the years. We've ridden a giant wave together—and we're still riding it! Lately, he's gone so far as to tell me he trusts my instincts on the food front and that he'd even consider opening a restaurant with me if I was so inclined—a far cry from the way he dismissed me after our first meeting as a total foodie newbie. I've turned the compliment right back on Gordon, reminding him that he's not only the most famous chef in the world as the result of his work on television, but he's also an amazingly instinctive producer and I'd be happy to partner with him on any type of television show.

The show was a reach from the very beginning. No one saw what Mike and I saw . . . what my partner Kent and I saw . . . what Gordon and I saw. Even the folks at ITV, who had the foresight to sign Gordon and build a show around him for UK audiences, didn't see what I saw. Most significantly, no one other than Mike at FOX really believed in the show in the way that we did—until, at last, they had a certifiable hit on their hands. One of the learned truths in television is that it's sometimes better to *zig* when everybody else is *zagging*, even if it can sometimes be a big ask to get a network to do so.

All of which reinforced what I already knew: good things happen when you follow your gut and reach for what you know.

13

WHOLE LOTTA SHAKIN' GOING ON

By the middle of 2006, we were on a big-time roll at our upstart production company—so much so that I worried we couldn't handle all the work. We had a new project at CBS, and we just finished *Skating with Celebrities*, while at the same time prepping *Kitchen Nightmares*, both for FOX and our favorite network executive, Mike Darnell. In fact, Mike and his counterparts at the other broadcast networks kept us so busy with prime-time network fare that we weren't able to take good and full advantage of the many opportunities that were out there for us in cable.

And so, as Kent and I reached to take our business to another level, I knew it was essential for us to bring in a like-minded and talented individual who could handle our cable business at A. Smith & Co. That person was Frank Sinton, who had been my right-hand man at FOX Sports. He'd recently left the network and was busy producing documentaries when I tapped him to run our new cable division. Within a very short time he was up and running with a dozen new cable shows under our banner, including *Trading Spaces*, *Pros vs. Joes*, and *American Gangster*. Frank was the perfect guy—a skilled, decent, and enormously kind soul. Our entire team just loved him. He continues to work at A. Smith and Co., now as our COO and president, and as my consigliere and trusted friend. It's because of Frank, as much as anyone else, that we have become one of the biggest producers of nonfiction television in the United States.

With Frank in place, I was able to turn my full attention to the next opportunity that crossed my desk courtesy of Mike Darnell. We had quite a streak going with Mike—three hits in a row!—only this one was more of a distress call than an invitation to help develop a new idea. Mike was having some trouble with a show that was already in preproduction, an elimination-type competition program called *Celebrity Duets* created by Simon Cowell, the British television personality and record executive best known in the United States for *American Idol*. At the time, he was probably the most important star in the FOX universe, and the network was scrambling to launch this new show, which from my perspective should have been relatively easy to produce.

Mike wanted A. Smith & Co. to jump in and hopefully set things right. Now, you might think that since I was in the business of making television shows, I would have been happy to receive a distress call from a network seeking our help on a television show already in preproduction, but my impulse in those days was to push back on these late-in-the-game repair jobs. Basically, I wasn't interested in stepping in to fix someone else's show. But Mike and I had become good friends, and we were looking forward to doing a ton of business together, which meant I should at least consider helping him out. Plus, it was tough to look away from the good money to be had in the form of producers' fees, so I didn't reject Mike's appeal straightaway.

Mike laid out the idea for the show, together with a wish list of celebrity names FOX was chasing to serve as contestants and another list of music-industry legends to serve as singers and judges. Trouble was, there was almost nobody booked—a scary place to be when you're doing a celebrity-driven, booking-dependent show. Mike also had some concerns about the format and the show rundown.

"We shoot in six weeks," Mike said. "I need you to come in and help fix the show."

"Six weeks? That's not a lot of time."

"I know. That's why I'm calling."

The executive producer attached to the show was a really good guy named Michael Levitt who had worked for me years before at Dick

Clark Productions as a talent executive. Because we had a history, I didn't think Michael Levitt would see me as any kind of threat. At least I hoped not. The real worry here was Simon Cowell, who had a reputation in the business for being difficult. He was a big personality on a huge momentum run with *American Idol*, the highest-rated show in the country and the kind of entertainment juggernaut that left people like Mike Darnell and his colleagues at FOX with no choice but to develop a follow-up project in hopes of another success that would keep Simon happy.

Mike knew full well that the relationship with Simon would need to be managed, so he'd already reached out to Gordon Ramsay, who'd been working with me for a couple years at this point. Gordon and Simon were friends, and Gordon took the opportunity to say nice things about me. Mike said some nice things of his own, but even once Simon signed off on the idea of bringing me on, it felt like an awkward situation waiting to happen.

The very first time we met, he shook my hand and said, "I didn't know you'd be so young and good-looking," so a part of me wanted to like him right away, while another part knew to trust that he hadn't earned his reputation as a "challenging" character for no good reason. Still, I agreed to do it—mostly because Mike was a friend and he needed me.

The production was a mess, just as Mike had advertised—mostly because we had a singing show without any singers. And yet after rolling up my sleeves with the hard-working Michael Levitt and getting into it, I was relieved to see that it was a fixable mess. Very quickly, we were able to get our talent bookings sorted out.

Wayne Brady, the talented improv comedian, signed on as host. He was a tremendous asset because he was funny, he could sing, and he could work extemporaneously—a triple threat. In short order, our contestants all fell into place—Alfonso Ribeiro from *The Fresh Prince of Bel-Air*, Lucy Lawless from *Xena: Warrior Princess*, comedian Cheech Marin, Olympic gymnast Carly Patterson . . . And soon, our duet partners did as well—Smokey Robinson, Kenny Loggins, Boyz II Men, Patti LaBelle, Michael Bolton, Belinda Carlisle, Gladys Knight, and on and on. As the show was taking shape, I started telling people it was like my CD collection from the '80s had magically come to life.

One of the keys to the show's success, we all knew, would be our panel of judges. If you look back at the early days of *American Idol*, for example, the give and take among the judges was undoubtedly one of the key drivers of the show's popularity, and we were looking to duplicate that dynamic in our own way. We wanted to bring together a group of music industry professionals who we hoped would genuinely like each other, feed off each other, and offer pointed notes and comments to our celebrity contestants.

We began with David Foster, the celebrated Canadian musician, composer and record producer, whose sixteen Grammy Awards lent instant credibility to the show. Joining David on the panel were Marie Osmond—the singer and spokesperson who, with her brother Donny, had once shone as one of the brightest stars in Hollywood—and Little Richard—one of the pioneering spirits of rock 'n' roll and a living legend.

What I loved about this ensemble was that each of our judges represented a different segment of the music business from different eras, each with their own style and personality. Little Richard stood out on our stage, just as he'd stood out on every stage he'd worked for the past sixty-plus years. He was funny, flamboyant, and a little insane. A lot of times, we'd have no idea what he was talking about—the man seemed to speak his own language—but David and Marie were good about letting him run off on one of his be-bop-a-loo-bop rants and then reeling him back in.

Though Simon's presence loomed large over our entire production, he wasn't exactly *present* as we ramped up and started taping. He came by to introduce himself early on. He participated in a few conference-call updates. I remember thinking there had been no reason to worry over any clash of personalities.

It was all smooth sailing . . . until it wasn't.

A chop in the water came when I turned my attention to the show open. One of the features I prided myself on was the way we opened our shows—what we called our "super tease." The open only ran for a couple minutes, but it was prime real estate in the show's landscape. It was our first and best chance to announce to viewers what we were about and what they were about to see. I thought it was essential in establishing the tone of each show and framing the story we wanted to tell.

Already, I'd developed a reputation in the business for the openers to my shows. Here I borrowed a page from the intros and openers we did at CBC Sports and FOX Sports, where we'd combine great music with stunning graphics and visuals and draw the viewer in with sharp writing and the promise of real human emotion.

For this open I wanted to highlight the incredible success of the music industry legends who'd signed on to sing with our celebrity contestants, so I used graphics and a dramatic voice-over to let viewers know that among them, they'd sold over 370 million albums, been nominated for over one hundred Grammy Awards, and recorded 250 number-one hits. (It was a pretty impressive lineup!) Michael Levitt loved the open. When we took it to Mike Darnell, he loved it too.

At some point it was decided that we should show it to Simon Cowell to get his take. I wasn't crazy about this idea, because we were only a day away from our premiere and there wasn't enough time to make any wholesale changes. Simon would either love it or he wouldn't, but I didn't see that it mattered all that much either way. Michael Levitt thought the open would help to get Simon excited about the show, but my thinking was, *Hey, if he's not excited about the show at this point, we're in trouble.* In the end, we agreed to hold back on showing Simon the opening . . . unless he asked to see it.

It fell to me to show Simon around on the day before our live shoot. I took him to meet Wayne Brady and some of our contestants, and there were a number of FOX executives on hand to greet him as well. Because this was peak-popularity Simon Cowell, when *Idol* was the most-watched show in the country, everyone was very deferential to Simon. It's like we were being visited by royalty. Simon had been very warm up to this point, like he was actually going out of his way to keep things positive.

Best I could tell, Simon was happy with what he'd seen on this eleventh-hour tour. The set, the lighting, the bookings, the format—he was satisfied with the way everything had fallen into place. But just as Simon was about to leave, Michael Levitt said, "You should see the open Arthur produced for the show."

"Right, let's have a look," Simon said—or something similarly British.

Oh, fuck! Really? I thought. I could have kicked Michael for bringing it up. (In fact, later on, I think I did.) In fairness to Michael, he was just trying to pump Simon up and get him excited about the show. But once he'd put it out there, we of course had to go to one of the edit bays to screen the open.

I sat huddled with Simon and the two Mikes and a handful of FOX executives. We dimmed the lights. We played the open. There were a couple oohs and aahs and general notes of enthusiasm. There was even a small smattering of applause. I let myself think we'd dodged a bullet and that my love affair with Simon would continue.

"I don't like it," Simon weighed in. That's all—just, *I don't like it.*

This was followed by dead silence. No one in that small editing room dared to contradict or step on Simon's comment and offer another point of view. Everyone was a bit terrified of him.

Me, I wasn't terrified, but he now presented a hurdle for me to get past. I tried to mask my frustration and keep my tone pleasant, professional. "What don't you like about it, Simon?" I asked. "We can adjust."

He waited what felt like hours but was probably only a few seconds before replying, "I don't like the way it feels."

I don't like it.

I don't like the way it feels.

I couldn't think how to react. These two generic comments were just about the worst notes ever. And it fell to me to act on them, to make things right in some way. It didn't feel like the right time or place to press Simon to be more specific. The moment he spoke, everybody else in that small room fell silent, so it's not like there was a resounding endorsement of the open to drown out his negative take, even though the folks who'd already seen it had weighed in previously with their enthusiasm.

And then, having dropped this little bombshell, Simon left.

I waited a few uncomfortable moments before turning to Mike Darnell and asking what *he'd* thought of the opening.

"The opening's great, Arthur," he said.

"So what the fuck am I supposed to do here?"

It was nine o'clock in the evening at this point, and the show was due to air live the next night. Whatever I was supposed to do, I would need to do it soon, but Mike had a different take.

"Don't do anything just yet. Let's think this through."

"Don't do anything? I can't just ignore his note. It's Simon Cowell!"

Mike was smart enough to coax me outside for a private walk-and-talk away from the others. He could see I'd been rubbed the wrong way by Simon's vague notes. We both knew I'd have to work with Simon going forward. We knew he was going to watch the show, and that I couldn't exactly slap the same opening on it after he'd announced that he didn't like it. There'd be no way to recover from that kind of insubordination.

I took a breath—a long breath, actually. As I let the air out of this tense situation, I saw that Mike was right about holding off on making any major changes. I wouldn't do *nothing*, but I'd find a way to make a few small repairs to the open without upsetting or upending the structure and images we'd already laid down. I would put a slightly different shine to it, change up the pacing a bit—enough, hopefully, to leave Simon thinking his notes had been honored and had made a positive difference.

I gathered with my staff and set about making the few small repairs. It took about a couple hours, and as I got into it, I thought, *Okay, this is not a big deal. This is just me jumping through some hoops to satisfy the biggest star on the FOX Network.* I was channeling my father, making an extra effort to keep his customers happy on those Saturdays when I used to go with him to work. I thought back to the way Mike Darnell had told me early on that Simon Cowell needed to be looked after and realized that this was just another way to keep this man's moods and emotions in check.

Simon watched the show live and called me up the next day to give me his take. "I loved what you did with the open." He sounded sincere.

"Really?" I'd dodged some kind of bullet, but I wasn't exactly sure how.

"It's just so much better."

I wanted to ask him *how* it was so much better, but I held back. As I hung up the phone, I thought, *Thank God*. Big personalities can be like that, don't you think? They can swoop in and offer a firm opinion on a matter, and then expect you to act on that firm opinion simply because they said so.

This was Simon's show after all, so naturally he needed to be heard. But I was able to satisfy him while sticking to my vision and trusting my instincts.

―――――――

As Simon Cowell occasionally brought the mood of the room down, Little Richard, in his own loopy way, brought a level of joy to the show that was infectious.

Little Richard was a strange dude, but I liked him enormously. Everybody did. Once, a few hours before our live show was to begin and we were going through the last of our rehearsals, he sat down at a piano we had onstage and started playing. He called over to me and demanded that I "sit my ass down" next to him at the piano—his words. It took everyone completely by surprise—although, looking back, I guess it shouldn't have been all that surprising that a rock 'n' roll legend would sit down at a piano and start playing. "Good Golly, Miss Molly," "Tutti Frutti" . . . he went through all his hits. Next thing I knew, Marie Osmond started singing some of *her* hits. Then David Foster sat down at the piano and began playing. At one point I looked up and saw the entire crew dancing and looking so damn happy.

For a half hour or so, we were enchanted by these enormous talents, treated to our own private, impromptu concert. It was wild—one of those special moments I'd have to always remind myself to step back and appreciate. When you've built a career on a series of reaches and challenges, it's easy to forget to live in the present, and this was one time where I allowed myself to set aside any worries of what was coming next, even though we had a live show to do in just a couple hours.

Little Richard surprised the hell out of me on an almost daily basis, but never more so than the time he called me to his dressing room one afternoon.

"I need to talk to you, man," he said.

"What's up?" I asked.

"What time we gonna be done, d'ya think?" He was concerned about our shooting schedule, which was now looking like it would stretch into a Friday evening. We were live, so there was a kind of hard stop to our shooting schedule, but it sometimes happened that we'd run over.

I said I was hoping to be done by seven o'clock.

"I don't know, man," he said. "I gotta be home by Shabbos."

"What?"

"Shabbos, man. We do Shabbos. Sundown. Like that."

It was just about the last thing I was expecting out of this man . . . but Little Richard was full of surprises. He'd actually converted to Judaism—or he embraced its traditions, at least. This was and remains astonishing to me, because there was a time in there when Little Richard had actually stepped away from his music career to devote his full attention to the ministry, and now here he was telling me he needed to be home in time to observe the Sabbath.

Apparently, his interest in Judaism stemmed from a years-ago car crash, when Bob Dylan reportedly visited with him at his hospital bedside and stressed the importance of keeping the Sabbath. After that, Little Richard told me, he'd only missed a couple Saturday mornings in synagogue.

"I'm serious, man," he said. "I can't be staying if we run long. It's against my religion."

As it happened, we did run long one Friday night, and when it started to look like we weren't going to break before sundown, he came to me and said, "It's like I told you, man."

"You're not really leaving, are you?" I said. "We'll be done in fifteen, maybe twenty minutes."

As I'd feared, we ran a few minutes over.

"I'm gone," he said.

And he was. We went to commercial, and he ducked out before our last act. I couldn't believe it, but it's not like the guy didn't warn me. And it's not like I could hold it against him, wanting to get home before sundown to observe the Sabbath—me of all people.

David Foster said something funny to explain away his absence, but Little Richard was true to his word and true to his faith, and the only thing that bothered me about this exchange was that he didn't wish me a *good Shabbos* on his way out the door.

Working with big stars means working with big personalities, and big personalities can present big challenges. Here the challenge was finding a way to diffuse the tension in the room brought by a guy like Simon Cowell in a way that honored his vision for the show. (After all, it was *his* show.) At the same time, there was a challenge to meet Little Richard's needs, even if they were presented to me at the last moment as a kind of *fait accompli*. I could only throw my hands up and think, *Oy*!

Looking back, I can see that *Celebrity Duets* was a risk for me because I was coming in to fix a show that wasn't mine—a show that was facing a number of issues. Was I worried about those issues? Absolutely, but I was willing to take them on because I wanted to add another high-profile show to our company's slate and to help out my good friend Mike Darnell.

No doubt, this one was a reach, but I understood that I wasn't the only one *reaching* on this project. It was a reach for Simon Cowell, who was determined to make a name for himself as a producer after establishing himself as a huge star on *American Idol*.

It was a reach for Little Richard—an opportunity for the music legend to show that he was still relevant and to grow his public profile by taking on this new role as a judge and mentor on a prime-time series that would hopefully appeal to a whole new audience.

Clearly, these two stars had a lot at stake, so it was to be expected that they might present a challenge for me and my production team. There was a lot on the line for our crew members and the dozens of artists and celebrities who appeared on the show. There were challenges all around—as everyone involved reported to work not only in service of the show, but mindful of their own missions.

That's often the case in any professional enterprise, in television as elsewhere, and it fell to me to navigate these various personal agendas with grace and good cheer. And with respect to Simon and Little Richard, I determined that the best course of action was not to fight them but to work with them in such a way that they felt heard and respected.

My thing, then as now, was to preserve and protect the quality of the production, while preserving and protecting the quality of the relationships I build on the back of each show. After all, television is a collaborative medium—*and* a business of relationships—and it takes knowing how to work with all different types of people in order to build and sustain a lasting career.

14

I SURVIVED A JAPANESE GAME SHOW

I never know where or when I'll find our next show, but I've been at it long enough to have some idea on the how and why. Inspiration hits at the unlikeliest times in the unlikeliest places, and I've found over the years that it helps to have a goal in mind whenever you start to reach. You've probably heard that great line from Zig Ziglar, the author and motivational speaker, that you can't hit a target you don't see. Well, in my experience, this often means thinking of a specific buyer when I'm kicking around an idea for a show.

We were seven years into our run at A. Smith & Co. and had some real successes with shows like *Paradise Hotel*, and *Hell's Kitchen* was well on its way to becoming one of our signature hits. On top of all that, *Kitchen Nightmares*, our second show with Gordon Ramsay, had debuted to great reviews and solid ratings. By every outward measure, we were a well-established production company. And yet when I stepped back and looked at the shows we had in development and the shows in our rearview mirror, I noticed that we were doing a disproportionate amount of business with my buddy Mike Darnell at FOX. That was great for the time being, but if we meant to be in it over the long haul, we'd need to develop stronger relationships with other networks.

I've always told people we're six or seven phone calls from being out of business. Even when things are going great for us, this is what I'm thinking. When I say a line like that, people invariably look at me like I've got two heads and ask me what in the world I'm talking about. I might have ten shows on the air and another ten in production, and it looks like things are going great—until or unless all these calls happen on the same day and all these shows are canceled.

It hasn't happened yet, and it's not likely to happen, but this very thought has kept me hungry for over twenty years at A. Smith & Co. As we were looking ahead to yet another show on FOX, I decided we needed to diversify and build a broader base of network partners—it's just good business, you know.

With this in mind, in late 2007 I reached out to John Saade, who was in charge of alternative series, specials, and late night at ABC. In the run-up to our meeting, I learned he had optioned a project called *Big in Japan* from a Danish production company. It was just a loose concept at this point, and John was trying to figure out what to do with it and who he could trust to develop it. There wasn't much there, but it did have the notion of foreigners going to Japan and attempting to be part of the unique world of Japanese entertainment—the seed of an idea we would grow into one of the most outlandish, creative shows I ever developed.

John was a big fan of Japanese television—Japanese game shows, especially. I was only dimly aware of that segment of Japanese culture, enough to understand the phenomenon, but I did a kind of deep dive and became fascinated with the genre. Japanese game shows at the time were over-the-top, anything-goes affairs—campy, outrageous, crazy. There was nothing like it on American television: wild music, colorful sets, and contestants who were willing to be completely embarrassed in front of a national audience. This last seemed to be an operating principle: find some silly, slapstick way to embarrass or blindside your contestants, and you're at least part of the way to a Japanese game show.

As I watched these shows with Kent Weed and our development team, I wondered what would happen if we took a group of Americans and press-ganged them into being on a Japanese game show. The idea was they wouldn't know what they were getting into until they were already into it. I filed this thought alongside another few concepts we had

percolating and went to meet with John. As we spoke, this one preposterous notion bubbled to the surface.

I think we both got a little carried away with the idea of breaking
the mold and coming up with a show so wildly absurd that no major
network would even consider putting any money into it. I can't remember ever laughing so hard at a pitch meeting, and when we ran out of
gas, John surprised me by telling me he wanted to keep the conversation
going. He offered us a budget to develop a show bible—a document
that spells out everything you hope a show could be.

In the pecking order of hopeful outcomes in series development, a
budget for a show bible is not any kind of green light or done deal. The
holy grail when you're pitching a show is to get a series commitment right
out of the gate, but that rarely happens. Short of that, you might get a
pilot commitment or money to develop a low-cost presentation tape.
And short of *that*, for a series in the genre we're still not calling *reality
television*, you might get a deal to write a show bible or a show outline.

In the business, we refer to this as "paper development." It's not everything, but it's something—certainly more than I expected in support of
this loopy, zany concept. (And this concept was not "pilotable" because
it would have been outrageously expensive.)

Kent and I went back to the rest of the team and started an even
deeper dive, this time watching as many Japanese game shows as possible, researching the market, looking at possible production facilities . . .
you know, seeing if we could take this pie-in-the-sky, pie-in-the-face
concept and make it real. Unfortunately, there wasn't enough room in
the very modest bible budget to send one of us to Japan, but we soaked
in what we could long distance and let our imaginations run.

As our loose idea for the show started to take shape, we stuck pretty
close to the premise I'd pitched to John Saade. We'd sign sixteen contestants to a blind-participation deal. All they'd know was that they were
agreeing to appear on a vaguely defined competition show and that
their schedules needed to be clear for a couple weeks and their passports
in order. We thought through different scenarios and set them down,
and what we kept coming back to was this: we'd meet our contestants

at LAX, where they'd be expecting to board a bus to take them on an hour drive to a location in Hollywood. On the bus, they'd learn instead that they were headed to the other part of the airport where they would board a plane to Tokyo. Our camera crews would film the reveal as our contestants made the quick trip from the domestic terminals to the international terminal.

Once in Japan, the group would be taken for a tour of the famous Toho Studios, where the Godzilla movies were made. While on the tour, they'd be led to a working sound stage, where a studio audience had been assembled. As they were led onto what they thought was an empty set, they would have their minds blown as they were introduced by a very loud and animated Japanese host and learn that they'd just walked onto their own game show . . . *live*!

Pretty *out there*, huh?

The show would be a wild hybrid of genres: a documentary of the contestants' journey, a game show, a competition show. We'd shoot all of the behind-the-scenes, docu life-in-Japan stuff with a distinct "film" look, and all of the game show stuff with a crisp videotape "live" look. We wanted to juxtapose the fish-out-of-water elements of life in Japan for our cast as they adjusted to the food and the culture with the outrageous game show elements.

Developing an outside-the-box show like the one we were imagining here, we focused on every little detail. Nothing like this had ever been done before, and as far as any of us knew, nothing like this had ever been *considered* . . . and so we considered the hell out of it.

After about a month, we sent the bible with our crazy idea for a show to ABC. A part of me figured they were going to think we are completely out of our mind and that would be the end of it. I swear, any sane network executive would have thought we were on drugs when we wrote it. We did bibles and outlines like this all the time, and that was often the beginning and the end of the project. You do them because that's the dance of our industry, and you're just happy to have a dance partner for the next little while. It's how much of television starts out. You give the folks at the network something to look at and discuss, and then you hope against hope that you strike just the right group of people in just the right way at just the right time. This one was so warped, so unlike anything else we'd ever seen, there was no reason to think anything would come of it. Plus, we knew the show would have been logistically impossible and ridiculously expensive to produce.

I put it out of my mind. I was preoccupied with the shooting of season two of *Kitchen Nightmares*, which was fast becoming our second franchise hit with Gordon Ramsay. I was on location shooting an episode, in a production trailer, when I got an unexpected call from John Saade. At first, I couldn't even think why he was calling.

"I read the bible," John said.

Oh, yeah, that, I thought.

Then he added that Steve McPherson, who was then the president of ABC Entertainment, had read it too.

"Ridiculous, huh?" I said, expecting he was about to lower the boom.

"We were both laughing hysterically. We want to do the series."

My jaw dropped all the way to the floor of the trailer. "You're kidding, right?"

He wasn't kidding. Not only that, he wanted to put the show on in June. It was the beginning of February, which put us on an impossible timetable given the sweep and scope and audacity of this project.

Fuck! I thought. Luckily, I didn't share this one thought with John. I'd been stunned into silence.

"You still there?" John said.

"I'm still here."

"Can you do that? Can we get the show on the air in June?"

"I don't know. I mean, I think so. I guess so. I don't know." I had no idea if we could do a show like this in just a few months. Honestly, I didn't know if we could do a show like this at all, but I was in the business of making television and making things happen, and I didn't have it in me to say otherwise.

"Well, that's our window," John explained. "We have the NBA playoffs in late spring, and we want to promote it during the playoffs, which will run until the end of June."

Okay, that's marginally better. The end of June gave us a couple more weeks to work with. But still, it was an extremely tight turnaround.

"So," John pushed, "can you do it?"

"I don't know," I said, still equivocating. "We wrote this bible in Burbank, not Tokyo." I thought it was a funny line, but John wasn't laughing—obviously, this was not the answer he wanted to hear.

"Look," he finally said. "I need to know by tomorrow. Twenty-four hours. Can you let me know by then?"

"I guess so."

I immediately got with Kent to talk it through. His thing was to say yes and worry about the details later. That was part of his charm. My thing was to make sure we could deliver. It was the difference between taking a leap and playing it safe. Kent was more of a dice-roller. Whatever it was, he was inclined to give it a shot, and if it all worked out to the good, that was great. If it didn't . . . well, that was okay too. I tended to take a more conservative, more risk-averse approach. That doesn't mean I wasn't prepared to take risks, but I paid more attention to the downside of risk. I wasn't prepared to risk everything, which in this case would have been our reputation. Our biggest asset as a production company was our ability to deliver shows on time, on budget, beyond expectations.

None of us had ever worked in Japan—other than the meetings I took on behalf of Paul Allen, which I wrote about earlier. We had no idea what it would take to shoot a show over there, how we'd overcome any language or cultural barriers, what kind of shooting schedule we could reasonably put in place. There were way too many variables, as far as I was concerned, and not nearly enough time to sort them out.

Ultimately, after doing every bit of due diligence we could squeeze into John's twenty-four hours, we decided to take the leap and go for it—a power move that doesn't always come from a place of power. Sometimes it comes from a place of being passionate about the challenge. In this case, it might have come from a place of ignorance or arrogance, but when you're in the business of reaching, sometimes you reach on faith alone.

The first hurdle was finding studio space in Tokyo on such short

notice. It turned out, there was a rare hole in the schedule at the famed
Toho Studios we were able to fill, but that just took us to our next
hurdle—finding a house to accommodate our unsuspecting contestants.
The housing market in Tokyo was tight to begin with, and homes tended
to be on the small side, so at the outset we didn't think we'd find a house
for fifteen to twenty people, which of course we needed as the setting for
the *Real World*–type elements of the show. Eventually, we hired a local
fixer to help us find a suitable house and sort through these logistical
hurdles, and a Japanese crew to keep the production authentic. We also
hired a Japanese director for the game show segments, and a Japanese
art director, because no American sensibility would have been able to
create what we had in mind.

We brought on an executive producer we'd worked with before, and
a head of challenges who would collaborate with us on growing our crazy
bible into a crazy show. I'd thought we were in good, capable hands, and
in one respect we certainly were. However, in another respect, these two
professionals were unable to shoulder this type of risk and uncertainty.
One of them came to me and said, "Arthur, it's not happening. There
are too many moving parts. There's not enough time."

They were capable, but not confident, and on a crapshoot of an
assignment like this one, they needed a heaping helping of both. In each
case, they quit because they thought it was only a matter of time before
things fell apart and they would have been let go anyway.

I was disappointed, but we were all having our own second thoughts.
Still, we would not be derailed. We hired another executive producer and
another head of challenges, and we kept pushing. We ended up with a
series of challenges that were completely nuts. One we called "Big Bug
Splat on a Windshield," in which a contestant dressed up as a bee, then
was slathered with a goopy, sticky liquid and flung against a target—
like a bug on a windshield. We had lots of games designed to make our
often-costumed contestants dizzy or to get them to slip or fall, including
one where they had to climb over three oiled-up Sumo wrestlers to reach
their goal . . . *insanity*, to say the least.

We created a fake Japanese game show within our show called

Majide—Japanese for *seriously?* or when said with emphasis, *seriously insane*—which resembled a real show, complete with its own host and studio audience. We did such a good job making *Majide* look authentic that most of our viewers thought this was a real show in Japan. Even industry people thought it was real, and we kept hearing how lucky we were to get the cooperation of an up-and-running production.

The idea was to follow the *Majide* game show *and* life outside the studio as our contestants adjusted to Japan. They were watched over by a *Mama-san*, who basically ran the group household and expected our contestants to respect Japanese culture and follow its traditions. The whole time they were in residence, the contestants had no idea that *Majide* was a fake show, so even though the dramas that inevitably unfolded in the house were very real, they were rooted in a staged game show that was anything but real. Of course, the competition was real, and so was the $250,000 prize money, but the challenges that were contained in this fictional game show only existed to drive the story of our show.

In the end, we shot the show on time and pulled off a television miracle, becoming the only American prime-time series to be shot entirely in Japan. The over-the-top game show elements turned out to be authentic and outrageous and very Japanese—and nobody got hurt. And the reality elements turned out to reveal some prickly personalities—some heroes, some villains, and enough unpredictable mood swings and flare-ups to make for compelling television. As it happened, watching these Americans adapting and experiencing Japanese life and culture was hilarious, intriguing, and *very* entertaining.

In almost every respect, the production could not have gone any smoother, especially considering the bits and pieces that were lost in translation behind the scenes. I was in Tokyo for about a month to oversee the shoot, and my partner Kent, who handled the directing duties on this one as well, was there for a bit longer. It was a crazy, thrilling adventure, apart from the fact that I could never find anything to eat because I'm afraid my taste for crazy, thrilling adventures doesn't extend to food.

We won a bunch of awards for our series, *I Survived a Japanese Game Show*, which was what we'd been calling it all along as a kind of placeholder title. In the end, we all agreed the name said it all, so that's what we went with, and people in television really paid attention. In and around the industry, it was hailed for its creativity and mold-bending format.

At the end of our first season of the series, we not only won the Best Reality prize but Format of the Year at the Rose d'Or, an international festival highlighting the best in broadcasting and programming. By almost every measure, the show was a success, enough so that we earned a second season. But by this point our "great reveal" had been revealed and the novelty that had been attached to our first season had since worn off, so we lost steam with viewers, and the network seemed to think it would be a good idea for us to focus more on the game and less on the contestants adapting to life in Japan. (It wasn't.)

Still, I put this one in the plus column. The great lesson it carried was a reminder to dig deep and reach, even if the thing I'm reaching for seems improbable or beyond my grasp. One of the reasons the show worked well and made such a splash was because it was so surprising, so completely unlike anything else on television. I wish my words could do justice to our ridiculous premise or the big, wild fun on display on our stage—but for that you can bounce over to YouTube and catch some episodes in full.

This was a reach with two key takeaways:

1. Evaluate your risk before diving in—and then, once
    you commit, stay focused on your goal and hang on
    for dear life. Kent and I were united on this one—true
    partners—even as members of our staff abandoned ship
    because they didn't think this crazy series was ever going
    to happen.
2. There are always going to be at least three oiled-up Sumo
    wrestlers blocking your path and trying to keep you from
    where you're meant to go.

15

CLIMBING MOUNT MIDORIYAMA

One thing I learned early on as an independent producer was that a lot of production companies aren't really *companies* at all. In many cases they are just a bare-bones operation with a small office staffed by one or two people with a single phone line and a framed promo poster of the one and only show they had a hand in producing.

That wasn't what I wanted (or expected!) for A. Smith & Co., and after our first decade in business, we'd succeeded beyond my wildest expectations. We were a full-fledged, up-and-running business with dozens of shows in development, a dozen in production, and dozens more in our rearview mirror. Sure, from time to time we staffed hundreds of freelance professionals to meet the temporary demands of a particular shoot, but we also employed a sizable full-time staff with nice offices, 401(k)s, and benefits—all the good stuff you expect to see in a going concern.

Getting to this place in our development as a company meant stacking one reach on top of another—building upon each success to bring us to the next one. Now that I had reached in this way, it fell to us to *keep* reaching. Success, in television as elsewhere, is never a one-and-done deal. It's not enough to turn the lights on; we had to work each day to keep them on and shining bright.

Each day Kent, Frank, and I came into work determined to nourish what we'd built, which meant maintaining a certain volume to offset our ongoing expenses, which in turn meant we were always looking for shows—big shows, small shows, in-between shows. Making it over the long haul as an independent producer means finding ways to keep the production pipeline flowing and being on the constant lookout for the next big thing, while at the same time acknowledging that it isn't always the next *big* thing that pays the bills. Sometimes it's the seeing-eye single that keeps a rally going.

In this context, with this mindset, I took a call one day in 2009 from an old friend named Neal Tiles, who'd been a vice president of marketing at FOX Sports during my tenure there. Neal was now running a small cable channel called G4, which ironically had once been owned by Paul Allen under a different name, Tech TV, before we convinced him to sell it.

Neal called me in frustration. His network was available in forty million homes, but his shows were struggling to find an audience. "The only show that's getting any kind of rating is this weird little show out of Japan," he told me. "Could you maybe take a look at it and let me know what you think?"

These distress calls from my friends and colleagues were never *just* to get my take on a show that may or may not have been working. Typically, they were meant to gauge my interest in signing on in some way, perhaps as a consultant or a producer, but I was always happy to take these calls and weigh in. After all, as I have by now made clear, television is a business of relationships, and it was on me to honor and serve those relationships at every turn.

The Japanese show was called *Sasuke*, a strangely produced obstacle-course show with subtitles. Yet as I watched, I was intrigued.

This show would ultimately morph into *American Ninja Warrior*, which has become one of our biggest, brightest, and most enduring hits—*and* a foundational piece of the NBC prime-time schedule. Over the years, some people have compared *American Ninja Warrior* to a syndicated competition show that ran in the late 1980s and early 1990s called *American Gladiators*, which pitted a group of amateur athletes against the show's self-styled gladiators in a series of challenges that tested strength, agility, and endurance. I never really liked the comparison because of one fundamental difference: the challengers on *Sasuke* weren't competing against each other or any larger-than-life gladiators; they were competing against the course itself.

Sasuke was a no-frills affair, but looking past the limited production values and the relative lack of creative supporting features, I saw an idea for a bigger show. Done right, it was the kind of show that could break out of its niche and find a wider audience—not a prime-time network show, by any stretch, but a solid cable performer. *Sasuke* showed ordinary people attempting to do extraordinary things, and I loved that the show celebrated the attempt. I knew if we did an American version, we were really going to lean into who these people were.

As I watched, I thought of my wife and two daughters, my sisters, my mother. The women in my life cared very little about sports, even though it had always been a big part of my life. In later years, when I had access to tickets to the biggest games in the best seats, they would sometimes join me, but if they walked through the room while I was jumping up and down and hollering in front of the television because the Lakers had just won a game in overtime or the Canadiens had just been whistled for a ridiculous penalty, they'd pass on through without even turning their heads to see what was going on. And yet they were addicted to sports movies—*Rudy, The Blind Side, Remember the Titans, Friday Night Lights.* They loved that stuff, especially my daughters, Rachel and Leah. Obviously, they were responding to the emotional elements of these stories, the human drama, the impulse to root for the underdog, the spirit of triumph and inspiration.

Back when I produced our packaged pieces for the Olympics at CBC, I considered how what I was working on might move my mom or my sisters. That was the broad audience I was always after. I knew I had the sports fans, but in order to get a big number, I had to draw beyond that core audience and attract a general audience as well. To do that, I reached for story lines and production elements I thought would encourage viewers of all ages and interests to care about these athletes.

Now I found myself doing pretty much the same thing, wondering if it was possible to inject this obstacle-course competition with the kinds of backstories and compelling human drama that might get my wife and daughters to watch.

I got back to Neal with my notes in just a couple days. I think I surprised him with how much time I'd clearly spent on it, but I saw something in the footage that excited me, so I went beyond his ask and grew my two cents into a couple bucks at least.

"The obstacle course needs to represent something," I said almost as soon as Neal picked up the phone, before we'd even gotten our pleasantries out of the way. "It has to be more than just a bunch of obstacles. And we have to show the viewers why these people are competing." I explained how the course needed to be a metaphor for life. "Find a way to do that," I said, "and you will have a more purposeful show that will connect with a bigger audience."

Neal wasn't sure what I meant by this—so Kent and I went over to his office and did a presentation for him and his senior execs. We explained that viewers were looking to root for real people, same as them—a plumber, a construction worker, a schoolteacher—everyday people chasing everyday dreams. For some, that dream could be tied up in the notoriety they'd receive from being on television in this empowering way. For others, it could be the validation they'd get from overcoming these physical and mental obstacles.

In the past year, Neal tried to launch an American version of the show, recruiting another independent producer to revamp the format, shooting a few episodes in an otherwise empty church parking lot. Those episodes were included in the package Neal sent over for me to watch, along with several Japanese episodes. The Americanized version fell flat. Without a real crowd cheering on these everyday people, it's like they were competing in a vacuum. Their extra efforts on the course, no matter how impressive, couldn't help but land with a thud. I told Neal he needed to layer in some excitement and stage the show in front of a sizable audience in a cool location—like, say, Venice Beach.

The more I talked, the more I saw the possibilities for Neal's show and all the different ways it could be adapted for an American audience. The problem was that my ideas weren't simple tweaks. They weren't suggestions on how to reframe or repackage the show for G4. What the show needed was a complete overhaul—the way the course was presented, how it confronted the athletes, and the athletes themselves—which in turn meant a substantial investment.

After many years of doing big events and network shows, I knew how much it would cost to stage this thing properly, but I wasn't interested in putting that kind of money into a pilot, even if it wasn't *my* money. It didn't make sense to build an elaborate course and go to all this trouble for the chance the show might get picked up. It would have been an enormously expensive pilot, and I couldn't see how Neal's fledgling network could afford it. You needed to be able to amortize these costs and shoot a bunch of episodes, and I said as much. "If you're looking to do a pilot, I'm not interested."

Okay, so that was the most compelling argument *against* doing the show. The most compelling argument *in favor* came from the son of one of our A. Smith & Co. development executives, Matt Miller. Matt came to me one day and said, "Oh my God, my kid loves the Japanese show. He's obsessed with this show." Matt's son was only about ten years old, but I knew that if this one little kid was so fired up about this one little show, there must be something to it, so I took his enthusiasm seriously.

Neal assured me that G4 would green-light an amped-up series based on how the Japanese version of the show was performing. The subtitled version of the show wasn't exactly lighting the world on fire, but it was pulling a decent number—big enough, certainly, for the network to find another way to keep a good thing going.

"If that's the case, we're in."

I knew full well that *all* our shows weren't meant to be network home runs and that we needed a bunch of cable singles in order to continue our growth plan. This would be something to add to our growing (and, by now, sizable) list of programming. I had no reason to think this obscure obstacle-course show would catch on, but when taking on a new project, it's better to ask "Why not?" than "Why?" And so we added Neal's G4 show to our lineup and went to work.

This Japanese obstacle-course show had a long history before it popped on my radar. I didn't just grab at this opportunity and make it my own. It wasn't like that, and it wasn't just me. It was a long, tough slog for a number of us—for a while, it even looked like our Americanized version wouldn't amount to anything more than a nice little show on a nice little network—but we kept at it, clearing different obstacles of our own.

We rebranded our version of the show as *American Ninja Warrior* and built an amazing course smack in the middle of Venice Beach. Initially, we designed our course based on the Japanese version, and the carrot at the end of the stick of our competition was that we'd send our top ten competitors to Japan to conquer Mount Midoriyama, the mother of all obstacles, which pretty much nobody ever completed. In later years, in success, we staged our own finale at our own Mount Midoriyama on the Las Vegas strip, but in the beginning, using the course at Venice Beach, we operated as a sister show to the original *Sasuke* version, sticking close to the Japanese format, and coordinating our schedule so that we could cap our season with a grand finale on the *Sasuke* set in Tokyo.

Soon enough, our souped-up version gained traction. Little by little, episode by episode, we found our voice and our audience. Perhaps the biggest contribution to our version of the show came from my partner, Kent. More than anyone else in-house, Kent *got* how to make the obstacle-course concept work for American audiences, and he was instrumental in developing and evolving our obstacles over the years. Very quickly, we went *way* beyond the Japanese version of the show in this area, and this was primarily Kent's doing in the beginning. He had an uncanny way of dialing in these memorable, relatable elements and setting up our cameras to allow us to capture the drama and excitement in a compelling way.

After three seasons, the show was starting to do really, really well—to where more people knew *American Ninja Warrior* than knew the G4 network—so viewers had to seek us out. Naturally, we were eager to get more eyeballs on our show, and around this time Comcast was purchasing a majority stake in NBC Universal. As good fortune would have it, G4 was already part of the Comcast family, bundled with a group of other niche cable networks like E, Bravo, and Oxygen. This, in the parlance of the television industry, was a moment of synergy just waiting to happen. At least, that's how it looked to us on the production side of things.

As we leaned into our third season, we pushed to get NBC to air our finale as a showcase episode. No one (including me!) thought our show would have a future on NBC—we did not see *American Ninja Warrior* as a prime-time network show. But getting on the network in this one-off way would be a tremendous billboard for our G4 show and drive more viewers our way for a hoped-for fourth season.

That's synergy. Trouble was, nobody on the network side saw it in the same way—at least, not at first. I reached out to a couple executives at the network and got back nothing . . . crickets. Neal, too, went at it through his bosses at Comcast from his perch at G4, and we still weren't getting anywhere.

Finally, some months into this effort, I got a call from Neal, telling me NBC had agreed to air our third season finale. I was on location for *Kitchen Nightmares*, sitting in the back of our production trailer— precisely where I was sitting on a number of other occasions when I got a good-news phone call. This can either mean that being on location in the back of a production trailer was a particularly lucky circumstance for me—or that I spent way too much time on location in the backs of production trailers. (I tend to think it was the latter—I mean, where the hell else was anyone going to find me?)

I was thrilled—but then the anxiety kicked in. I worried that now that we'd been given this tremendous platform, we'd wind up doing a terrible number. I decided we needed to broaden the show to make it more appealing to a network audience. G4 was a network targeted to young males, and here we were about to be showcased on the broadest of all platforms: network prime time! *Yikes!*

Fear can be a powerful motivator, don't you think? Fear of bad ratings can be *particularly* powerful, so I switched into full-on, hard-charging producer mode. Looking back, my reaction to this opportunity at NBC exposed the qualities many successful television producers have in common:

1. *We worry.* Even when we don't yet have a reason to worry.
2. *We sweat the details.* Even the ones that don't need sweating over.
3. *We're impatient.* When we see something that needs doing, we tend to think it needs doing immediately. No matter what.
4. *We like to be in control.* Which is often why we become producers in the first place.

Taken together, these are not exactly the best qualities—they're certainly not what you'd consider areas of strength in most other occupations—but they've worked out pretty well for me.

So I put on my producer hat and called NBC. "Listen," I said. "Now that we're going to be on in prime time on your network, I have some ideas to broaden the show."

"What do you have in mind, Arthur?"

I answered that we should probably spruce up our opening and do more at-home pieces featuring our athletes, focusing on who they are and what they have overcome. The network wanted to know how much it would cost, so I said we could get it done for $100,000—not a lot of money in network-television terms.

"Nah, it's okay, Arthur. We're fine with the show as it is." For a one-off show from the little G4 network which the giant NBC network had essentially been strong-armed into airing, it was $100,000 more than they were willing to pay.

In the end, Kent and I decided to invest our own money and make some upgrades—not because we hoped to score a big number in the ratings so much as out of fear of winding up at the very bottom of the ratings pile. We didn't spend $100,000, or even get close to that number, but we made a significant investment and rounded out the show in the ways we could with the time we had.

That's the thing about reaching: you aren't always able to hit your target in just the right way on your own terms. Sometimes you can only get close on someone else's terms. When that happens, you have to find it in you to be grateful for the opening and then double down and power through the challenges to fight your way closer to your goal. That's how we chose to play it here. We stretched our budget as far as it would go, doing what we could to give the show the fresh look we wanted.

Next, we turned our attention to the backstories of our contestants. This didn't take a whole lot of money, just a shift in focus. We'd already been doing this to a certain extent for our G4 episodes—and best I could tell, the emphasis on the human drama was a big reason for our growing appeal. Neal and I were convinced that our showcase episode would live and die on our ability to present real, relatable people in pursuit of real, relatable dreams. So I reached back to the Olympic profiles I used to do at CBC and looked for ways to highlight the emotions behind each contestant's relentless push to beat our course and to remind viewers that our big competition was built on many small moments of personal triumph.

As it happened, NBC put our *Ninja* showcase on its Monday schedule, up against our long-running prime-time hit *Hell's Kitchen* on FOX. *Hell's* ran from 8:00 p.m. to 10:00 p.m., and *Ninja* ran from 9:00 p.m. to 11:00 p.m., so we had all of prime time covered. I no longer remember what was on the other networks that first night. I only cared about our two shows.

There was nothing I could do that night but hold my breath and hope for the best—which, quite honestly, would have simply meant avoiding the worst. I wasn't worried about *Hell's Kitchen*. The real worry was what *Hell's* would do to *Ninja* in hour one and whether anyone would stick around to watch *Ninja* in hour two. NBC wasn't doing any promotion for *Ninja*, which I guess was the network-television equivalent of throwing spaghetti at the ceiling to see if it sticks.

Hell's won the eight o'clock hour on FOX, and then *Ninja* showed up at nine and gave Gordon Ramsay a run for his money. *Hell's* ended up winning the nine o'clock hour as well, but *Ninja* came in a strong second, and then finished up the night with a really strong number in the ten o'clock hour.

First thing the next morning, I heard from Paul Telegdy, who at the time was running NBC's alternative and nonfiction programming effort. "Mr. Monday Night!" he said.

I had no idea what he meant, but it sounded good.

"Your company won every time period last night," he explained.

"Wow. That's great." And it was—it surely was.

"Maybe we should do more of this *Ninja* thing," Paul said.

In the end, we did. Paul believed in us and he believed in *Ninja*. In Season 4, NBC and G4 negotiated a *Ninja* time-share arrangement. NBC aired a third of our *Ninja* episodes, and G4 showed the rest. By Season 5, the show had grown in popularity, so NBC flipped the arrangement and aired two-thirds of our shows. Soon the powers that be at the network realized they had a runaway summer hit and decided to take on the show outright—the final twist on the long, unlikely path to a spot in the network lineup. Being on NBC at all had taken everyone by surprise, including us, and now here we were on the network's regular schedule. Against all odds and expectations, we had reached into the big time—albeit along this circuitous, unorthodox path—and we were determined to stay there.

Of course, we weren't done reaching. Early on, we sweated our renewal each year. It was not a slam dunk yet that we would be back for another season—until, at last, it was. We were gaining traction and finding our audience on the strength of the compelling human drama at the heart of our competition when a contestant came along with a backstory that was like gasoline on our low flame.

Early on in our *Ninja* run at NBC, most of our competitors were ordinary people from all different backgrounds. Some of them had to jump through a lot of hoops to make their way through our audition process, and some were able to walk on and impress us with their story or their potential to navigate the course.

Over the years, the makeup of our competitors would change to a degree as the show become more of a phenomenon, and appearing on our air held its own appeal. Inevitably, applications surged, and we started pulling from a more well-rounded, more representative pool of aspiring humans—most of them astonishingly fit and incredibly focused. We continued to attract our share of truck drivers, CEOs, entrepreneurs, nurses, teachers, mailmen, bouncers, marketing executives, construction workers—you name it. Add some top gymnasts, personal trainers, parkour specialists, mountain climbers, and even some former professional athletes into the mix, and we had a cast that truly reflected the full spectrum of human achievement.

Our operating principle in casting a wide net for competitors was to never trust a book by its cover because appearances (and backstories!) can be deceiving. Strength and agility were a given for our wannabe Ninja warriors, but beyond that we always looked to mix it up with athletes from all walks of life with all kinds of reasons for appearing on our show.

From the beginning, I've thought of *Ninja* as a singular sporting event. Really, it's unique in so many ways. It's the only athletic competition where men and women compete together on the same course with no handicap or adjustment to level the playing the field—a signature element that's baked into the show, along with a number of other broadening techniques and strategies. Without these elements, we'd just be the *X Games*. Nothing against the *X Games*—or any of the niche cable offerings that ask our most fearless, most extreme athletes to push themselves in fearless, extreme ways—but I believe our show is so much more than that. We tell great stories. We shine a light on the many ways people overcome not just obstacles, but real hardships . . . real difficulties. Through them, we show our viewers what's possible instead of what's impossible.

The course is the course, and it's on our athletes to dig deep and *reach* and find it in themselves to beat it . . . or not. It's the only sport where the athletes are "cast" in a purposeful way, giving them an opportunity to demonstrate their skills while at the same time sharing their story. It's the only sport where the athletes root hard for each other—a very un-American concept when you think about it—but then, it's the only sport where there's *typically* no winner. In our first fourteen seasons, we've only had three athletes successfully conquer Mount Midoriyama, our ultimate challenge.

Our athletes are amazing, but it's what they bring to our obstacle course that's *truly* amazing, as Kacy Catanzaro, a tiny powerhouse of an athlete from Texas, proved in Season 6. We all knew there was something compelling in Kacy's push to qualify for a spot on our show—but then, to us, everyone who fought their way to our obstacle course had an exciting story to share. What we couldn't *really* anticipate was the way her backstory would light something in our audience and reinforce the all-important message at the heart of our show: *Anything is possible if you put your mind to it . . . if you commit to it . . . if you work tirelessly and fearlessly and relentlessly to make it so.*

Kacy was five feet tall and weighed ninety-five pounds. She worked at an obstacle-course gym in San Antonio, had been a Junior Olympic gymnast, and had competed at the Division I collegiate level for Towson University. In pursuit of her dream, she'd trained for two years with her then-boyfriend Brent Steffensen, who was also a strong competitor on our show—his 'n' her reach moments where each one helped to lift the other.

Kacy Catanzaro captured the spirit of our competition and struck a chord with viewers. American television audiences love to root for the underdog. She was a tremendous athlete with a dynamic personality—in a lot of ways, she was no different from the other competitors on our show. But she was the first woman to complete our iconic Warped Wall obstacle, an insane fourteen-foot-high wall that was all but impossible to climb. And it's not just that she was the first woman to conquer the wall—no athlete shorter than five foot five, male or female, had ever accomplished it.

Kacy's assault on our Warped Wall went viral. It was featured on the *Today* show, on *SportsCenter*'s "Play of the Day" . . . all over. Almost overnight, she became a social media star; clips from her obstacle-course run were viewed over one hundred million times on Twitter and Instagram, most of them accompanied by the hashtag #MightyKacy.

We felt the impact in our production offices almost immediately. We'd had approximately ten thousand hopefuls try out for spots in our current season—an impressive number, we all thought—but by the next year, that number was up to over seventy-five thousand, with a 40 percent jump in the number of women applicants. (Contrast *those* numbers with the couple hundred applicants who tried out for our very first G4 season.)

Obviously, there was more to our rapid success than this one Kacy Catanzaro moment, but her run represented what we'd tapped into at *American Ninja Warrior.* I share her story to underscore the all-important lesson that to reach without patience is to reach without a plan.

Sure, it sometimes happens that you grab at a goal and achieve it straightaway, but more often than not you'll need a measure of persistence to help you along. You'll need to play the long game and wait for the marketplace and the moment to align with your vision. You'll need a strategy too. Our decision to focus on the hopes and dreams of our competitors, and not just the challenges and pitfalls of our wild obstacle course, is what makes *Ninja* such a compelling watch. When you set those elements against the backdrop of a distinct sporting event, where *everyman* and *everywoman* is able to compete on a level playing field . . . well, then you might just have something truly special.

We've had a lot of incredible "moments" like that of Kacy Catanzaro, but she was definitely the spark. You could draw a line from Kacy's appearance to Michael and Enedina Stanger, fans of the show, who'd been struggling through a devastating health crisis. Enedina had Ehlers-Danlos syndrome and used a wheelchair, with a grim prognosis. Michael had devoted himself to caring for her and their two daughters, and Enedina encouraged him to enter our Kansas City event as a walk-on.

Friends and family drove through the night to watch him compete, but by the time Michael's number was called, we were about to shut down production. We had a truncated schedule due to weather delays earlier that evening, but our alert production team found a way for Michael to run the course as the last runner of the night, so his wife and kids could watch him compete. Sure enough, he shocked everyone by completing the course and gave us one of our most emotional moments of triumph!

In addition to heartfelt stories like Michael and Enedina, there was Brian Burk who struggled socially with autism but found a welcoming community at his local *Ninja* gym. Encouraged by family and friends, he applied for the show and completed the course in his first-ever run. And then there are stories like Gary Weiland, a Texas firefighter whose leg was amputated. He worked hard to get his job back and then set a goal of competing on *Ninja*, inspiring millions with his heroic run.

What a joy it has been for us to share hundreds of amazing stories like these, episode after episode—real people from every walk of life and circumstance, putting themselves through their paces on our courses and tugging at the heartstrings of our viewers.

After *Ninja* went viral with Kacy Catanzaro, millions of people were moved to check out our little obstacle-course show with the crazy title. Kacy's inspiring run helped to vault us to our first Emmy nomination in the Outstanding Reality-Competition Program category the following year in our seventh season. (There's that pesky *reality* term rearing its ugly head!) There hadn't been a new entrant in that category for a decade, so we were thrilled to break through and be counted in.

I don't think anyone was more surprised by that Emmy nomination than yours truly—not because I didn't think our show was deserving. It *absolutely* was. No, the shock was that we were recognized in such a meaningful way, alongside all of those other influential competition shows. The space between where we'd started and where we were in this moment was astonishing—like we'd jumped the Snake River Canyon on a motorcycle. I'd be remiss here if I didn't offer a shout-out to the hundreds of talented professionals who, in addition to Kent, made this show a success.

On our list of *Ninja* MVPs are our guys in the booth, Matt Iseman and Akbar Gbajabiamila—our chief hype-men, cheerleaders, and storytellers. It's no surprise that NBC has redeployed this dynamic duo in a variety of ways, including featuring them in their own daily show during the Tokyo Olympics. Zuri Hall, alongside the course, provides gripping and uplifting interviews, knowing when to be dramatic, funny, warm . . . and even silly. Of course, our show wouldn't exist without the "mayor of *Ninja*," Kristen Stabile, our executive vice president who's in charge of our traveling circus, overseeing twenty-three trucks of equipment as we make our way from city to city. In almost every way, Kristen is responsible for this logistical monster, the production, and our technical crew. Since Season 6, we've been joined by Anthony Storm and Brian Richardson as executive producers—two talented guys who have gone through walls for the show and know how to deliver all the key elements that make *Ninja* special.

Today *American Ninja Warrior* is seen in more than one hundred countries all over the world, with local versions in England, Germany, Australia, Spain, Italy, Israel, and twenty other countries. Here at home, we've become one of the mainstays of NBC's prime-time schedule—and along with *Hell's Kitchen*, the show stands as one of our tentpole productions at A. Smith & Co. We are a Critics Choice winner and we've been nominated for a People's Choice Award, a Nickelodeon Kids' Choice Award, a Producers Guild of America Award, and seven Emmy Awards.

Along the way, there have been tie-in *Ninja* books and *Ninja* Halloween costumes. Every week our production office is flooded with reports of families all across America having *Ninja* parties, building their own *Ninja* courses in their backyards, gyms, and basements. There are full-on *Ninja*-inspired gyms in every major American city—and in some out-of-the-way places too—as well as *Ninja* leagues, pitting athletes of all ages against each other in organized and homespun competitions. Most incredible of all, as of this writing there is talk in and around the International Olympic Committee that a *Ninja Warrior* course could be tested for possible inclusion in the 2028 Olympic Games in Los Angeles.

We've even been parodied on *Saturday Night Live*, with Drake as the announcer and a hilarious Bobby Moynihan falling and flailing all over a miniaturized version of our set on the *SNL* stage. Let me tell you, nothing says you've arrived like a bunch of talented performers making fun of you on such a staple of late-night television. The very same weekend, the *Ninja* sensation was featured on a National Public Radio segment, making us one of the few network shows to be parodied and probed at virtually the same time by two leading arbiters of pop culture phenomena.

We stand atop Mount Midoriyama not just because we reached . . . but because we *kept* reaching, stretching ourselves just a little bit more each time out. In this way, *Ninja* offers the ultimate lesson in perseverance, at least in television terms, because nobody involved in the show ever expected it to become such a sensation. At no point along the way could you have made the argument that we were an *overnight* sensation. No, this was a slow build with incremental gains at every step. We took a nugget of a niche show and brought it to a whole new level, and when we outgrew that level, we took it to another . . . and then another. It was reach after reach after reach.

And get this: we're *still* reaching on behalf of this show. I'm pleased at the other sports-entertainment opportunities that have come our way on the back of our *Ninja* success: working with the National Football League to help reimagine their Pro Bowl skill competitions to make them appeal to a wider television audience; the development of *The Titan Games* with Dwayne Johnson at NBC (more on that later); the launch of *The Dunk King* series on TBS, *Spartan: Ultimate Team Challenge* on NBC, and *Floor Is Lava* on Netflix . . . and on and on. There have been countless *Ninja* specials, like *USA vs. The World* and *Ninja All-Stars*, and numerous spin-offs, like *Team Ninja Warrior*, *Ninja vs. Ninja*, and *American Ninja Warrior Junior*.

Of course, we were producing sports-infused entertainment programming before *Ninja*, with shows like *Pros vs. Joes* and *UFC Countdown*, but *Ninja* proved that we could tap a far bigger audience with this type of content than anyone in television had ever imagined—audiences made up of people like my wife and daughters and sisters, who don't really care a ton about sports but who find inspiration and uplift in the stories of real people pushing themselves in inconceivable ways.

The positive messaging at the heart of the show is what allows us to reach such a wide audience across so many markets. At its core *American Ninja Warrior* is a show for the entire family—one that parents happily make time to watch with their children and one that kids don't seem to mind watching in the company of their parents. In a strange way, it's like the two most successful animated shows of all time, *The Simpsons* and *The Flintstones*, which were both conceived as prime-time shows meant to appeal to adults before turning out to be wildly popular with kids as well.

That's *Ninja* in a nutshell. We're known for our heartwarming stories, but at the same time there's the tension and excitement of a challenging athletic competition—a competition that signals to viewers that they themselves can achieve a certain level of success on our obstacle course, a course that in its own way has come to represent the challenges and hurdles we face in our everyday lives. You might never take a snap from center in the Super Bowl or sink a birdie putt to win the Masters . . . but you might have what it takes to complete the Warped Wall. We give armchair athletes an opportunity to *reach* . . . in front of millions of people.

We give kids a chance to dream. That's one of the reasons we've seen such a surge in the popularity of local *Ninja* gyms, as more and more kids embrace *Ninja* as their sport of choice. It presents them with a series of barriers they can successfully climb. It's also one of the reasons we lowered the age-eligibility requirements for our flagship show in Season 13 to fifteen years old! Turns out there were tens of thousands of kids who'd grown up watching our show, who'd been training for years for the chance to compete on our show—and not only are they deserving of the opportunity, they're capitalizing on it in a big-time way. We witnessed a teen invasion that season. The top fifteen- and sixteen-year-olds in America blew everyone away with their amazing athletic abilities, and the last *Ninja* standing (the competitor who went the furthest at the national finals) was a fifteen-year-old named Kaden Lebsack, who picked up a check for $100,000—confirming to all of us who work on the show that the future of *Ninja* is remarkably bright.

Looking back, I can't help but marvel at the genesis of this show, starting out on a small cable network and blossoming into hundreds and hundreds of hours of prime-time network television. So many things had to fall into place for us to be where we are today, starting with the happy accident of Comcast, the G4 network's parent company, buying NBC Universal. The resulting act of corporate synergy that placed us on the network schedule on a Monday night in August not only gifted us the opportunity to take *Ninja* to a whole new level, but it transformed our company into the leading producers of sports-entertainment programming—or what I sometimes refer to as physical-entertainment programming.

No question, this one was a reach. That's an expression you hear frequently, in all contexts. *This one was a reach.* Typically, you hear it when an unlikely goal has somehow been met or a far-fetched vision comes into view. But sometimes when you reach, you end up in a place you never could have imagined.

16

SAVE OUR BUSINESS

"How's the picture business?" The voice on the other end of the line was unmistakable. Although back in 2013 I only knew it as that of one of reality television's most confounding personalities—and, for a while, the man who was slated to be my partner.

Donald Trump had starred in Mark Burnett's competition show *The Apprentice* since 2004, and it had quickly become one of the most talked-about series on television. In its own way, the format was similar to Burnett's signature series *Survivor*, a season-long elimination process that would ultimately leave one contestant standing. The prize for winning *The Apprentice* was an unspecified job within the Trump Organization with a first-year starting salary of $250,000.

The Apprentice had an outstanding run but waned in popularity after its breakout first season. Still, it was a major blockbuster hit, seeping into the culture and establishing its host as a national personality complete with his own catchphrase. Almost ten years after its debut, *The Apprentice* was trending down, and we were developing a business show of our own that we thought might be a good fit for its star. And so I found myself in discussions with the man who would become the forty-fifth president of the United States. Of course, I didn't know that future back then.

I have made an extra effort over the years to keep ideology out of our shows. Our objective is to offer viewers an escape from their own realities, so I've been careful to steer clear of events and issues that might somehow date our programming or alienate a potential audience.

And yet this one telephone conversation was particularly revealing. I'm not out to make a statement about the fitness for office of a man who would go on to upend many of the societal and institutional norms I had come to embrace since arriving in the United States to work for Dick Clark in 1990. This is not a political book. But my life and work sometimes placed me at the intersection of popular culture and world events—a front-row seat that often caused me to reflect on the power of reach in an entirely new way.

It was unclear from his tone if he was kidding with the old-fashioned term *picture business* or if he was simply out of touch. I decided to give him the benefit of the doubt and play along.

"We're doing talkies now," I said. "And everything's in color."

He laughed—perhaps to let me know he was aware I'd been making a joke. "That show of yours, *Hell's Kitchen*. It does really well."

I thanked him for noticing. "We're on a good run."

"Not as well as my show, though," he said. "Talk about a good run."

At the time, *Hell's Kitchen* was actually doing a little better than *The Apprentice* in the ratings, so I kindly pointed this out, but Trump wasn't buying it.

"My show's the number-one show in the country," he said, as if stating it as a fact would somehow make it so.

Here again, I kindly pointed out that it was not, but Trump was insistent. When I mentioned that *American Idol*, with over thirty million weekly viewers, was far and away the most-watched show on network television, he doubled down. "I'm told my show beats *American Idol*," he said.

I suppose it's possible that this was what Donald Trump had been told, but weekly viewership numbers for *The Apprentice* were down from over twenty million viewers in its debut season to just under six million, and *Hell's Kitchen* was outperforming *The Apprentice* in the key 18–49 demographic, so I couldn't see how what he'd been told carried more weight than what had been widely reported in the trades. And yet for some reason we went back and forth on this for an uncomfortable while, so I tried to move our conversation onto common ground.

"Why don't we talk about the show we're doing together?" I said.

The show we were developing at A. Smith & Co. was a business makeover program that would match a successful tycoon with struggling small business owners in the hope that together they would find a way to turn things around. Admittedly, the premise of the show borrowed a bit from our critically acclaimed *Kitchen Nightmares* series with Gordon Ramsay, where we'd send our *Hell's Kitchen* chef on a rescue mission to help failing restaurants around the country. However, there was clearly an appetite for shows appealing to aspiring (and often struggling) entrepreneurs. There were *Kitchen Nightmares* rip-offs all over the place during this period. It was the genre of the moment, and I figured if all these other producers were pinching our successful format, we might as well get in on it too. The bending and borrowing of a popular format appealed to many network programmers, so we were on the lookout for a Gordon Ramsay–type from the business world to star in a show we were calling *Save Our Business*.

Hair salons, furniture stores, karate schools—every small business was ripe for a makeover, and we'd been able to sell Michael Wright of Turner Broadcasting on this latest iteration of our workhorse concept. In fact, it was Michael who would suggest casting Donald Trump in the Gordon Ramsay role. Looking back, I see why Trump was an obvious choice to host our effort. Since we were only one booking away from a series pickup, I said, "Okay, then. Let's book the Donald."

Trump and I were both clients of William Morris Endeavor, so it was relatively easy to get together with him on this—and, as I recall, we reached a deal in principle fairly quickly. It was at this point that he reached out to me on this phone call, a final opportunity for us to check each other out and go over our planned shooting schedule. I'd already seen what he could do in front of the camera, so this wasn't any kind of audition. We'd already negotiated our deal.

All that was left, really, was for the two of us to forge some kind of working relationship. For me, I was mostly concerned about the tone of our program. I wanted the focus to be primarily on the mom-and-pop business owners we would highlight in each episode, and I worried that, in the mind of Donald Trump, the emphasis might be off. As the world now knows, I was probably right to worry, but at the time I assumed that if the "script" called for Donald Trump to let other people shine, he would have followed it.

And yet Trump had a different agenda for this phone call. We'd already agreed to terms, our contracts all but signed, but he was out to sell himself. Only, it wasn't entirely clear why he was selling himself to *me*. He kept telling me what an asset he was on *The Apprentice* set, how he could improvise and write his own material and get everything done in one take. "Nobody's ever seen anything like it," he said. "I don't need to rehearse. You just throw me out there and I deliver."

He rambled on and on about how great he was, like he had something to prove. As he spoke, I started to think how difficult it was going to be to rein him in. Gordon Ramsay was so willing to take direction; his work ethic was unmatched, and his enthusiasm for great food, best kitchen practices, and overall excellence were infectious. I could not imagine Donald Trump bringing any of these same qualities to our enterprise. But since Michael Wright had pushed for him on this and TNT had already bought the show with Trump attached, I could only hang back and find a way to make things work.

At some point we'd exhausted the time each of us had allotted for the call—*exhausted* being the operative word for me; it was a wearying thing to be on the wrong end of so much self-congratulation.

There were red flags to this partnership all around. Could a guy like Trump ever step up and be a real lifeline to the struggling entrepreneurs on our show or would he just pop in for an appearance and phone it in? Could we dial down his larger-than-life persona in such a way that would allow him to give the nurturing advice our small business owners needed to move forward?

In the end, Trump himself decided to kill our deal. On reflection, I find it telling that our "done deal" was undone so easily. One day he was all in, and the next he was done. He said it was going to be too much work and he didn't see why he needed to commit more than a single shooting day for each episode, so we shifted gears and hired Peter Jones to do the show instead.

Peter was a successful British businessman and one of the original hosts of *Dragons' Den*, the inspiration for ABC's *Shark Tank*. He was already known to the networks as one of the stars of a show called *American Inventor*, which he'd developed with Simon Cowell, and his personality and professionalism were so markedly different from Donald Trump's that when I look back on the development of our show, I find it hard to believe I'd considered them for the same role.

Save Our Business ran on TNT for just one season. It was a good little show, but it never found enough of an audience to warrant a second season. Plus, the show didn't exactly fit with the drama-rich programming schedule TNT was showcasing at the time. When we pulled the plug, I filed it away as a modest success—another show in a string of many that nurtured what I hoped would be a long and fruitful relationship with the Turner networks. Truth be told, I'd have no reason at all to look back on this show were it not for the man I'd briefly entertained as a potential star, who years later cast himself in his own reality show when he decided to run for president.

I can't shake the feeling we dodged a bullet. The call hadn't been meant as an audition, and yet with his bluster and arrogance on full display, it turned me off to the idea of working with him. This one strange phone call has been a cautionary reminder for me to trust my gut, even when it's telling me to go against the wishes of my partner—in this case, the network head who was backing our show. I know full well that hiring Donald Trump for *Save Our Business* might have launched our show in a more meaningful way. We might have made it to a second season. He was a bigger name to American television audiences than Peter Jones. Signing him would have been a big deal.

Then again, maybe we would have never gotten on the air at all. It would have cost us a lot more money to get Trump, making it a reach hire. When you're reaching, you need to extend yourself from a place of confidence. It's not enough to throw money at a project and believe you have things covered or attach the brightest star to your show and expect it to make you shine.

In addition to trusting your gut, you need to trust that the pieces you're assembling will ultimately fit together in a way that gives you the greatest chance for success. It's the dilemma a lot of movie producers face when they're casting a big-budget film—do you reach for a name-above-the-title star who might not be suited for the part or an unknown who might have been born to play the role?

When it starts to look like your reach might leave you holding the bag and hurting your overall mission, adjust your thinking and move on.

17

CHASING THE ROCK

I'm not a big fan of rules of thumb: rules are made to be broken—thumbs too, in some cases! And yet in television it rarely pays to play it safe. If you keep using the tried-and-true, proven formula that happens to be the flavor of the moment, you'll never stand out in a crowded field.

Our two longest-running shows at A. Smith & Co., *American Ninja Warrior* and *Hell's Kitchen*, were built on long-shot concepts that seemed to target niche audiences. An obstacle-course show on network television? Are you kidding me? A food show, built around a relatively unknown chef from the UK, at a time when no food show had ever successfully worked on network television? Forget about it. But viewers crave freshness. The setups for these shows were not only groundbreaking at the time, they were also individually tailored to reach a broad audience.

Of course, there's a whole lot more to making a hit show than simply being out in front of a trend. In my experience, the *whole lot more* comes down to four specific ingredients that need to be in the mix for every successful television show, scripted or unscripted. These aren't rules of thumb so much as component parts, and you'll need to line up all four if you want to give your show the best possible shot.

The four ingredients:

1. *A great format, concept, and script.* The foundation of the whole enterprise—everything flows from this right here.
2. *A great cast.* The right person in the right role can mean all the difference. They don't have to be the most famous person, but they need to connect with your concept and your audience in just the right way, and if you're working with an ensemble, you'll need just the right mix of personalities.
3. *A great production team.* Without a talented group of people to execute an idea, you're nowhere.
4. *A great fit with the right network or platform.* Put your show in the wrong environment or the wrong time slot, or fail to give it the support it needs, and audiences might never find you.

Every once in a while, these general truths collide in a way that leave those of us on the producing end trying to reverse engineer a hit show from the upfront interest of one of our network partners and the long-shot interest of one of the biggest names in the entertainment industry. At least, that's how it kinda, sorta happened with *The Titan Games*, hosted by Dwayne "The Rock" Johnson.

Without *American Ninja Warrior* there would be no *Titan Games*; without my unusual background in sports (unusual, that is, for an entertainment producer) and my firm belief that viewers can be drawn to an athletic competition whether or not they're familiar with the athletes (or even the nature of the competition itself), there would be no *Titan Games*; and finally, without an invitation from one of our network partners to think about partnering on a show we could develop and own together, there would be no *Titan Games*.

The story of how *The Titan Games* came to be is shot through with examples of what can happen when you reach above and beyond what you previously thought possible, but it starts with the way some of our productions have been summoned into existence—with a simple phone call from a network partner who came to us with the not-so-crazy idea that we should work together on something at some point in some way. It was a vague pitch—more of a desire than a plan—but it was built on that learned truth that television is a business of relationships. When things go well with an initial partnership, you want to extend the run. If you've worked together on a hit show, you're inclined to work together again— same way you'd look to keep a good thing going in any business. You'd be amazed at how many shows get spun from this basic impulse to re-up with someone you know and trust, to build on a previous success, and that's what happened here.

It started with a phone call from Meredith Ahr, who reached out on behalf of NBC. At the time, Meredith was the president of Universal Alternative Studio—the primary in-house production arm of NBC Universal for all non-scripted, non-dramatic programming. We'd been on a great run at NBC with *American Ninja Warrior*, and Meredith and I had developed a friendly working relationship. From time to time, I'd hear from her about extending that relationship to a new show.

For as long as I'd known her, Meredith had been on the network side. She'd started as a page at NBC and worked her way up, so she knew the business upside down and inside out. She'd recently been promoted to run the new in-house division, reporting from her post at Universal Alternative Studio to Paul Telegdy, the head of alternative/reality programming at NBC. Meredith was sharp, smart, savvy—all qualities I loved to see in a network studio partner, and she was determined to make her mark. We'd been on a great run with *Ninja*, which took everyone by surprise, and the idea of continuing that good relationship with Meredith and Paul had tremendous appeal.

"We're all doing really well with it," Meredith said of *Ninja*. "But you don't own it and the network doesn't own it. You're making good money with your fees, and we're making our money from advertising and other promotions and tie-ins, but we don't own the show."

When you own a show, you have the rights to sell the format to other territories—or sell the show itself. It's possible to build a billion-dollar platform from a hit network show, as has happened with shows like *American Idol* and *Who Wants to be a Millionaire?* Our own *Hell's Kitchen* was getting close to that level. *Ninja*, which, as Meredith pointed out, we did not own, had been sold into 133 countries, with twenty-six foreign versions of the show—all because we helped make the show a prime-time hit in the United States, the largest and most influential television market in the world.

"What do you have in mind?" I said.

Meredith allowed that she wasn't quite sure what she had in mind. Her *idea*, basically, was that we should come up with something in the athletic/fitness space and try to replicate the success of *American Ninja Warrior*. The network was always looking to develop its own physical competition show. After all, they're the ones who ultimately put *Ninja* on in prime time to great success, so it made sense for them to develop a program of their own in the arena they had helped build. They'd had some similar success in the dance space just a couple seasons before with *World of Dance* with Jennifer Lopez, and now they were back at it, eager to establish a franchise they could own. And there was nobody better in the physical competition space than us—Meredith and the folks at NBC knew it, reaching all the way up to network chairman Bob Greenblatt.

We knew it too. We regularly fielded calls from the other networks—Netflix, FOX, USA Network—asking, "What's our *American Ninja Warrior*?" A cynic might say Meredith was simply angling for some kind of competitive edge or an inside track, and I suspect this was true to some extent. However, it was also true, and particularly interesting to me, that she came to me as a potential partner, which meant that NBC Universal could absorb a lot of the development costs of a show, as we figured out what we wanted to do.

Neither one of us wanted to do something that felt like a *Ninja* rip-off. Those attempts rarely work, and the last thing we wanted was to water down the original with a similar show on the same network. And yet, as always, my thing was to look for opportunities to tell compelling human-interest stories. If I could find a way to do that within the context of a sports-entertainment program, I was all over it, so that's where we placed our focus at the outset.

Sports-based programming is typically a tough sell to network prime-time viewers. When I was younger, it was hard for me to get my head around this fact of television life—because I'd come up in sports and I was a huge fan—but sporting events generally appeal to a narrow segment of the market. We were always mindful of this in our *Ninja* brainstorming sessions. Internally, we were always focused on broadening the show, looking for compelling elements that would appeal to all members of the family.

I should note here that there are two main outliers to this learned truth about sports being a tough sell. One of them is football. It's part of the culture, and there's a big gambling component to it, so there's a built-in audience, even in prime time. Plus, the game itself is ideally suited to television, with camera angles that actually make for a richer viewing experience at home than in the stadium and natural stoppages in play to allow for replays and analysis.

Another outlier is the Olympics, which of course only comes around every two years. The appeal comes from the special-event nature of the wall-to-wall coverage, a shared surge of national pride among viewers eager to feel a part of something far bigger than themselves, and the way producers cultivate so many emotional and inspiring story lines from all over the world as the Games unfold. On the annual miniseries front, the NBA Playoffs and the World Series are two other outliers—but that's a whole other ball game!

Meredith proposed a fifty-fifty partnership on whatever show we ended up doing together, which was certainly fair, especially considering that the network would underwrite our development costs. This was enormously helpful to us, but it wasn't essential. We were a formidable production company with an outstanding track record, so we were certainly in a position to pitch and sell shows without a partner. But at the same time, there was comfort in knowing that your show had a landing spot and that there were deep pockets at your disposal.

In this case, there was the cost of the development team that identified a number of potential formats, the art team that came up with a design and renders of a set, and the challenge team that created and storyboarded dozens of obstacles. The longer it takes to hit on just the right idea in just the right way, the more money you're likely to spend in pursuit of that idea, and it took us about a year to come up with a concept everybody liked.

Even though we were partners, there was still very much a producer-network dynamic in our working relationship. We'd come up with the idea and work it out in our offices and then we'd pitch it to Meredith and the studio. It wasn't a *direct* pipeline to the network, but it was pretty damn close. Meredith knew Paul Telegdy's tastes. Their offices were in the same building. We knew that if Meredith and her team were on board with the idea, there was every reason to think Paul would be as well. Whenever we had something we all thought was viable, we'd take it to him and his network colleagues to see how they reacted.

After going round and round on a number of ideas, we finally landed on an epic event series called *Herculeague*. Whereas *American Ninja Warrior* was human-versus-course, the course serving as a kind of metaphor for life's obstacles, our *Herculeague* concept was human-versus-human, giving everyday people a chance to become superheroes.

NBC loved the idea of setting up a league of some kind, but they worried a city vs. city element would alienate viewers in markets with no rooting interest in a given week, so we built the show around some of the principles and legends of Greek mythology. I envisioned a king-of-the-hill competition, crowning a winner one week who would return to defend their title the following week. In this way, the show could drive viewers to the next episode when a new set of everyday-warrior-type competitors with a new set of story lines would emerge to knock off the reigning champ.

I've always thought this king-of-the-hill format was one of the reasons for the long-running success of a show like *Jeopardy!* Yes, the show is addictive and intellectually challenging, and after so many years, it's become a nightly routine for so many. Without question, the enduring appeal of the show is the game itself. But folks also tune in to see if the challengers can knock off the returning champion, and when a terrific player is on a good long run, there's an added level of excitement. That's what I was after here.

However, the conceit of the show went beyond its competition format. We were about taking everyday people and presenting them as larger-than-life characters—almost like superheroes. Our competitors would be that one person you'd spot at the gym and do a double take because you were struck by their energy or work ethic—men and women who pushed themselves to peak performance. They'd come from all walks of life: dental hygienists, teachers, warehouse workers, and on and on. The idea was to portray these everyday people as characters in an epic Greek myth and surround them with a ton of showmanship on a massive stage.

When casting began, we identified one prospect who drove a delivery truck for Budweiser, a single dad who somehow found the time to train and keep himself in tremendous physical shape, and ended up winning our first men's title. And we found a physical trainer/life coach with a heart ailment who won our first woman's title.

Our creative team came up with amazing challenges for our competitors—the Lunar Impact, the Power Vault, the Herculean Pull—all of which culminated in our final challenge, Mount Olympus, which would feature half a dozen menacing obstacles rolled into one massive challenge. Next, we created an arena to highlight the Greek theme. Our design team came up with an epic set, spectacularly unlike anything viewers would have seen on any other show. In almost every respect, it was shaping up to be a strong pitch.

For months, all these moving parts came together in just the right way, and we had support for the show at the network. By the summer of 2017, the project had quietly moved from our back burners to a spot out in front, but we weren't there just yet. We were all super excited about the show, on both sides of our partnership, and we'd talked about who we might get to host. *American Ninja Warrior* didn't have a famous face out in front, and when long-running franchises like *Survivor* and *The Bachelor* started out, television audiences didn't know Jeff Probst from Chris Harrison, but here it was felt that we would benefit from a name-above-the-title host to help us launch the show—somebody who embodied the striving, competitive spirit we were looking to celebrate in each episode and who could also drive viewers to the program. We were going for the gold here—a global hit! We all believed the right star would tie the whole project together and help us shine.

I sat down with Meredith one day to kick around some names, and it quickly turned into one of those classic spitballing sessions where we took turns saying whatever popped into our heads.

"You know who would be great?" I said when it was my turn to add a name to the mix. "Dwayne Johnson."

I'd been thinking of Dwayne for a couple weeks on this, but I hadn't said his name out loud until this moment. He'd become such a megastar with a number of wildly successful movies to his credit. His brand seemed exactly right for the program we had in mind. His social media platform was *huge* with over 270 million Instagram followers, and his empowering messages of inspiration, of never giving up, of putting in the hard work resonated with fans around the globe. Plus, Dwayne's backstory was so compelling and in a lot of ways symbolized the hopes and dreams we knew our competitors would bring to the show. He'd started with nothing and lifted himself up by always being the hardest-working person in the room, whether he was playing football for the Miami Hurricanes or making a new name for himself on the professional wrestling circuit or leaning into a Hollywood career. Dwayne's production company was called Seven Bucks, because that was the amount of money he had in his pocket when he got cut from the Calgary Stampeders of the Canadian Football League, which in turn led to his new ambition of becoming a professional wrestler.

His "blood, sweat, respect" philosophy embodied the spirit of the show we had in mind, and I started to see him as more than just the star or host. He'd be more like the commissioner of the league we were hoping to fashion—the spirit of our enterprise.

Meredith literally fell over when she heard his name. She was sitting on the couch, and she made this grand show of being knocked to the floor by this idea. "Oh my God," she said, almost shrieking with excitement. "That would be the best."

Her reaction was so exaggerated, I think, because the idea was so far-fetched; The Rock was one of the biggest stars on the planet. What in the world made me think he'd want to sign on to host a television show? But that's the thing about *reaching*, right? Sometimes you have to give voice to a dream, even if it seems like an impossible dream, because until you put it out there, you can't begin to make it so.

"Get off the floor, Meredith," I said, laughing, joining her in her silliness but at the same time bringing us both back to reality. "We haven't even approached him on this."

"I know," she said, calming down and switching into hard-nosed studio president mode. All of a sudden, she was dead serious. "But we've got to get him. He'd be perfect."

Yes, he would be. In so many ways, he was exactly right, and the more we talked about him, the harder it was to think of anyone else in the role. Dwayne was represented by William Morris Endeavor, so I went to my own WME agent, David Sherman, and said I wanted to make a run at him.

"For what?" David asked. He knew all about our *Herculeague* project, of course, and this partnership with NBC, but he didn't see the connection.

"For the NBC thing. To be our commissioner."

I can't be sure, but I thought I heard David laugh on the other end of the phone—one of those *oh boy!* exhalations, the kind you always hear from someone letting you know you've got no idea what you're getting yourself into. I could picture him rolling his eyes; that's how outlandish it was for me to think we could get Dwayne Johnson to sign on for an on-camera role and to be on set every day.

"Dwayne doesn't do this type of television anymore," David said, telling me what I already knew. "Maybe if you're lucky you can get him and his company to executive produce, but that's it."

"Still," I said. "We need to make a run at him. If we can get this in front of him, we can convince him."

As long as I had David's ear, I went on to explain exactly why Dwayne was so perfect for this project, so on brand, and how the show would dovetail nicely with the work Dwayne was doing on his social media platforms, inspiring millions of people. Attracting A-level talent to your project is never about the money—or, at least, it's never *just* about the money. The money, in many ways, is a given.

The differentiator is the nature of the project itself. It has to speak to them; it has to work directionally with their career and their brand; it has to fit into their work schedules; and perhaps most importantly, it has to be consistent with the message they're putting out into the world.

David was doubtful, even with my passionate appeal—but he's a great agent and to his credit he was willing to champion the fight with us at WME. I came out of that conversation thinking we were at least taking a step in the forward direction.

In truth, I had no reason to believe we could make this happen, but I felt in my bones that Dwayne Johnson was the right fit. Meredith and I had come out of that fall-on-the-floor meeting with only one name on our wish list, and I'd learned over the years that when you focus on a single target, you sometimes give yourself the best possible chance of hitting it. (On the flip side of that, you also leave yourself without a fall-back position and no room to fail, but some of our best deals happen when we have no choice but to succeed.)

Now it was not enough for me to tell my guy at WME to arrange a meeting with a superstar and expect it to happen right away . . . or even happen at all. There are hoops you need to jump through and other agents who need convincing—some with competing agendas. We sent materials to his agents and understood that the executives at his production company were intrigued.

In the end, it took three or four months for a meeting to materialize. During that time, Meredith and the rest of the NBC brass kept getting more and more excited at the prospect of signing The Rock to star in our Greek-themed competition show. A couple times a week, it seemed, she'd call and gush over the possibilities. We'd have other business to discuss, but she'd invariably find a way to bring the conversation back to *Herculeague* and where we were with Dwayne Johnson. She'd say, "This is what prime-time television should be!" or "This is going to be great, Arthur! This is the key piece we've been missing!"

Each time, I'd remind Meredith that we weren't there just yet—but I've got to admit, her enthusiasm was infectious, and I suppose it's possible that together we put out enough positive energy that we finally got our meeting.

Actually, our initial meeting was with Dwayne's ex-wife, Dany, who continued to manage Dwayne after they split up. Dany Garcia, a part-time bodybuilder, was a savvy businesswoman, who had helped to shepherd Dwayne Johnson's career from the time they were college sweethearts. She and Dwayne were partners in their production company. She knew her stuff and she knew Dwayne's mind, and yet she went out of her way to make an impression on *me*.

I'd flown to Florida with an entourage that included Paul Telegdy and a couple WME agents, including my own agent, David Sherman, and Dwayne's agent, Jason Hodes, but as far as I was concerned Dany was the only person in the room. She knew all about the shows we were doing at A. Smith & Co. and made it seem like it was an honor for her to take the meeting and that it would be a privilege to be in business together. She was so warm, so wicked smart, so complimentary—and as I went into my pitch, I got the feeling she'd already been inclined to like the idea.

I sat around the kitchen table at Dany's ranch and walked her through some of the challenges we'd come up with, talked a little bit about the everyday people we planned to tap as competitors, what a successful appearance on our show could mean for them. Dany listened with great interest and kept jumping in with committed, forward-looking questions. The more we talked, the more excited I became about partnering with *her* on this, as well as with Dwayne. Really, the meeting couldn't have gone any better.

Paul Telegdy chimed in with the network perspective and let Dany know that NBC was prepared to support the show—an easy sell for Paul, not only because he believed in the show but because he had a major man-crush on Dwayne. Guys like Paul, who run the major television networks, are stars in their own right, but he was just so tickled at the prospect of doing a show with The Rock, the rest of us couldn't help but tease him about it—and he was more than happy to own it.

Dany still needed to talk it over with Dwayne, but we left her ranch that day thinking all that was left was to bang out the details. One of those details had us revisiting the working title for our show. As readers will surely remember, Dwayne had appeared in the big-budget movie *Hercules* some years earlier, and even though he'd been a consistent box-office dream, this one didn't exactly set any attendance records when it was released. It had come out with great fanfare, which usually meant there were hopes of establishing a kind of *Hercules* franchise on the back of an initial hit, so there was a bit of a concern from Dany about attaching Dwayne to a project like ours, with a name like *Herculeague*, that tracked so closely to a movie that was only a modest success.

Dany and I eventually landed on *The Titan Games* as a title, while still leaning on our Greek mythology theme, and came up with a tagline we all loved: "Titans aren't born . . . they're made."

Another detail was Dwayne's fee, but because of our unique prepitch partnership, this wasn't my direct concern. It was, however, *a* concern. In the car back to the airport, Paul went back and forth with David Sherman, while the two of them theorized how much this was going to cost NBC. It wasn't a negotiation so much as a strategy session.

Weeks after our trip to Dany's home in Florida, Dwayne and the team at Seven Bucks signed on officially as our partners, and of course all of us at A. Smith and everyone at NBC were ecstatic.

We still had to figure out a way to match Dwayne's availability—as the biggest, hardest-working movie star in Hollywood—to our hoped-for production schedule. We needed Dwayne on set for at least ten shoot days. We were hoping for twelve, but that was looking out of the question. As we mapped out a budget and shooting schedule, it was looking more and more like we'd be working without a net. Still, we were determined to make it happen, although as we got closer and production costs were running into the tens of millions, the network was becoming concerned. Meredith too. What would happen if there was an unforeseen delay in shooting and we couldn't get it done in ten days?

A couple days before we were due to start shooting, Meredith suggested we reimagine our format. All along, I'd thought we would shoot the show linearly—from beginning to end—in service of the king-of-the-hill format at the heart of the show. But now she wanted us to shoot in a more modular way—meaning we would shoot all of our competitors on each grouping of obstacles at once, to avoid the painstaking process of breaking the set each time, and edit the footage together in a way that allowed us to tell the story of the competition in a dramatic way. Her idea was that we could make a compelling production by crowning a "titan" after each episode, and then bringing back all the titans to battle it out over the final two episodes to determine the overall male and female winners. Shooting modularly would save us a ton of staging time and allow us to shoot challenges for multiple episodes consecutively.

She had a point: the challenges were massive, the sets were massive, the entire production was massive, Dwayne was massive . . . and so was the risk. I wasn't crazy about this solution, and I pushed back on it initially, but Meredith and Paul felt strongly about it. They'd been such big supporters of the show that I went along with them on this. It wasn't ideal, but Meredith believed there was no other way to ensure that our star would be available to us for every episode—the last thing we wanted was for him to be waiting in his trailer while our crew broke down and set up these challenges.

In each of our challenges, there was the chance we could run long, but the Mount Olympus challenge that capped the competition had so many different elements to it that we could have run longer still. We didn't have that luxury. We had to get it done in ten days or Dwayne wouldn't be there to crown a champion and we would have a very expensive runover. Still, I hated to lose the drama of challenging and potentially knocking off our reigning champion from one episode to the next. If it had been up to me, I would have taken the chance and hoped for the best—*Reaching 101*.

But I had already pushed everybody involved on the show. Paul was out on a limb because he was the one who'd approved the show. Meredith was out on a limb because she'd championed it at the outset and was staking her new post with this new division on this show. Dany was out on a limb because she stood behind what we were doing and helped to make it happen. And Dwayne was out on a limb because he was attaching his reputation and carefully cultivated brand to this effort—owing in part to the fact that he and Dany were both big fans of *American Ninja Warrior* and thought we could create some of the same magic here working together.

I didn't get around to meeting Dwayne in person until a preproduction meeting and a casting callout shoot for competitors at one of his Iron Paradise gyms, this one in Burbank. We'd had a few conference calls where we went over our thoughts for the show and began the creative part of our collaboration, but this first face-to-face meeting didn't happen until we were signed and sealed and good to go.

What struck me was how warm and genuine Dwayne was from the moment we met. Normally, when you work with a star of such magnitude, it takes a while to develop trust and familiarity, but here it happened right away, and Dwayne deserves all the credit. It just so happened that I'd recently hurt my elbow and was wearing a brace around my forearm, so that was the first thing Dwayne asked me about, and once we got into it, it was like we were lifelong gym buddies, trading workout routines and physical therapy strategies like I even belonged in the same conversation with him.

I liked him immediately.

During the promo shoot that afternoon, I was also struck by Dwayne's professionalism and his ease in front of the cameras. Oh, man . . . this guy was a producer's dream. We'd given him a script, which he looked at for no more than five minutes before delivering his lines with ease and throwing in a couple trademark Dwayne-isms I would come to so appreciate.

On a second take, he looked over at me and said, "Arthur, thoughts?"

To be honest, my only thought just then was how grateful I was to have Dwayne on board and to have all of our logistical problems apparently sorted out. But since he asked, I gave him three or four adds. Without missing a beat, he did the second take without a hiccup, complete with my new material. After forty years working with the best ad-libbers in sports broadcasting and consummate professionals like Gordon Ramsay, I had to put Dwayne right up there.

I could tell from the outset he'd be a breeze to work with, and I guessed his poise and polish flowed from his WWE days. You don't speak off the cuff in front of arenas or stadiums filled with thousands of screaming fans, going off on your own rants while at the same time following the overall script, without learning a thing or two about playing to an audience and being quick on your feet. He carried the reputation in the business of being the hardest worker in the room, and now I knew why. But it wasn't just the hard work that stood out—it was the *quality* of that hard work. He could have given a master class in composure and likability.

I was excited as hell coming out of that promo/casting callout, convinced that *The Titan Games* would be the next big thing, and that Dwayne was absolutely the right guy to lift us to next-level success. Our NBC partners were also pumped, and we looked ahead to a post-holiday launch, sometime in early January 2019. Working backward on the calendar, we had to scramble to make good and full use of Dwayne's ten-day shooting window in September 2018 and to make sure we were in position to do our edits and work our postproduction magic in time for our premiere.

The show was a monster to stage. We determined early on to shoot outside under the lights at night, which meant we needed a sprawling parcel in or around Los Angeles where we could build an arena. The biggest piece of flat land we could find was the Irwindale Speedway, about an hour outside of town (not counting traffic), where there were over five acres for us to spread out and do our thing. Our compound was massive, unlike anything else on television short of the Olympics. There were trailers everywhere and a giant stadium we'd built to house the competition and accommodate the audience. It felt a little bit like we were staging our own mini Olympics—a setting fit for a megastar like Dwayne Johnson.

With all that room to work with, and that big financial commitment from NBC, we really went to town. Hands down, it was shaping up to be one of the most expensive, most elaborate shows I'd ever produced, but we all believed that in order for us to achieve the epic success we envisioned, we needed to design the show to epic proportions.

On a personal level, the production schedule was brutal. Because we were committed to shooting at night, I couldn't justify the long drive back and forth to my house, so I camped out at a Sheraton hotel on the outskirts of Irwindale. I worked three weeks of overnights—one week of prep and two weeks of shooting—with just a few hours of sleep from 8:00 a.m. to 11:00 a.m. each day. It was draining. I think I lost close to ten pounds over the run of the shoot. And underneath and alongside *The Titan Games*, I still had to find time to run my production company.

Dwayne, too, felt the effects of our intense production schedule. The location and overnight shoots nearly did him in, same as me. For the run of the shoot, he lived in a home all the way on the other side of Los Angeles, in Encino, but he insisted on making the drive each day. He liked sleeping in his own bed and squeezing in some family time. I offered to send a chopper for him because the traffic was just miserable in late afternoons when he was headed to set for his 6:00 p.m. call, but he had his routines. We'd work late into the night—most nights he wouldn't get home until four or five in the morning. His kids would wake him up early and he'd spend the morning with them, then he'd hit the gym for a couple hours and deal with whatever business matters Dany and his team had lined up for his attention.

A word on Dwayne's team and our partners at his production company: they were a group of loyal, creative, and abundantly talented individuals who really had Dwayne's back and a vision for what lay ahead. Brian Gewirtz, Dwayne's head of television, had been with him since his WWE days; Kevin Hill had come over from WME; and Hiram Garcia, Dany's brother and the president of the company, oversaw all of Dwayne's film projects as well as his television work. All three worked seamlessly with Dany Garcia to collaborate effectively with us and to make sure Dwayne had what he needed to do a tremendous job.

Dwayne was not a big fan of the overnight schedule, but he gutted it out. He never complained. In fact, he was so excited about the arena and the look of the show, he tried to match the intensity of his effort to the intensity of the production—and it really was a crazy, over-the-top production.

Nobody involved on the production side had ever seen anything like it. One NBC executive, astonished at all the technical gear, the massive scale of the challenges, and the grandeur of our busy set, came up to me on the first night of taping and said, "You have a lot of balls."

I hadn't been nervous about how things would go . . . until this one presumably well-meaning comment. I'd convinced myself that each separate piece of craziness was something we could handle, but taken together and viewed from this outside perspective, I considered for the first time the enormity of what we'd undertaken.

Big movie star + big production + big budget = big risk.

In the moment, I wasn't really liking this equation.

Because we were shooting outside, we were completely dependent on the weather. We'd built a small buffer into our shooting schedule to accommodate a half day or so of rain, but if it rained at all, we'd be well and truly screwed. We would have had to shift to daytime, which would change the entire look of the show. So we had to trust that the old saying that it never rains in Southern California would hold true for us . . . at least for the next little while.

The one time I stepped away from the set was to attend the Emmy Awards. *American Ninja Warrior* had been nominated that year for Best Reality Competition Program—for the third year in a row! I really wanted to attend the ceremony, believing wholeheartedly in the old gambler's theory that the third time's the charm. Also, I was tremendously proud of the show, and the thought of not being there with our team would bother me. It would have been a drag on the *esprit de corps* I had worked so hard to cultivate in our *Ninja* offices if we actually won the Emmy this year and I wasn't there to share in the celebration. I had to find a way to be there.

Timing was on my side. The ceremony began at 5:00 p.m., and we didn't really get going on set until 8:00 or 9:00 p.m. Still, it was a schlep with the stress of fighting traffic in both directions. Our *Titan Games* director, Alex Rudzinski, was also nominated that year and made the trip as well. The thing about the Emmys, though, is you never know when your category is going to be scheduled. I worried I might not make it back to the speedway in time, but I went for it anyway.

As it happened, our category came up in the first hour—and we lost again that year, this time to *RuPaul's Drag Race*, but I was glad I'd made the effort. I kissed my wife and kids—who'd go off to the Governors Ball following the ceremony without me—changed out of my tux, got back in the car, and drove back to Irwindale.

Turned out I only missed some rehearsal and setup shots, so it all worked out—other than the fact that we lost out on the Emmy—but the mild disappointment allowed me to see a side of Dwayne Johnson that most people don't appreciate.

He was the first person to greet me when I got back to the set. He knew where I'd been, and he came up to me all excited. "Did you win?"

I shook my head. "Not our year."

"Oh, man," he said. "I'm so sorry. We were all rooting for you. Everybody here. It's like they say, 'It's an honor just to be nominated.' And it is. It's incredible."

"Thanks," I said. "I guess it is."

It was sweet of him to ask about the award and console me over our loss. I got the sense that this wasn't just something to say with Dwayne. He was genuinely disappointed for me that *Ninja* didn't win the Emmy that year, and at the same time he wanted me to know it was a real accomplishment that we'd been honored with a nomination.

Then he turned the conversation back around to *The Titan Games*. "We've got to get our show nominated," he said. "Next year. You and me."

It struck me as the most generous gesture. He went out of his way to lift me up and point me forward, an aspect of his character that had surely served him well in his career.

In the end, it all worked out to the good, and for the most part, the ten-day shoot went smoothly.

The show did well enough to get picked up for a second season, and this time we figured out a way to do the king-of-the-hill format I'd been pushing for all along. We staged and shot the second season on a massive fifty-thousand-square-foot sound stage in Atlanta. (Dwayne's idea.) There was no more overnight shooting. (Also Dwayne's idea.) He has a home in Atlanta, and we squeezed the shooting in when

Dwayne had a break while shooting the Netflix film, *Red Notice*, with Gal Gadot and Ryan Reynolds.

Dwayne's hard-charging work ethic is legendary—he's got one of those full-speed-ahead personalities that has obviously been one of the key drivers of his success. His career has been all about the *reach*. But he also has this thoughtful, magnanimous side, and he's quick to bring others along with him. He reminded me that it's not enough to reach and stretch and light your own fire in pursuit of your goals. You also have to reach out to those around you and help them to stretch and ignite their own fires.

Dwayne's example resonated with me because it reflected the ways I've always tried to live my life and reinforced the importance of reaching back and extending kindness. At A. Smith & Co., I'm not only proud of the shows we've put on the air and the awards and honors we've collected along the way. Mostly, I'm proud of the ways we've helped our people reach their goals—freelancers and full-timers alike.

After all, we don't get where we're going on our own.

CLOSE

The more you try, the luckier you get . . .

I'm repeating myself here, I know, but as I write these final few words, I feel I should reinforce this book's all-important point.

I've told some wild stories of my time on the front lines of television. I've shared the story of my family and showed how the values of my parents and the legacies of my grandparents shaped me. I've written about my lifelong love affair with television and the decision I made early on to find a way to work in the entertainment industry. I've presented a collection of stories about television that hopefully entertained and enlightened you—but ultimately, I hope it inspired you to reach . . . to not be afraid to put yourself out there . . . to remember to reach back and help others.

What prevents people from reaching?

- Building on a weak foundation
- Fear of failure
- Unwillingness to be vulnerable
- Overanalyzing the next move
- Looking too far ahead
- A lack of commitment or desire

Many times, during the writing of this book, I felt like an old man sharing the hard lessons and learned truths of a lifetime. I'd sit down at the computer and think of the stories I wanted to include in these pages, always on the lookout for insights and takeaways that might help readers grow their games or learn from my experience. My head was filled with what I started calling *teachable, reachable moments*—and I took to carrying a notebook with me to jot down my ideas.

Here's a page from that notebook, just to let you see what's been on my mind during this process:

"If you let fear be your guide, you will most likely be stuck in neutral . . . If you're not sure what you want, or what you want to do, take your best guess . . . Once you start moving in a direction, even if it's the wrong one, you will learn what you don't like . . . Be prepared to stumble into a new job or a new field or a new project you never thought you would like . . . It's important to get going, get moving . . . We don't learn if we don't try . . . Life is a series of experiments—some of them are failed experiments, but we can learn from them anyway . . . Accept the fact that if you're reaching, you're going to be at least a little bit vulnerable . . . Being dedicated, working hard, and having a positive attitude will make you less vulnerable . . . Failure is not the end of the road—it's a detour, a redirect . . . As you look ahead, visualize where you want to go . . . The mind, as we all know, is a powerful tool . . . You will be surprised by how comfortable you will be 'when you get there' if you have spent quality time visualizing it."

Many of these thoughts and ideas are not original to me, of course. But they run like a current through my life and career, and I would be holding back if I didn't share them here. Sometimes that current was switched on as I was living these moments, but sometimes I didn't recognize the power in these stories until I started writing them.

And yet . . . there it was. The *power* of reach. Running all the way from that moment on the ice when I was nine years old, just trying to fit in, to this present moment, as I look over my shoulder at a body of work that in its own way has reshaped, reimagined, and reinvigorated the television landscape.

There is a danger to *overreaching* and being overly ambitious. Admittedly, this has been my biggest challenge. If, like me, you are committed to reaching in your personal and professional life, take your foot off the gas every once in a while. If you're always reaching, always looking ahead to what's around the next bend, you'll never be fully in the moment. In *this* moment. Remember to enjoy the ride—be grateful for the journey and the stops along the way. It's a good and welcome thing to reflect on your past, as I have attempted to do here, but let these reflections act as a reminder to enjoy the present.

And now, if you don't mind, I think I'll look for a copy of this week's "TV Times" supplement and see if there's anything good to watch on television.

ACKNOWLEDGMENTS

There is a danger that this section could be longer than the book itself because there are so many people to thank for helping me on my journey—a series of reaches that would not have been possible without the support and love of the people I have counted on. But I'm going to keep this brief.

As I said early on in this book, it is significantly easier to reach when you are reaching from a strong foundation. I am fortunate to have had the best parents, who provided that strong base for me. I am extremely thankful for my loving family, close friends, loyal colleagues, patient collaborators, and hard-working coworkers—way too numerous to mention. I treasure these relationships. They are without question my most cherished assets.

I want to acknowledge the good people at Blackstone Publishing, who found enough things to like in my story of perseverance and chutzpah to take it on. I am grateful for their keen editorial insights and creative professionalism, but mostly for their enthusiasm and belief that readers might find insight and inspiration in these pages. Writing and publishing a book, like developing and producing a television show, is a collaborative effort, and it's an honor (and a kick!) to work with such a talented, dedicated team. Special thanks to my editor Christina Boys, who kept me focused and targeted—and to WME's Sabrina Taitz, for championing this project and working so tirelessly to find it the perfect publishing home.

An enormous thank-you to Dan Paisner, whose wisdom I relied upon greatly throughout this process. His guidance, pithiness, and partnership made this book possible.

And thank you to all of you who decided to read this book. I hope it entertained you but also inspired you to REACH.

ABOUT THE AUTHOR

Arthur Smith, the chairman of A. Smith & Co. Productions, is a pioneering veteran of nonfiction television, known for creating and producing some of the longest-running unscripted series in history, including *Hell's Kitchen* and *American Ninja Warrior*. Smith was honored as one of *Variety*'s "Titans of Unscripted TV" in 2022, inducted into the Realscreen Awards Hall of Fame in 2021, awarded *Broadcasting & Cable*'s "Producer of the Year" in 2020, nominated for several Emmy Awards, and received dozens of awards, including NAACP Awards, Realscreen Awards, and Critics Choice Awards. Smith embarked on his career in television as a twenty-two-year-old wunderkind, talking his way into sports production at CBC in his native Canada. He quickly distinguished himself as a rising star at the network, where he produced three Olympic Games among countless other high-profile events. At the age of twenty-eight, Smith was named the youngest-ever head of CBC Sports. His successful run at the network ended when American broadcasting icon Dick Clark lured him to Hollywood to develop and produce a wide variety of entertainment programming. Then as the head of programming and production at FOX Sports Net, Smith played an instrumental role in the launch and growth of this massive entity, before the biggest reach of his life—the creation of his eponymous production company that has since thrived for more than twenty years and counting. He lives in Los Angeles.

My motion picture debut in *Pinball Summer*. The movie itself wasn't much, but it was a key pivot point for me. At the time, I thought I'd find my way as an actor, but the more hours I logged on film and TV sets, the more I was intrigued by what the director and the producers were doing behind the scenes.

Then and now. Here I am sandwiched between my sisters—my two biggest supporters and lifelong confidants. That's Sheryl on the left, and Marylin on the right. I still speak to them every day!

At the controls. Here I am at our command center at the 1988 Seoul Olympics—one of the most consequential sporting events I ever covered. It was during these games that our CBC host, Brian Williams, famously said I whispered into his ear more frequently in sixteen days than his wife had in sixteen years of marriage. And here I am again in 2013, in the *Hell's Kitchen* control room, where I haven't missed a day in our twenty-two seasons. The equipment might have changed over the long run of my career (and my hair!), but I am still in my element.

A life among heavy-weights. On the set of ABC's *Jim Thorpe Pro Sports Awards* with the greatest of all time, and behind the scenes at *Hell's Kitchen* in Las Vegas with the scariest—two champs who need no introduction.

Another shot from the *Pro Sports Awards*—this one capturing the moment in 1992 when Magic Johnson presented Michael Jordan with the "Player of the Year" award. The photo was taken just after I'd stumbled in on Magic and Larry Bird practicing in an otherwise empty gym, offering a compelling reminder to keep *reaching* . . . even when no one is watching. That's our head writer, Larry Wilmore, on the left, who'd go on to create or produce *The Bernie Mac Show*, *Insecure*, and *Black-ish*, and to host his own talk show.

With Dick Clark at the Oakland Hills Country Club in Birmingham, Michigan. The sixteenth hole at Oakland Hills was the first hole in our *Great 18* golf championship—a tournament and show Dick thought was the stupidest idea he'd ever heard when I pitched it to him in our Burbank office. The show offered me a lifelong lesson on the importance of chasing your dreams, even when everyone around you thinks your dreams are nuts.

This was the photo I found on my dad's nightstand after he passed away. I'm making a presentation at one of our *Great 18* holes, while my dad is beaming proudly in the background. I never knew the picture meant so much to him—now it means so much more to me.

With my dad at Pebble Beach in 2003, walking up the fairway to the eighteenth green, reliving our trip-of-a-lifetime ten years after the whirlwind *Great 18* shoot. This time, we actually got to play the iconic course.

The Icemen Cometh. Sandwiched between two of the greatest to ever put on a pair of skates, in the green room at the *Jim Thorpe Pro Sports Awards* show. On the left, Olympic gold medalist, Scott Hamilton, who'd go on to host our production of *Skating with Celebrities* for FOX. On the right . . . well, that's the Great One, Wayne Gretzky, who was quick to remind me of the time I convinced the network heads to air a special midweek edition of *Hockey Night in Canada* four years earlier, to capture his Edmonton homecoming.

A rare quiet night home with my girls in 1997, during a particularly crazy time for me as head of programming, production, and news at FOX Sports Net—*a reach* that saw us launch twenty-two sports networks! That's Rachel with me, and Leah in Wendy's arms—we've got the whole world in our hands!

One of my favorite photos of my mom and her "favorite child." I love the way she's looking at me, which was pretty much the way she *always* looked at me.

With the brilliant Gordon Ramsay on the set of *Hell's Kitchen*. The two of us have been in sync for twenty-two seasons and we're not done yet!

Just how wild and *out there* was our 2008 *I Survived a Japanese Game Show* production? Well, this picture gives you some idea.

(see above) Our *I Survived a Japanese Game Show* shoot in Tokyo marked the first time a prime-time American show was shot entirely in Japan. Here I am with my partner-in-crime, Kent Weed, celebrating what was truly a unique experience.

You never know who's watching. I was thrilled to learn that Stan Lee, the genius behind Marvel Comics, was a fan of *Hell's Kitchen*. Here I am giving Stan the "cook's tour" on a 2012 visit to our set. He was fascinated by the way we covered every conceivable angle (and some *inconceivable* ones!) with over eighty cameras.

"You must be *this* tall to ride the roller coaster of my life." Here I am being brought down to size by Shaquille O'Neal, a giant of a man and an outsized talent on the court and off. We'd met a bunch of times over the years, before we worked together in 2015 as producer and judge of *The Dunk King*. Also pictured: Brent Barry, Charles Barkley, Kenny Smith, and Terrence J.

Celebrating our second Emmy nod for *American Ninja Warrior* on the red carpet, with my sister Marylin; my wife, Wendy; and my daughters, Rachel and Leah.

With one of the nicest guys in the entertainment business, on our massive *Titan Games* set. That's the buzz on Dwayne "The Rock" Johnson, and he justifies his reputation in every encounter. A class act!

The show must go on—even in the midst of a global pandemic. One of the many shows we shot under our strict COVID-19 protocols was *Floor is Lava*, a competition show for Netflix. On set with (from left) Netflix executives Lou Wallach and Derek Wan, and executive producer Anthony Carbone and executive producer and A. Smith president, Frank Sinton. Lou and Derek thought we might be kidding when we told them we needed room in the budget for a working volcano—but who jokes about such a thing?

A shot with my cherished wife, Wendy—surely the most understanding and supportive wife in all of human history. Of all the many *reaches* that have stamped my life and career, this one has yielded the most blessings. And the greatest blessing of all . . . she *reached* back!